Career Planning
AND
Succession Management

D0209866

Career Planning

AND

Succession Management

Developing Your Organization's Talent—for Today and Tomorrow

William J. Rothwell

Robert D. Jackson

Shaun C. Knight

John E. Lindholm

with Wei Aleisha Wang *and* Tiffani D. Payne

Westport, Connecticut
London

Library of Congress Cataloging-in-Publication Data

Career planning and succession management : developing your organization's talent—for today and tomorrow / William J. Rothwell, Robert D. Jackson, Shaun C. Knight, and John E. Lindholm ; with Wei Aleisha Wang and Tiffani D. Payne.
   p. cm.
  Includes bibliographical references and index.
  ISBN 0-275-98359-5 (alk. paper)
  1. Career development. 2. Executive succession—Planning.
I. Rothwell, William J., 1951–
   HF5549.5.C35C39   2005
   658.3'124—dc22   2004028378

British Library Cataloguing in Publication Data is available.

Library of Congress Catalog Card Number: 2004028378
ISBN: 0-275-98359-5

First published in 2005

Praeger Publishers, 88 Post Road West, Westport, CT 06881
An imprint of Greenwood Publishing Group, Inc.
www.praeger.com

Printed in the United States of America

∞™

The paper used in this book complies with the Permanent Paper Standard issued by the National Information Standards Organization (Z39.48-1984).

10 9 8 7 6 5 4 3 2 1

William J. Rothwell dedicates this book to his wife Marcelina, his daughter Candice, his son Froilan, and to the coauthors below with whom it was a delight to work.

Robert Jackson dedicates this book to his gracious wife, Marcia Jackson.

Shaun Knight dedicates this book to his wonderful wife Sandy, Ryan and Amy, and his daughter Abby for their inspiration, patience, and never-ending support.

John Lindholm dedicates this book to his father, John Victor Lindholm, for his guidance and modeling of a faith-based life.

CONTENTS

I
Making the Business Case for Moving Beyond Career and Succession Planning: Why They Must Be Integrated

II
Foundations for Integrating Career and Succession Planning

III
Strategies for Integrating Career and Succession Planning

IV
Concluding Thoughts

Appendixes

TABLES AND FIGURES

TABLES

FIGURES

PREFACE

M any organizations today are scrambling to prepare for an expected wave of retirements. Between 1998 and 2008, almost twice as many job openings are occurring or will occur from people retiring rather than from economic expansion. This change is the result of the U.S. labor force—and, indeed, the global workforce—simply growing older. The average age has been increasing for some time. The aging population, like a glacier carrying all before it, is enormous.

What are the practical consequences of this massive shift in the average age of the workforce? Consider the following statistics:

- One in five of all senior executives in the Fortune 500 is eligible for retirement within the next few years.
- About 80 percent of all the senior executives and about 70 percent of all middle managers in the U.S. federal government are eligible for retirement during the current administration's term in office.
- About 50 percent of the entire federal government workforce is eligible to retire now.

- One million college professors will soon be eligible for retirement.
- One million schoolteachers will soon be eligible for retirement.

To cope with these daunting challenges, many organizations are establishing and implementing organized succession planning programs, while others have experienced renewed interest in career development programs. Indeed, *career planning*—known by various names, including *employee development*—has experienced a rebirth of interest, emerging in a new form that differs from widely used approaches in the 1980s.

A great need exists today to integrate succession planning programs with career planning programs. Succession planning programs help to ensure the continuity of talent needed to preserve economic growth and organizational viability. Career planning programs help individuals discover their career goals and provide reasons to qualify for advancement—or simply keep their skills current, as employability in a new economy places more responsibility on individuals to remain competitive in a dynamic labor market. Integrating career planning and succession planning is essential because career plans give individuals goals to develop themselves and methods by which to do so, while succession plans give organizations ways to focus on meeting their talent needs over time and provide direction to development efforts. Both career planning and succession planning share development as a means to an end but approach it from different directions: career planning tends to be bottom up (from individual to organization); succession planning tends to be top down (from leaders to individuals). Career plans give individuals reasons to develop themselves; succession plans shape the efforts of organizational leaders to identify the talent needs of the organization and systematically develop that talent.

THE PURPOSE AND CONTRIBUTION OF THIS BOOK

The key purpose of this book is to describe a systematic approach by which to integrate career planning and succession planning programs. Succession planning, on the one hand, provides for an organization's continuing talent needs. However, it is an inherently top-down process in which the organization's decision makers select potential replacements as well as identify talent requirements for all job categories, functions, and geographical locations in which the organization operates. Talent is, after all, key to an organization realizing its strategic objectives. Career planning, on the other hand, gives individuals an opportunity to identify their career goals and develop themselves to achieve those goals. Without career planning, succession planning is a wish list; without succession planning, career planning can be a roadmap leading to an uncertain destination.

THE INTENDED AUDIENCES OF THIS BOOK

This book is written for vice presidents, directors, and managers of human resources, HR practitioners and specialists, and line managers. This book is intended to be a practical, how-to guide to help readers understand how to integrate career and succession planning programs. As such, it meets a growing need experienced by today's HR practitioners and line managers alike.

THE KNOWLEDGE BASE OF THIS BOOK

The book has a fourfold knowledge base. First, the authors are (collectively) experienced in establishing and implementing career and succession planning programs. Hence, one base of knowledge stems from the authors' experience.

Second, the authors have assembled, reviewed, and distilled research and literature about succession planning and career planning from 1995 until the present. This thorough literature review provides the basis for supporting assertions about effective practice.

Third, the authors have designed, developed, conducted, and analyzed results from a written questionnaire survey of 500 HR practitioners about typical organizational practices to integrate career planning and succession planning programs. The goal of this survey was to assess common challenges, common practices, and useful strategies to integrate career and succession planning programs across a broad spectrum of organizations.

Fourth and finally, the authors conducted select interviews with practitioners involved with establishing and implementing succession planning and career planning programs. The goal of these interviews was to "dig deep" into what the interview respondents had learned from experience and share that with the book's readers.

THE ORGANIZATIONAL SCHEME OF THE BOOK

This book is organized in four parts and consists of 14 chapters. Part I is "Making the Business Case for Moving Beyond Career and Succession Planning: Why They Must Be Integrated." The two chapters in this part make the case for integrating career planning and succession planning efforts in organizational settings. Chapter 1 is titled "Why Career and Succession Planning Must Be Integrated." Chapter 2 is "An Approach to Integrating Career and Succession Planning."

Part II, "Foundations for Integrating Career and Succession Planning," consists of four chapters. Chapter 3 describes how to establish an infrastructure in an organization to support career and succession planning programs. Chapter 4 focuses on competency models and value systems as foundations for career and succession planning programs. Chapter 5 describes how to use assessment and evaluation in career and succession planning. Chapter 6 describes essential elements in individual development planning and career advising.

Part III, "Strategies for Integrating Career and Succession Planning," consists of six chapters. Chapter 7 explains how training and development can be used to narrow developmental gaps between competency models, which describe "what should be," and the results of assessments, which describe "what is" for individuals. Chapter 8 reviews mentoring programs as tools for narrowing developmental gaps; Chapter 9 reviews coaching programs as tools for narrowing developmental gaps; Chapter 10 reviews self-learning programs as tools for helping individuals narrow developmental gaps; Chapter 11 explains how self-assessment programs can help individuals pinpoint their own developmental gaps and narrow them; and, finally, Chapter 12 explains how other approaches may be used to narrow developmental gaps and thereby help to implement career and succession planning programs.

Part IV, "Concluding Thoughts," consists of two chapters. Chapter 13 provides questions and answers about integrating career and succession planning programs. Chapter 14 points the way toward the future, offering predictions about the future of integrating career and succession planning programs.

The book ends with four appendixes. Appendix 1 addresses the question *what is an employee?* Appendix 2 describes competency statements for career counselors. Appendix 3 provides a case study. Appendix 4 clarifies the difference between a coach and a mentor. The book ends with biographical sketches of the authors and contributors.

Taken together, the chapters in this book provide a starting point for considering how to build competitive synergy by integrating career and succession planning programs. Our advice: enjoy—and use—the information in this book.

ACKNOWLEDGMENTS

I t is difficult to thank all the people who had a hand in writing this book, since so many were involved. Simply stated, this was a team effort—which, admittedly, was led by a benevolent dictator.

First, the authors should take time to congratulate each other. Everyone worked hard. It was worth it.

Second, the authors wish to thank those who completed and returned our survey. Wei Aleisha Wang took the lead on that. She sent out the surveys, followed up on them, and compiled the results. And she did it in record time. Good job—and thanks for demonstrating the sense of urgency that is so key to success in the HR field today!

Third, the authors want to thank the HR practitioners who participated in the in-depth interviews conducted by Tiffani Payne. Thanks, Tiffani, for taking the lead to pull useful information out of those who are trying to do what we are talking about in this book.

Fourth and finally, the authors wish to thank those who read various drafts of this book and offered their helpful comments. You know who you are.

William J. Rothwell
University Park, PA

Robert Jackson
Harrisburg, PA

Shaun Knight
University Park, PA

John Lindholm
Sterling, MA

MAKING THE BUSINESS CASE FOR MOVING BEYOND CAREER AND SUCCESSION PLANNING

Why They Must Be Integrated

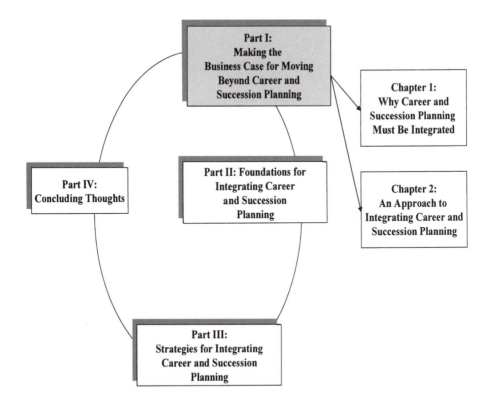

ONE

REFLECTIONS ON THE CONTEMPORARY
BUSINESS SCENE

Why Career and Succession Planning
Must Be Integrated

In this chapter, we deal with several issues facing everyone with career development and succession planning responsibilities at every level:

- How does your organization currently measure up to employee development initiatives? You will find a self-assessment questionnaire to measure your organization's focus on valuing employees and aligning "people policies" to support your organization's performance goals.
- Where is the "puck" really going? Or why it is imperative to anticipate changes in the workforce and not be forced to react due to lack of understanding and preparedness?
- Do the math—why there will be 10 million more jobs than people in the labor force available to fill them by 2010. It is a replacement needs crisis, too.
- How to deal with employee turnover, employees with low to high potential, and employees with low to high performance characteristics.

- Read how the federal government is tackling serious human capital shortfalls that could erode the ability of many agencies to economically, efficiently, and effectively perform their missions.

In this chapter, the realities of the future workforce are revealed and the business case for career development and succession planning is made. The stage is set to begin the journey into developing the future workforce by using career development and success planning concepts, principles, and practices.

Organizational leaders must be prepared to cope with a looming workforce crisis in the United States: the lack of sufficiently prepared workers to fill future job openings. Leaders must begin to ask some important questions: What are the projected retirement dates of the organization's workers, and what percentage of workers is eligible for retirement over time? Does the organization's workplace climate encourage or discourage worker satisfaction, since dissatisfaction is related to absenteeism and turnover? How do employees interpret their "psychological contract" and such concepts as "lifetime employment" and "lifetime employability"? The answers to these and other difficult questions about human capital are essential if organizational leaders are to strategize effectively for the future. Jack Welch, GE's former chairman and CEO, put people and strategy in perspective: "Getting the right people in the right jobs is a lot more important than developing a strategy."[1]

Use the self-assessment checklist shown in Table 1.1 to establish a baseline for developing employees through career development and succession plan programs. The checklist can assist in creating a *human capital organization*—understood to mean an organization that focuses on valuing employees and that aligns people policies to support the organization's performance goals.

PREPARING FOR THE FUTURE

Secretary of Labor Elaine L. Chao has stated that, "to succeed in the 21st century, our workforce must be able to anticipate and swiftly adapt to changes in our economy—changes in how we work, where we work,

TABLE 1.1 Self-Assessment Questionnaire About Your Organization's Employee Development Program

Directions: Read each item below. Then, place a check mark (✓) in the appropriate column: *Yes, Sometimes,* or *No.*

My Organization:	Yes	Sometimes	No
1. Monitors head count on a regular basis to measure and track workforce requirements.			
2. Monitors employee turnover to track any unusual "spikes" that could result from either internal or external factors.			
3. Makes an effort to plan for workforce needs in advance for reasons such as promotions and retirements.			
4. Makes appropriate investments in education, training, and other developmental opportunities to help employees build their competencies.			
5. Makes appropriate investments in individual development programs for employees at all levels.			
6. Provides adequate opportunities for career advancement that take into account supervisory and managerial needs.			
7. Encourages employees to take control of their learning so they will possess the necessary skills to be employable throughout their working life.			
8. Provides flexibility, facilities, services, and programs to enhance employee satisfaction and commitment to the organization.			
9. Makes flexible use of the workforce—such as putting the right employees in the right roles according to their skills or using "virtual teams" to focus on the right talent for specific tasks.			
10. Provides career advisement and developmental services to employees at all levels.			
11. Implements creative ways to recognize and reward employees.			
12. Creates a workplace climate that allows and encourages employees to become more involved with or engaged in their work.			

TABLE 1.1 *(Continued)*

My Organization:	Yes	Sometimes	No
13. Has in place, and ready to activate, a plan for the replacement of the organization's key leadership positions in the event of sudden tragedy affecting an individual or a group.			
14. Provides high-potential employees with developmental (stretch) assignments to prepare them for larger roles in the organization.			
15. Consistently provides employees with opportunities to become part of the talent pool from which key leadership positions are drawn.			

Scoring: Add scores based on this scale:
Yes responses = 2 points; *Sometimes* responses = 1 point; *No* responses = 0 points.

If the Score of Your Organization Was:	Then:
24 to 30 points	Congratulations! You and your organization are on the right track to ensuring the future through efficient and effective interaction with your employees.
15 to 23 points	More work needs to be done to improve organizational effectiveness in interacting with employees.
14 points or below	Pull out all the stops! Begin immediate improvements to the organization's efforts to interact with and develop employees.

and how we balance our professional and family lives. Many of the changes are dramatic. We cannot simply react to these changes; we must anticipate them."[2]

In the 1980s, as John Naisbitt was introducing his ten new directions for transforming our lives,[3] Tom Peters was either searching for excellence[4] or thriving on a chaotic management revolution.[5] Joel Arthur Barker was helping us understand paradigms and how they figure into discovering the future.[6] New business strategies established new paradigms for many workers. In the early 1990s, Hal Rosenbluth, then CEO of

Rosenbluth Travel,[7] revealed a key secret behind his organization's century of success by proclaiming that customers come second while employees actually come first.[8]

Clearly, the "rules" of modern business have been changing. Observers of the contemporary business scene have witnessed a fundamental paradigm shift as organizations such as Wal-Mart, FedEx, Dell, and Microsoft developed by breaking all the old rules. In Tom Peters's most recent book, he calls the operating environment of today's business the "New War. New Business."[9] Peters fondly quotes Paul Allaire, former CEO of Xerox, about the state of the contemporary business scene: "We're in a brawl with no rules."[10]

From the mid-1970s to the present, another revolution has affected virtually every organization and worker. Traditionally, the term *career* implied "a series of upward moves, with steadily increasing income, power, status, and security."[11] Douglas T. Hall introduced a new concept, the *protean career*, in which individuals (rather than employers) are the driving forces behind their careers.[12] This idea ran counter to many traditional assumptions about loyalty, mobility, and job security. Currently, the business world is hearing much about "wars" for talent,[13] how to win these wars,[14] and how to solve talent issues.[15] Concepts such as the *boundaryless career*,[16] the *boundaryless organization*,[17] the *emotional economy*,[18] and the *free agent worker*[19] are clear indicators that the business world is experiencing radical transformation.

In its most basic form, the U.S. economy is driven by the relationship between population, demand for goods and services, and the labor force. The concepts presented in this book are meant to educate the reader about the development of the U.S. labor force. A solid understanding of this development is crucial to success in the twenty-first century (see Table 1.2).

BY THE NUMBERS

According to projections from the Bureau of Labor Statistics,[20] by 2010 there will be 10 million more jobs than people in the labor force available to fill them. In 2000, there were 5 million more jobs than there were people in the labor force. In just 10 years (2000 to 2010), the number

TABLE 1.2   The Relationship Between Population, Demand for Goods and Services, and the Labor Force

	Effects
Population (Trends for 2000 to 2010)	• The U.S. population is expected to increase by 24 million. • Age group 35 to 44 will be the only one to *decrease* in size. (This reflects the decrease in births following the baby boom.) • Age group 55 to 64 will increase by 11 million persons—more than any other group (aging baby boomers).
Goods and services	• Continued population growth influences the demand for goods and services. • Changes in population influence the demand for goods and services. (A growing and aging population increases the demand for health care services.) • Demand for various goods and services determine employment in the industries providing them. • Services is the largest and fastest growing major industry group. (By 2010, this group is expected to account for three out of every five new jobs created in the U.S. economy. Over two-thirds of the projected job growth is concentrated in only three service industries: business, health, and social services.) • Goods production has been relatively stagnant since the early 1980s. (Employment in this group is expected to grow 6.3 percent over the 2000–2010 period.)
Labor force	• Population is the single most important factor in determining the size and composition of the labor force (people who are either working or looking for work). • Population ultimately limits the size of the labor force which constrains how much can be produced. • Demand for various goods and services determines employment in the industries providing them. • The civilian labor force is projected to increase by 12 percent to 158 million over the 2000–2010 period. • Employment is expected to increase by 15.2 percent (to 168 million) in 2010. (The 22 million jobs to be added will be determined by changes in consumer demand, technology, and other factors that continually change the U.S. employment structure.)

Source: U.S. Department of Labor, Bureau of Labor Statistics. (2002, January). *Occupational Outlook Handbook*, Bulletin 2540. Washington, DC: Author.

of jobs in the United States will double while the labor force will have grown by only 12 percent (see Table 1.3).

To compound the problem, many organizations are preparing for a tidal wave of retirements as the baby boomers age (see Table 1.2). For several years, labor economists have been predicting a replacement needs crisis. Between 2000 and 2010, more job openings are expected to result from replacement needs (36 million) than from employment growth in the economy (22 million). This means that nearly two-thirds (62 percent) of the job openings over that period will result from people retiring—or leaving the labor force for other reasons—than will be created by economic expansion.[21] Figure 1.1 depicts the relative distribution of job openings in the United States resulting from economic expansion and replacement needs between 2000 and 2010.

Put simply, the U.S. labor force is growing older. The median average age of the labor force has been rising since 1980, when it was nearly 35; it will approach age 41 by 2010. The median average age of the entire U.S. population will be even older (almost 45) in 2010.[22] That translates into millions of retirements in the near future by workers from all occupations, industries, and economic sectors. The U.S. Government Accountability Office (GAO) projects that more than half of the members of the Senior Executive Service—which are the equivalent to senior corporate executives in private sector firms—employed in 2000 will have

TABLE 1.3   Civilian Employment Opportunities and Available Labor Force: 2000 to 2010

Year	Civilian Employment Opportunities	Available Labor Force	Results
2010	168,000,000	158,000,000	10,000,000 jobs exceeding the available labor force
2000	146,000,000	141,000,000	5,000,000 job exceeding the available labor force
Results	22,000,000 jobs added to the U.S. economy in the next 10 years	Available labor force has grown by only 17,000,000	Question: How will your organization plan for, and manage, a shortage of workers?

Source: U.S. Department of Labor, Bureau of Labor Statistics, (2002, January). *Occupational Outlook Handbook*, Bulletin 2450. Washington, DC: Author.

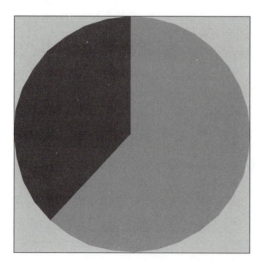

FIGURE 1.1 Two major reasons for 58 million job openings between 2000 and 2010. *Source: U.S. Department of Labor, Bureau of Labor Statistics.* (2002, January). *Occupational Outlook Handbook,* Bulletin 2540, Washington, DC: Author.

left the service by October 2007 and that about 15 percent of the total federal workforce will retire between 2001 and 2006.[23]

GETTING SMALLER

More people are becoming entrepreneurial and working in a self-employed status. According to the *Wall Street Journal*, the ranks of the self-employed increased by 400,000 in 2003 alone. There has also been a surge in "proprietor's income," up 8.6 percent from 2002.[24] Some strategists speculate that this increase is caused by corporate outsourcing, a process in which organizations trim their labor forces to slash payroll and then rehire released workers as independent, self-employed consultants who are responsible for their own (increasingly expensive) health insurance and other benefits.[25]

In many instances, workers who experienced a corporate "reduction in force" and are rehired as consultants use the opportunity to establish themselves as free agents. According to Daniel Pink, some become "soloists" who work from their homes, use the Internet as their business platform, and create an independent business that may or may not be connected to other small, medium, or large businesses.[26] Others choose to become temporary employees (temps) and, through association with temporary employment agencies, work on short- or long-term assignments for different organizations. Yet other "independents" join other free agents and start small businesses or "microbusinesses" made up of only a handful of people.[27]

Since the mid-1990s, small establishments[28] of fewer than 100 workers have employed more than half of the total U.S. private sector. Medium-sized establishments of 100 to 999 workers have employed around one-third of private workers, while large establishments with 1,000 or more workers now employ just over 10 percent of the private sector.[29] Table 1.4 provides more information about this trend. Note that a worker may be in both a contingent and an alternative work arrangement at the same time. That can produce complex, interconnected work assignments and potential conflicts in employment relationships.

What follows is a list of various nonstandard positions that stand in stark contrast to the (until recently) so-called permanent employment relationship that was once expected to endure from postschool employment to retirement:

- Self-employed knowledge workers
- Proprietors of home-based businesses
- Temps
- Permatemps
- Freelancers
- E-lancers
- Independent contractors
- Independent professionals
- Micropreneurs and infopreneurs
- Part-time consultants
- Interim executives
- On-call troubleshooters
- Full-time soloists[30]

Appendix 1 provides additional information on defining an employee.

The population and workforce statistics provided above clearly indicate that there is—and will continue to be—a serious shortage of

TABLE 1.4   Workers with Nonstandard Work Arrangements

Contingent Worker	
Definition	Number in Workforce
Worker who does not have an implicit or explicit contract for ongoing employment and who does not expect their current job to last	5.4 million (4% of workforce)

Alternative Work Arrangements		
Name	Definition	Number in Workforce
Independent Contractor	Worker who contracts to do a piece of work according to his own methods and is subject to his employer's control only as to the end product or final result of his work	8.6 million
On-call worker	Worker who is available literally when the phone rings to supplement a permanent workforce when additional work requires or in an emergency.	2.1 million
Temporary help agency worker	Worker who is actually employed by a temporary staffing agency but is assigned to one or more organizations on an "as needed" basis.	1.2 million
Contract company worker	Worker who is "under contract" with an organization to work either as a specialist or during a high-demand period.	.6 million

Source: Muhl, C. J. (2002, January). What is an employee? The answer depends on the federal law. *Monthly Labor Review,* 3–10.

qualified workers in the United States. These facts and figures help to build a compelling case for organizational leaders to consider establishing and integrating career planning and succession planning programs. After all, career planning programs help people plan for the future so that they can be flexible in a turbulent work environment, while succession planning programs help managers prepare for the future by developing people for key positions throughout organizations.

HIGH PERFORMERS AND HIGH POTENTIALS

Perhaps the most popular decision-making matrix used to identify and categorize the caliber of employees in an organization is based on individual potential and performance (see Table 1.5). The benchmarks for the *performance* axis are employees' "demonstration of values, competencies, and achievement of results," while "the ability to move up the organization structure" is the benchmark for the *potential* axis.[31]

Jack Welch, former chairman and CEO of GE, and his corporate executive office relied heavily on their famous Session C human resource reviews "to show how [their] human resources strategy is being applied to all the major initiatives of the business."[32] GE's Summary Assessment is a customized decision-making matrix and a component of the Business Leadership Dashboard.[33] A decision-making matrix simplifies the selection of high-performance and high-potential employees (known as *HiPers* and *HiPos*). HiPers and HiPos are among the most valuable employees because they are productive and are thus highly attractive to other employers. They may leave an organization on their own and attract the attention of corporate headhunters who seek them out for other organizations.

During an era of high unemployment, managers know that employees will be reluctant to leave organizations; they therefore make considerable work demands and ignore the need to maintain employee retention programs. In bear markets and tough economic times, employers will not replace a separated or retired employee—or will instead simply hire one of many eager, sometimes hungry, applicants on a waiting list. John Sullivan notes: "Over 75 percent of firms have no separate retention department, and most HR retention systems are either rusty or have been dismantled altogether."[34] Human resource (HR) leaders predict that a projected upswing in the economy will cause managers and human resource professionals to reexamine employee retention in a bid to reduce the consequences of a coming tidal wave of departures that stem from retirements and from dissatisfied people who seek better work–life balance than they had earlier experienced.

TABLE 1.5 Decision-Making Matrix

		Potential	
	Low	**Medium**	**High**
Performance **High**	Solid Citizen Performer (High performance/low potential) Gets all of the important things done Is a real pro in his or her position Is seen as a leader in his or her area of expertise Has reached potential	Strong Performer (High performance/medium potential) Gets all of the important things done May act at a level of capability of the next level in the organization Acts as a leader and role model Exhibits many leadership and organizational competencies beyond current role responsibility Some leadership development issues	Star Performer (High performance/high potential) Gets all of the important things done Acts at a level of capability of at least the next level in the organization Acknowledged as a skilled situational leader and role model Exhibits many leadership and organizational competencies Has widespread influence beyond current role
Medium	Action required: Continue developing skills in current job; is in right job Questionable Performer (Medium performance/low potential) Gets most of the important things done Is very proficient in his or her position	Action required: Look for opportunity to display leadership; qualified in current job Solid Citizen Performer (Medium performance/medium potential) Gets most of the important things done Shows signs of being a leader and role model	Action required: Look for stretch assignments to prepare for larger roles Strong Performer (Medium performance/high potential) Gets most of the important things done Acknowledged as a leader and role model

Performance	Low Potential	Medium Potential	High Potential
Medium	Is not seen as a leader in his or her area of expertise Action required: Work on improving performance in current job; may be candidate for lateral move	At times, exhibits many competencies beyond current role responsibility May be new in position Action required: Leave in current job; continue developing skills and improving performance	Exemplifies leadership and organizational competencies Acts at a level of capability of the next level in the organization Action required: Short term: focus on improvement Longer term: focus on development opportunities
Low	Low Performer (Low performance/low potential) Isn't getting most of the important things done Difficulty performing satisfactorily in current position Action required: Consider reassignment to more appropriate position, including a lower level or exit option	Questionable Performer (Low performance/medium potential) Isn't getting most of the important work done Probably capable of making higher contribution May be in wrong job or having nonwork distraction Action required: Focus on improving performance	Solid Citizen Performer (Low performance/high potential) Has been acknowledged as a team player and role model Has exemplified leadership and organizational competencies May be in wrong job or having nonwork distraction Action required: Address root cause of performance issue; worthy of investment in development

Source: American Productivity and Quality Center. (2001). *Succession management: Identifying and cultivating tomorrow's leaders* (p. 95). Houston, TX: Author. Reprinted with permission from APQC.

A CAPITAL IDEA

The people working in any organization are its human capital. Jack Welch always impressed on other GE business leaders: "You own the businesses. You're *renting* the people."[35] Although referring to people in economic terms may sound cold, employees truly are organizational assets or human capital: they contribute to the creation of economic and social outcomes and support the continued development of goods and services.[36] In 1999, U.S. Comptroller General David Walker assessed the importance of human capital: "The key competitive difference in the 21st century will be people. It will not be process. It will not be technology. It will be people . . . the stakes are high."[37]

In 2003, ASTD published *The Human Capital Challenge,* a white paper prepared by the ASTD Public Policy Council that focused on the critical fact that public and private organizations alike need "skilled and knowledgeable workers" to be successful in the "knowledge-based economy of the 21st century." Indeed, "improved performance and productivity, increased competitiveness, and more" will be the rewards for organizations that subscribe to the human capital concept, while those that do not will face potential failure.[38] Vincent J. Seritella articulated the human capital challenge: "Now, more than ever before, organizations will drive results through the alignment and integration of people processes and systems with business strategy."[39]

Acquiring, developing, and retaining talent (human capital) is now acknowledged as a paramount initiative for executives in all private, public, and nonprofit organizations. A GAO document explains that "an organization's people define its character, [and] affect its capacity to perform and represent the knowledge-base of the organization. Effective strategic human capital management approaches serve as the corner-stone of any serious change management initiative."[40]

THE FEDERAL GOVERNMENT HUMAN CAPITAL INITIATIVE

In early 2001, strategic human capital management was identified as a government-wide high-risk area. The GAO indicated that "serious human capital shortfalls are eroding the ability of many agencies . . . to economically, efficiently, and effectively perform their mission."[41] Federal employees were not the major problem; rather, the lack of a consistent strategic approach was identified as the cause of the breakdown in marshaling, managing, and maintaining sufficient human capital to (1) maximize government performance and (2) ensure its accountability to its customers.[42]

The strategic human capital management model adopted by the GAO identifies four pervasive human capital challenges or cornerstones:

1. Leadership, continuity, and succession planning
2. Strategic human capital planning and organizational alignment
3. Acquiring and developing a staff with the size, skills, and deployment to meet agency needs
4. Creating results-oriented (sometimes called high-performance) organizational cultures[43]

Though there are certain fundamental differences between the public and private sectors,[44] many basic management functions are interchangeable.[45] One consistent factor is that human capital management alone cannot ensure high performance. Proper attention to human capital is essential to achieving an organization's mission and goals.[46]

To identify private sector human capital strategies that could transfer directly into the federal government, the GAO studied nine private sector organizations[47] and identified 10 underlying and interrelated principles of human capital management (see Table 1.6).[48] These principles can serve as a foundation for organizational leaders to build corporate cultures that encourage peak performance by supporting human capital management and development.

MAKING THE BUSINESS CASE

Retaining, rather than replacing, high performers and high potential talent decreases replacement costs and minimizes employee turnover. Jac Fitz-enz thoroughly examined the costs of terminating an employee, which can vary greatly depending on the type and size of an organization, and categorized those costs as follows:

TABLE 1.6 Principles of Human Capital Management Common to Nine Private-Sector Organizations

Principle	Description
Treat human capital management as fundamental to strategic business management.	Integrate human capital considerations when identifying the mission, strategic goals, and core values of the organization as well as when designing and implementing operational policies and practices.
Integrate human capital functional staff into management teams.	Include human capital leaders as full members of the top management team rather than isolating them to provide after-the-fact support. Expand the strategic role of human capital staff beyond providing traditional personnel administration services.
Leverage the internal human capital function with external expertise.	Supplement internal human capital staff's knowledge and skills by seeking outside expertise from consultants, professional associations, and other organizations, as needed.
Hire, develop, and sustain leaders according to leadership characteristics identified as essential to achieving specific missions and goals.	Identify the leadership traits needed to achieve high performance of mission and goals, and build and sustain the organization's pool of leaders through recruiting, hiring, development, retention, and succession policies and practices targeted at producing leaders with the identified characteristics.
Communicate a shared vision that all employees, working as one team, can strive to accomplish.	Promote a common understanding of the mission, strategic goals, and core values toward which all employees are directed to work as a team to achieve. Create a line-of-sight between individual contributions and the organization's performance and results.
Hire, develop, and retain employees according to competencies.	Identify the competencies—knowledge, skills, abilities, and behaviors—needed to achieve high performance of mission and goals; build and sustain the organization's talent pool through recruiting, hiring, development, and retention policies and practices targeted at building and sustaining those competencies.
Use performance management systems, including pay and other meaningful incentives, to link performance to results.	Provide incentives and hold employees accountable for contributing to the achievement of mission and goals. Reward those employees who meet or exceed clearly defined and transparent standards of high performance.

TABLE 1.6   (*Continued*)

Principle	Description
Support and reward teams to achieve high performance.	Foster a culture in which individuals interact and support and learn from each other as a means of contributing to the high performance of their peers, units, and the organization as a whole. Bring together the right people with the right competencies to achieve high performance as a result of—rather than in spite of—the organizational structure.
Integrate employee input into the design and implementation of human capital policies and practices.	Incorporate the firsthand knowledge and insights of employees and employee groups to develop responsive human capital policies and practices. Empower employees by making them stakeholders in the development solutions and new methods of promoting and achieving high performance of organizational missions and goals.
Measure the effectiveness of human capital policies and practices.	Evaluate and make fact-based decisions on whether human capital policies and practices support high performance of mission and goals. Identify the performance return on human capital investments.

Source: U.S. General Accounting Office, (2000, January). *Human capital: Key principles from nine private sector organizations*. GAO/GGD-00-28. Washington, DC: Author.

- *Termination expenses* incurred in out-processing (including staff time)
- *Replacement expenses* (assuming the employee will be replaced), such as the costs involved in the hiring process
- *Vacancy costs* or the value of lost revenue the former employee would have generated
- *Productivity costs* or the amount of revenue lost before the new hire's productivity is equivalent to that of the departed employee[49]

Associated costs may also include the following:

- *Advertising* the vacancy
- *Agency fees* incurred if a headhunter is used

- *Travel expenses* if candidates are interviewed in person
- *Relocation costs* if provided to move the selected employee
- *Recruiter costs* involved in the employee search[50]

These costs (potentially amounting to hundreds of thousands of dollars per employee) can be saved if visionary organizational leaders establish and implement effective retention programs.

EMPLOYEE TURNOVER

Simply stated, employee turnover occurs when an employee leaves an organization and is replaced by someone else. The concept is simple, but its implications can be devastating based on a variety of factors, including: *why* employees are departing, the *number* of employees leaving and at what *frequency*, and at what *level* within the organization. Departing employees are typically replaced, but this is not always the case. An economic downturn can cause a reduction in force (RIF) as departing employees are not replaced and the workload is redistributed among remaining workers or is outsourced.

The transformation of an organization from a traditional to a futuristic structure is another reason why employees may not be replaced by direct hires. The traditional employee structure relies on a large core of permanent employees, sometimes supplemented by employees available for extraordinary or seasonal requirements. Specialty work may be contracted out to organizations with core competencies that are able to perform that work best or at the lowest cost. A futuristic structure maintains the same three categories of workforce, but their size is essentially reversed. The core group of (so-called) permanent employees becomes the smallest in number, while supplemental employees and outsourced organizations become the largest. This structure results in a lower turnover ratio, but each individual plays a more significant role in the organization. One implication is that organizational leaders are well advised to establish retention programs geared to keeping people who possess critically sensitive (and often proprietary) knowledge. Corporate mergers, which can prompt reductions in force, and globalization, which can prompt some work to be sent offshore, can also profoundly impact employee headcount and influence turn-over rate.

Why an employee leaves an organization can be clarified by differentiating two categories of turnover: voluntary and involuntary (preventable and unpreventable losses). *Voluntary* refers to an employee's act of separating from an organization on his or her own volition (this would normally be categorized as a preventable loss from the organization's standpoint). An *involuntary* departure is one that is not the choice of the employee but results from a decision made by the organization. It is usually considered an unpreventable loss. For example, retirement may be either voluntary or involuntary. An organization with a mandatory retirement age would categorize an employee's retirement as involuntary, because it was not the worker's choice to separate. If no mandatory retirement policy is in place and an employee chooses to retire, this is classified as voluntary because it is a preventable loss.

The number of employees leaving an organization over a given period must also be monitored and analyzed by a retention management program. If many employees are separating voluntarily in a short time span, these preventable losses must be investigated further. Are job opportunities surfacing elsewhere at a higher rate of pay or with more attractive benefits? Do employees harbor pent-up frustrations with current working conditions or supervisors? Such questions must be examined to stabilize the workforce and retain key talent. If employees at high levels of responsibility are separating voluntarily, it could be a symptom that an organization's succession planning program is not functioning properly—or is nonexistent.

No matter how much effort and care is put into developing a sound retention management program, there will always be employee turnover. The key is to minimize turnover through an effective career development program, ultimately stabilizing the organization's bottom line. Integrating a career development program with a succession planning program secures an organization's financial investment in human capital so that other business strategies and initiatives may be aggressively pursued.

The National Institute of Standards and Technology echoes clearly in their issue sheet to chief executive officers that "with a sharp focus on human capital, employees are no longer considered a cost, but rather an investment. And, [corporate] executive officers are expected to present clear strategy and direction for staffing their respective organizations. Their own value to their organization is, in part, measured by how skilled they are at recruiting and retaining key employees."[51] That topic is addressed in Chapter 2.

NOTES

1. Welch, J. F., Jr. (2001). *Jack: Straight from the gut.* New York: Warner Books, p. 383.

2. United States Department of Labor. (n.d.) *Working in the 21st century.* Retrieved November 6, 2003, from http://www.bls.gov/opub/working/stmtosecretary.htm.

3. Naisbitt, J. (1984). *Megatrends: Ten new directions transforming our lives.* New York: Warner Books.

4. Peters, T. J., & Waterman, R. H. (1984). *In search of excellence: Lessons from America's best-run companies.* New York: Warner Books.

5. Peters, T. J. (1987). *Thriving on chaos: Handbook for a management revolution.* New York: Harper & Row.

6. Barker, J. A. (1993). *Paradigms: The business of discovering the future.* New York: HarperCollins.

7. On October 7, 2003, American Express completed the acquisition of 111-year-old Rosenbluth International, a leading global travel management company. Both American Express and Rosenbluth Travel have been ranked by *Fortune* among the 100 best companies to work for in America.

8. Rosenbluth, H. F., & McFerrin, D. P. (1992). *The customer comes second: And other secrets of exceptional service.* New York: Quill.

9. Peters, T. J. (2003). *Re-imagine: Business excellence in a disruptive age.* London: Dorling Kindersley, p. 12.

10. Ibid., p. 23.

11. Hall, D. T. (Ed.). (1996). *The career is dead: Long live the career.* San Francisco: Jossey-Bass, p. 1.

12. Hall, D. T. (1976). *Careers in organizations.* Glenview, IL: Scott, Foresman, p. 201.

13. Michaels, E., Handfield, H., & Axelrod, B. (2001). *The war for talent.* Boston: Harvard Business School Press.

14. Tulgan, B. (2001). *Winning the talent wars: How to manage and compete in the high-tech, high-speed, knowledge-based, superfluid economy.* New York: Norton.

15. Gubman, E. L. (1998). *The talent solution: Aligning strategy and people to achieve extraordinary results.* New York: McGraw-Hill.

16. Arthur, M. B., & Rousseau, D. M. (1996). *The boundaryless career: A new employment principle for a new organizational era.* New York: Oxford University Press.

17. Ashkenas, R., Ulrich, D., Jick, T., & Kerr, S. (2002). *The boundaryless organization: Breaking the chains of organizational structure.* San Francisco: Jossey-Bass.

18. Coffman, C., & Gonzalez-Molina, G. (2002). *Follow this path: how the world's greatest organizations drive growth by unleashing human potential.* New York: Warner Books.

19. Pink, D. H. (2001). *Free agent nation: How America's new independent workers are transforming the way we live.* New York: Warner Books.

20. Bureau of Labor Statistics, U.S. Department of Labor, *Occupational Outlook Handbook, 2002-03 Edition.* Bulletin 2540. Washington, DC: U.S. Government Printing Office.

21. Ibid.

22. Fullerton, H. N., Jr., & Toossi, M. (2001, November). Labor force projections to 2010: Steady growth and changing composition. *Monthly Labor Review*, 36.

23. U.S. General Accounting Office. (2003). *Succession planning and management is a critical driver of organizational transformation* (GAO-04-127T). Washington, DC: Testimony of J. Christopher Mihm.

24. Hilsenrath, J. E. (2003, December 2). Self-employed boost the economic recovery. *The Wall Street Journal Online.* Retrieved from http://www.startupjournal.com/howto/soundadvice/20031202-hilsenrath.html.

25. Ibid.

26. Pink, *Free agent nation,* pp. 10-11.

27. Ibid., p. 39.

28. An "establishment" is defined by the U.S. Department of Labor as an economic unit that produces goods or provides services, typically at a single physical location and engaged in one type of economic activity.

29. U.S. Department of Labor. (1999, February 11). *Small establishments employ the largest share of workers,* Retrieved from http://www.bls.gov/opub/ted/1999/feb/wk2/art04.htm; U.S. Department of Labor. (2001, March 8). *Majority of private-industry employees work in small establishments.* Retrieved from http://www.bls.gov/opub/ted/2001/ Mar/wk1/art04.htm.

30. Pink, *Free agent nation.*

31. American Productivity and Quality Center. (2001). *Succession management: Identifying and cultivating tomorrow's leaders.* Houston, TX: Author, p. 95.

32. Welch, *Jack: Straight from the gut*, p. 162.

33. Ibid., pp. 164-165, 454.

34. Sullivan, J. (2003, September 22). *The turnover tidal wave is coming: Are you ready?* Retrieved November 8, 2003, from http://www.erexchange.com/articles/db/EDD8FD06E17F4658BE65BAFE2A2AE6E5.asp.

35. Welch, *Jack: Straight from the gut*, p. 388.

36. National Round Table on the Environment and the Economy. (2003). *The state of the debate on the environment and the economy: Environmental*

and sustainable development indicators for Canada. Ottawa, Ontario: Author, pp. 15–16.

37. Figura, S. Z. (2000, March 1). Human capital: The missing link. *GovExec.com.* Retrieved from http://www.govexec.com/gpp/0300hr.htm.

38. ASTD. (2003, August). *The human capital challenge* (A white paper by the ASTD Public Policy Council). Alexandria, VA: Author, p. 2. The ASTD (formerly known as the American Society for Training and Development) Public Policy Council is a consortium of senior learning executives representing corporations and educational institutions. The council assists ASTD in shaping national discussions and public policies that encourage the development and support of a high-skilled, high-performing workforce.

39. Ibid., p. 5. When this white paper was written, Serritella was the ASTD Public Policy Council Chair as well as vice president for employee development and director of the Grainger Learning Center with W. W. Grainger, Inc.

40. U.S. General Accounting Office. (2002). *A model of strategic human capital management* (GAO-02-373SP) Washington, DC: Author, p. 4.

41. Ibid.

42. Ibid.

43. Ibid.

44. Not only does the government not operate for profit, but it also takes on duties (such as defense) that are prescribed by the Constitution, is subject to statutory requirements that do not apply to the private sector, and takes actions in the public interest (such as securities or environmental regulations) that the private sector is not empowered to take.

45. U.S. General Accounting Office. (2000, January). *Human capital: Key principles from nine private sector organizations* (GAO/GGD-00-28). Washington, DC: Author, p. 4.

46. Ibid., p. 2.

47. Nine private sector organizations benchmarked by GAO from April to October 1999: Federal Express Corp. (now FedEx), IBM, Marriott International, Merck, Motorola, Sears, Southwest Airlines, Weyerhaeuser, and Xerox Document Solutions Group.

48. U.S. General Accounting Office, *Human capital,* pp. 2–4.

49. Fitz-enz, J. (2000). *The ROI of human capital: Measuring the economic value of employee performance.* New York: AMACOM, pp. 104–105.

50. Ibid., p. 103.

51. National Institute of Standards and Technology. (2001, Summer). *Baldrige: For hiring and keeping the best employees,* p. 1. Retrieved from http://www.quality.nist.gov/Issue_Sheet_HR.htm. The National Institute of Standards and Technology is a nonregulatory federal agency within the Commerce Department's Technology Administration. NIST's primary mission is to develop and promote measurement, standards, and technology to enhance productivity, facilitate trade, and improve the quality of life.

TWO

AN APPROACH TO INTEGRATING CAREER AND SUCCESSION PLANNING PROGRAMS

Understanding the total impact that corporate scandals, terrorist attacks, aging, and sudden illnesses have upon an organization's workers is key to maintaining competitive viability in a global marketplace. Implementing a strategy to retain, develop, and recruit employees that can make the most substantial impact on the bottom line requires an organization that is committed to the successful integration of career and succession planning programs. This chapter examines multiple questions relating to this issue:

1. What are the benefits of succession planning, career planning, and integrating career and succession planning in an organization?
2. What model can aid in conceptualizing succession planning?
3. What model can aid in conceptualizing career planning?
4. Why is there a need to integrate career planning and succession planning?
5. What model can help to integrate career planning and succession planning?
6. What action steps are necessary to integrate succession planning and career planning successfully?

To start off this chapter, you will be asked to complete a strategic self-assessment relating to your organization's current state of employee development and how successfully your organization's career development program and succession planning program has been integrated. Understanding your organization's current state is the first step in moving to a fully integrated business model that will not only maximize your employees' contributions to the organization but will provide a rich source of talent that can be leveraged in the future.

Effective succession planning and career planning practices are essential to the survival of today's businesses. Succession planning has surged to the forefront of executive attention due to recent corporate scandals, the disastrous loss of key people due to terrorist attacks or sudden illnesses, and growing awareness of widespread aging among the leadership ranks in businesses, government agencies, and nonprofit organizations. As Guinn has noted, "the increased use of technology and the globalization of the economy has increased competitiveness in the marketplace, with increasing demands for quality and added value to products and services to grow market share, forces company leaders to be highly future oriented and flexible in the organizations."[1] Implementing an effective succession planning program decreases the risk of losing key people, increases employee job satisfaction, and improves the likelihood of matching the most qualified individuals to the most crucial work.[2] Further, succession planning offers a competitive advantage over other organizations that are not farsighted enough to possess an effective succession strategy.[3] A comprehensive succession planning process enhances typical human resources tasks by clarifying what talent is available in the organization's talent pool.[4]

The results of a Society for Human Resource Management Retention Practices Survey revealed that 61 percent of over 450 HR experts believe that the lack of career planning activities poses an employee retention risk.[5] One reason is that dynamic, and shifting, workplace requirements have fostered a change in employee values and expectations of their employers. Individual workers want to participate in career planning activities that enable them to do their daily tasks better, remain employment-ready in a dynamic labor market, and position them for internal promotions.[6] A succession planning program, combined with a career planning program, can minimize retention risks while developing talent poised to meet the organization's future competitive challenges.

This chapter examines the key benefits of integrating succession planning and career planning. It opens with a self-assessment activity. The remainder of the chapter addresses such questions as these:

- What are the benefits of succession planning, career planning, and integrating career and succession planning in an organization?
- What model can aid in conceptualizing succession planning?
- What model can aid in conceptualizing career planning?
- Why does a need exist to integrate career planning and succession planning?
- What model can help to integrate career planning and succession planning?
- What action steps are necessary to integrate succession planning and career planning successfully?

INTRODUCTORY ACTIVITY: INTEGRATING CAREER PLANNING AND SUCCESSION PLANNING

Pause a moment to rate your organization on how well its career planning and succession planning efforts are aligned with the organization's strategic objectives. Use the assessment appearing in Table 2.1 for that purpose. When you finish, continue reading the chapter.

THE BENEFITS OF SUCCESSION PLANNING

Organizational leaders are realizing that the long-term viability of their organization is at stake as they seek to recruit and retain qualified talent to meet strategic objectives. Succession planning consists of a systematic, long-term approach to meeting the present and future talent needs of an organization to continue to achieve its mission and meet or exceed its business objectives.[7] The succession planning process takes time, persistence, and consistent review. Organizations tend to fail in their succession efforts and ability to invigorate their corporate culture

TABLE 2.1 Rate Your Organization on the Integration of Career Development and Succession Planning

Directions: Rate how successfully your organization's career development program and succession planning program has been integrated by using this rating form. For each characteristic of a best-practice career development program or a succession planning program appearing in the left column below, circle a number in the right column to indicate how well you believe your organization manages that characteristic. Use this scale for your ratings: **1 = Very Poorly; 2 = Poorly; 3 = Neither Poor nor Good; 4 = Good;** and **5 = Very Good.** Ask other decision makers in your organization to complete this form individually. Then add up the numbers from the right column and compare notes. See how others rated the relative success of your organization's career development program or succession planning program.

Characteristics of an Effectively Integrated Career Development and Succession Planning Program	How Would You Rate Your Organization's Integration of Career Development and Succession Planning?				
Your organization has successfully . . .	Very Poorly 1	Poorly 2	Neither Good Nor Poor 3	Good 4	Very Good 5
1 Defined the purpose and goals of an integrated career and succession program for your organization.	1	2	3	4	5
2 Determined what performance is presently needed for job categories through the creation of competency models.	1	2	3	4	5
3 Established a formal career planning structure to identify and address employee competency needs, career planning needs, and goal actualization.	1	2	3	4	5
4 Created a methodology to assess employee performance and current competency requirements as a means for comparing competency models and career development activities.	1	2	3	4	5

TABLE 2.1 (*Continued*)

Characteristics of an Effectively Integrated Career Development and Succession Planning Program	How Would You Rate Your Organization's Integration of Career Development and Succession Planning?				
Your organization has successfully...	Very Poorly 1	Poorly 2	Neither Good Nor Poor 3	Good 4	Very Good 5
5 Specified what future performance will be needed through future competency models.	1	2	3	4	5
6 Implemented a specific individual development plan (IDP) to address skill gaps, monitor career planning activities, and identify future training needs.	1	2	3	4	5
7 Formalized a recurring evaluation strategy to monitor career planning and training activities as a means of establishing expectations for accountability.	1	2	3	4	5
8 Used a structured evaluation tool or approach to document present individual competence and career goal achievement to identify organizational talent on demand.	1	2	3	4	5
9 Maintains a clear and consistent employee advancement/reward system that aligns with career development efforts and succession planning efforts.	1	2	3	4	5

TABLE 2.1 *(Continued)*

Characteristics of an Effectively Integrated Career Development and Succession Planning Program	How Would You Rate Your Organization's Integration of Career Development and Succession Planning?				
Your organization has successfully . . .	Very Poorly 1	Poorly 2	Neither Good Nor Poor 3	Good 4	Very Good 5
10 Performs frequently evaluations of the integrated career and succession program as a means to pinpoint areas needing improvement.	1	2	3	4	5

Scoring

Now add up all the scores you circled in the right column and put the sum on the line at right

Interpreting Your Scores

If the score for your organization was . . .		Then that means . . .
1	50–40	You and your organization deserve congratulations. Your organization has effectively integrated career and succession planning programs.
2	39–30	Your organization is doing pretty well. Your organization's career program and succession planning programs are reasonably well-integrated. Examine areas with lower scores so that you know what areas should be the focus of improvement efforts.
3	29–20	Your organization is doing a fair job of integrating career and succession planning programs. You have some important efforts in place but may need to spend some time to fix some others. Steps should be taken to become more effective at integrating career programs and succession planning programs.
4	19–0	Your organization deserves a failing grade. To have an effective and integrated career and succession planning program, you and your organization should take immediate steps to improve what is being done. Get to work!

with new talent and ideas when they do not continually use a systematic succession planning process.[8]

Effectively managing succession planning yields many benefits, including the following:

- Enables the organization to assess its talent needs by establishing competency models or job descriptions
- Allows leaders to identify, and tap in record time, key people who are available to fill critical work functions
- Provides avenues for present and future succession planning and discussions about how to develop talent
- Defines career pathways through an organization
- Provides for a higher return on investment from employees
- Leads to the appropriate promotion and preselection of people to meet organizational goals

Benefit 1: Enables the Organization to Assess Talent Needs by Establishing Competency Models or Job Descriptions

Understanding an organization's business needs can be difficult due to global competitive issues, available talent pools, and general uncertainties in consumer demand. Few organizational leaders take a proactive stance to attract and retain talent through comprehensive succession planning until gradual turnover escalates or the organization experiences the sudden loss of high-profile talent.[9] A major benefit of the succession planning process is that it leads to a formal evaluation of current job functions and people. This facilitates the development of competency models that provide profiles of ideal performers by job category, department, or hierarchical level. Mismatches of people and work challenges severely affect retention rates and work results. Turnover alone can be a costly issue, since studies indicate that the cost of replacing individuals can range from 70 to 200 percent of an employee's annual salary.[10]

Benefit 2: Allows Leaders to Identify Key People Who Are Available to Fill Critical Work Functions

A second benefit of succession planning is that it encourages organizational leaders to evaluate the key people available to fill critical work functions at present and in the future. An examination of employee competencies can surface individuals who can meet mission-critical organizational tasks, perhaps on short notice. Many organizations spend valuable time filling vacancies ("plugging holes") as they arise rather than inventorying talent resources and building the talent pool. A thoroughly developed job competency model pinpoints the competencies essential to satisfactory or exemplary job performance in the context of a person's job roles, responsibilities and relationships in an organization and its internal and external environments.[11] While competency models describe the people who do the work, they do not measure how well individuals are performing in a given time span. The best practice in succession planning and management programs is to integrate competency models (which describe the people who do the work) with their measurable work results in a given time span.[12] In many instances, job competency models can identify underlying characteristics of employees—that is, motives, traits, skills, aspects of self-image, social roles, or bodies of knowledge—leading to effective or superior performance in a specific job. Subsequent evaluations of individual expertise (performance measure) will likely uncover many transferable skills that can fit into other mission-critical work functions. The succession planning process also provides key stakeholders with information on high potentials in the organization and identifies developmental gaps (differences between individual competencies and those needed for subsequently higher levels of responsibility) and thus helps to underscore future training or employee development requirements. The analysis of developmental gaps (gap analysis) also provides valuable information for career planning programs by dramatizing to individuals what differences exist between their existing competencies and what they need to realize their career goals. A key point worth emphasizing here is that the competencies essential to success at one level do not necessarily qualify individuals for advancement—nor does a long tenure with the organization.

Benefit 3: Provides Avenues for Present and Future Succession Planning

The third benefit stemming from the succession planning process is that it provides a comprehensive inventory of available talent that can be tapped, perhaps on short notice. This invaluable information plays a key role in realizing future talent needs to meet strategic objectives by facilitating the development of talent to fill important positions as needed. Conversely, this information can assist in limiting growth objectives due to an identified lack of star (exemplary) performers. Identifying future talent needs is an important responsibility of key stakeholders. "Decision-makers should examine how the organization will respond to external pressures by structuring responsibility and organizing work processes...key positions will emerge—and the old ones will fade away."[13] Understanding present and future human resource needs provides a clear competitive advantage over other organizations that fail to do so. It also facilitates discussions to guide individual development to meet individual career goals.

Benefit 4: Defines Career Pathways

The definition of career pathways is often an important by-product of assessing organizational needs, identifying key personnel, and establishing a succession planning effort aligned to the organization's strategic business plan. Clarifying career pathways throughout an organization allows employees to understand where they currently fit in the business unit, and more importantly, where they can go in the future if they take initiative to acquire essential competencies. Clear career pathways make it easy for individuals to see what they need to do to develop themselves to qualify for advancement. That also takes away a common cause for employee attrition.

When career pathways have been clarified, managers can also better understand what coaching and other developmental experiences they must provide to their workers to help them qualify for advancement. That also makes succession planning more effective, thereby establishing credibility and support for the effort.

Benefit 5: Provides for a Higher Return on Investment from Employees

Most organizational initiatives require some kind of change. But a well-planned succession effort can prepare people more effectively for the challenges they will face as the future unfolds in the present. A well-planned succession effort also leads to more effective use of resources to build talent. That leads to a higher return on investment in employees and their development. Research indicates that organizations that plan for high-level executive succession realize improved fiscal returns.[14] Most of these cost savings are attributable to reduced attrition and less need for employee retraining that can result from capricious, vague, or nonexistent succession planning efforts. Additionally, a properly implemented succession plan provides employee incentives (promotions) through the clarified career pathways discussed previously. This clarification of career pathways can also offset salary expenditures by increasing productivity as individual employees try to move up the corporate ladder.[15] As many organizational leaders attempt to cut costs and measure the benefits of all human resource efforts, this benefit alone can help to build a convincing case for succession planning.

Benefit 6: Leads to the Appropriate Promotion and Preselection of People to Meet Organizational Goals

The intended overall benefit of succession planning is to identify, develop, and properly place qualified individuals into key positions to meet present and future strategic needs. A clear and attainable promotion process is a proven workplace motivator.[16] This process can be one direct result of an effective succession planning effort. Promotions can serve a dual role, increasing the ability to properly match organizational needs with qualified talent and providing a means to monitor and reward employees' contributions to the organization.

Organizational leaders have many reasons to promote internally once they have established a formal succession plan. One reason is to retain star performers and show the value of clarified career pathways. Organizational leaders tend to tap into their own internal labor force for key positions—especially when employees undergo specific in-house training for that purpose.[17]

Another important issue is the ability to remove individuals from a succession plan. Employees expected to be key players in the future, based on their competencies, are motivated to sustain their performance and develop themselves for the future. Competency models play a crucial role in identifying the monitored progress of a specific employee. Return on investment from employees can be maximized by avoiding the placement of unqualified or unmotivated employees into positions for which they are not qualified. That is especially important when considering the negative impact an improperly placed person—especially a manager—can have on the people reporting to him or her.

Traditional approaches to succession planning provide some strategies to align an organization with best-practice models. But many organizations suffer from the lack of adequate internal career planning programs simply because, while many organizational leaders make it a practice never to tell people if they are successors or are in the talent pool, the organization's leaders never have a chance to compare their intentions for a person to his or her own career goals. Career planning can be integral to an effective succession planning program. It can provide many benefits directly linked to succession planning. What follows in the next section is an examination of these benefits.

EMPLOYEE NEEDS AND THE BENEFITS OF CAREER PLANNING

Employee development should be given more attention as employee retention becomes increasingly important for many organizations. Career planning, as a field, has evolved from the vocational guidance movement first created with the publication of *Choosing a Vocation* by Frank Parsons in 1909.[18] While rapid technological advancement has affected career planning activities, the basic philosophical precepts of this process have evolved relatively slowly. Many issues influence the individual career planning process, including (but not limited to) the following:

- The individual's educational background
- The individual's physical abilities to perform certain job functions
- The individual's psychological stability and awareness
- The individual's economic situation
- Circumstances that help to shape the individual's career identity[19]

Individual career planning is also affected by an individual's exposure to activities that "enhance a person's career planning or enable that person to make more effective career decisions."[20]

Of course, it is worth emphasizing that career planning is only a subset of life planning. What people choose to do in their careers can be shaped by their life decisions about where they want to live, when they want to marry, how they will partner with a mate or significant other, how many children they wish to have, and other such issues. Career planning is effective only with people who know what they want—and what they do not want—in their lives.

As work-based career planning models have evolved due to technological advancements, the fundamental tenets of career planning theory have become inadequate.[21] Constantly changing work creates the need to refocus on career planning as a tool for retaining and improving the competencies of the present workforce. To be effective, career planning activities need to occur while the employee is engaged in work to ensure that maximum transferability of work-specific knowledge and applications can take place. It is easier for employees to learn and adapt to work functions when they occur in real time, within a natural state, as this necessitates an ability to address change as it occurs.[22]

A relationship clearly exists between career planning and employee development. After all, employee development focuses "on identifying, assuring, and helping evoke new insights through planned learning. It gives individuals opportunities to grow; it gives organizations employees who are capable of working smarter rather than harder because they have a burgeoning storehouse of creativity, experience and knowledge from which to draw as they do their work."[23] In short, employee development—having a broader meaning than training and development—is a tool for building the competencies needed to help people prepare themselves for the future.

Ample evidence exists to suggest that people want those competencies. A 1999 Nierenberg Group study revealed that 86 percent of surveyed workers felt that it was important to obtain career-enhancing work training as a model for self-improvement, while 97 percent felt that having the most current, applicable skills needed to perform their jobs was imperative. When employees take the initiative for career planning activities, they are best able to align their own personal growth and job competencies with the organization's strategic objectives.[24]

Due to the changing nature of workforce demographics, basic education levels, and legislative mandates, workers' expectations of individual, focused, skill set enhancement has come into clear focus.[25] A career planning program provides a treasure trove of benefits, especially when tied to a succession planning program. Three major benefits of a comprehensive career planning system are described below.

Benefit 1: Career Planning Improves Retention

One way to improve employee retention is to offer a comprehensive employee development program. Employees have evolved in their workplace values. Today's employees want training, a clear understanding of the competencies needed in their places of employment, and opportunities for upward mobility. Employers that choose not to offer a career planning program may face higher rates of turnover and dissatisfaction from their workers.

Benefit 2: Career Planning Improves Employee Morale and Job Satisfaction

Organizational employee development initiatives are integral to employee morale and job satisfaction,[26] which illustrates the importance of supporting such activities in the workplace. Managers who have successfully participated in their own professional career planning processes tend to encourage that practice in those they supervise.[27]

Benefit 3: Career Planning Improves the Organization's Bottom Line

A career planning program contributes to the bottom line. Companies with high levels of employee satisfaction and morale have lower turnover than organizations that have lower levels of satisfaction and morale. That, in turn, cuts costs.

High retention rates can have other benefits to an organization. First, the need is reduced to train new employees on basic operations, policies, procedures, and work expectations. It can take up to six months before a company receives a return on the investments in salary for a new hire. Increased retention rates thereby maximize corporate returns on workers. Second, organizations that support employee development see the payoff in that workers are prepared for change, having been developed for it. An organization with a fully supportive leaning culture builds a sustained competitive advantage.

A properly selected, well-trained, and heavily committed workforce makes it easy to build a succession planning program that taps into internal talent. As in any effective initiative, a well-defined action plan is crucial to successful implementation. A half-hearted succession effort has the potential to destroy itself and any career planning program by building worker cynicism. The next section reviews the steps in establishing and maintaining a succession planning program.

THE ORGANIZATIONAL SUCCESSION PLANNING MODEL

An effective organizational succession planning model provides a roadmap for action. An effective succession effort is not a one-shot effort. Instead, it requires long-term commitment across several long-term change efforts that are designed to build a culture that encourages development. See Figure 2.1 for a 10-step succession model created by William J. Rothwell in 2002 that can be used to guide succession planning efforts in any organizational setting. Then read the details about that model below.

Step 1: Clarify the CEO's Expectations

Almost any organizational change effort demands support from the top. But a succession program requires an extraordinary commitment from the CEO to make things happen. It is not enough for the CEO to pay it glib lip service and then delegate this "people program" to the HR department. That is a guaranteed recipe for failure. A succession program is unique in that it demands not just support but participation from the top if it is to be successful. The CEO—and increasingly the board of directors—as well as senior leaders reporting to the CEO must take a hands-on approach to making things happen.

All too often, CEOs agree with the notion of succession planning and its potential benefits, but they do not support it through fiscal, personnel, and procedural practice—let alone drive the daily operations

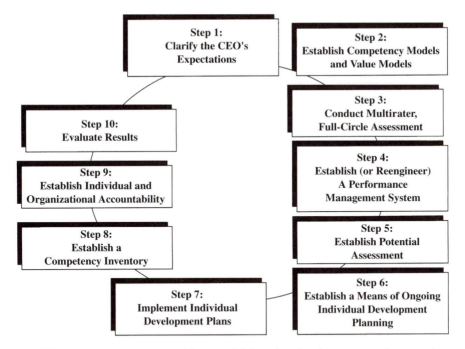

FIGURE 2.1 A step-by-step model to establish and maintain a systematic succession planning program. © copyright 2004 by William J. Rothwell.

of the effort personally. While many organizational leaders are beginning to see the value in succession planning, few are willing to see it through with the commitment it requires. However, increasingly, succession planning is being driven by corporate accountability, global economic issues, and efforts to manage the organization's human resources strategically.[28] Boards of directors are not only guiding corporate policies and procedures but are demanding to see how CEOs are personally involved in succession issues.[29]

Step 2: Establish Competency Models

Competency models are key to succession planning. They provide profiles of ideal performers at present and in the future. In that way, they make it clear what talent needs to be developed at each level. They also provide a way to align what people are selected, and how people are developed, with the organization's strategic objectives. Competency models go further than describing the characteristics of employees and what they need to have to be successful on the job. The models also define how they should be applied within the workplace and work settings.[30]

But competency models are not enough for the simple reason that successful work results are no longer enough. Due attention must also be paid to values and ethics. Corporate leaders are under the gun as never before to articulate what ethical standards they expect, what values they espouse, and then make sure that future leaders at all levels are the kind of people who will get results but will do so only by playing by the rules, complying with laws, and embodying and modeling ethical behavior. The succession planning process must not only focus on realizing strategic objectives but also on ensuring that the people selected and developed are ethical.

Step 3: Conduct Multirater, Full-Circle Assessment

A competency model describes what should be. But it does not indicate how well individuals compare to the model. One way to do that is by conducting a multirater, full-circle assessment, sometimes called a 360-degree assessment. Gathering information on individual potential is essential—and makes it very clear (for example) that success at one level (such as supervisor) does not necessarily guarantee success at higher levels (such as executive) for the simple reason that the competency models for each level are different, reflecting real differences in expectations.

Gathering detailed information about individuals can be time-consuming and expensive. But it is essential to do so. Only by doing so is it possible to pinpoint developmental gaps between an individual's present repertoire of competencies and those necessary for success at higher levels of responsibility (vertical advancement) or broader levels of responsibility (horizontal advancement along a continuum of professional or technical abilities). Those gaps must be identified if individuals are to be developed for the future.[31]

Increasingly, it is insufficient to compare individuals to competency models alone. After all, work performance alone is not enough. Individuals must also demonstrate that they behave in accordance with corporate codes of conduct, are ethical and moral people, and embody the value system that the organization's senior leaders espouse. To do that, it may be necessary to compare individuals not just to the competencies required for success but also to the behaviors, values, ethics, morality, or code of conduct of the organization.

Step 4: Establish (or Reengineer) a Performance Management System

Performance management, while sometimes a term in search of a meaning, should measure how well individuals are acquitting the performance expectations at their level of responsibility. Performance management is thus intended to measure individuals' success at their levels of responsibility. Without measuring success, organizational leaders would not know how well people are doing their present jobs. They might therefore be inclined to break a cardinal rule of succession planning—which is to promote only those who have been successful at their current levels of responsibility. (Nobody wants to promote losers.)

However, performance management systems are fraught with many problems in today's organizations. One problem is that they are not taken seriously, and so everyone is rated high. A second problem is that they do not measure people on the same basis as the competency models established for each level or job category, and it is thus impossible to tell how well people are doing in their current jobs relative to the requirements identified for success at their levels. A third problem is that organizational leaders may not uniformly require performance management forms to be completed at all levels—with the result that executives are exempt when, in fact, they may be exactly the ones whose performance track record is needed most to make informed succession decisions.

Step 5: Establish Potential Assessment

While a performance management system accounts for present performance, it does not compare an individual to requirements at higher levels. While a multirater, full-circle assessment can do so, some means must be established to compare individuals to the requirements at higher levels. There are many ways to achieve this comparison, such as assessment centers, psychological profiles, and other methods that may be used individually or collectively.

Potential assessment also offers individuals a chance to make their wishes known. (Career planning programs can also help with that.) There is no point in identifying successors who do not wish to be considered for higher-level responsibility. Increasingly, employees are opting to stay put so they can enjoy their work–life balance. Without asking individuals what they want to do in the future—which is an important role of a career planning program—organizational leaders may make costly, foolish mistakes by assuming all people will accept promotions when, in fact, some may have no interest whatsoever in doing so.

Step 6: Establish a Means of Ongoing Individual Developmental Planning

Effectively implementing the succession planning model should reveal two individual gaps. One gap may exist between present performance and present expectations. These are managed during the performance management process. Only after problems with present job performance have been addressed should the second, and future, developmental gap between future potential and present performance be addressed.

Narrowing the developmental gap requires an action plan. Individual development plans (IDPs), sometimes called individual learning plans, provide that action plan. IDPs should identify what developmental activities should be undertaken to help an individual prepare for the future. IDPs should clearly identify what the individual should do, how the individual should do it, how success will be measured, and when the efforts are to be measured and completed. IDPs may also necessitate an honest dialogue between individuals and their immediate supervisors (or others, such as mentors) about individual career goals and interests.

Step 7: Implement Individual Development Plans

It is important to clarify what is required to implement an IDP. When asked to think of developmental efforts, many managers think first of "shipping the person off to a training program or an executive development experience." But the reality is that 90 percent of all development occurs on the job and in the work setting. If a person is to learn budgeting skills, the best thing to do is to make him or her accountable for doing the department's budget and then coach the person through the effort. If a person is to learn about the company, then shipping him or her on long-term rotations or short-term task force assignments is more likely to achieve that objective than sending them off to a training program somewhere else. In short, a staggering number of ways exist to develop people right where they are. It simply requires managers to experience a paradigm shift in their thinking about where development happens and how it is carried out. Development is interwoven with doing work.

Step 8: Establish a Competency Inventory

Many organizational leaders closely monitor production levels to maximize revenue. Most production goals involve providing enough goods to meet demand while minimizing excess inventory. Human capital inventory is quite similar. The formulation of a competency inventory provides decision makers with real-time competency data on their current workforce. Ideally, this system is tied to technological support.

To spell this out more clearly, how do the organization's leaders scramble talent when they need it in a crisis? How do they know where their in-house experts can be found beyond personal awareness and familiarity with some people in the organization? The point here is that it is increasingly important to know where the in-house experts can be found. If the problem is a production problem on the floor of a plant, then how do the organization's leaders find the most skilled person to address the problem? While that may be a simplistic example, the point is that organizational leaders—particularly in large organizations—do not know where the talent is for the simple reason that they cannot know everybody in the organization. To find talent, they must devise ways of inventorying it and cataloging it. Their efforts must go beyond simplistic, old-style skill inventories that track individuals by their education, job titles, self-professed foreign language fluency, and other superficial criteria. Instead, an inventory must be established around what competencies employees have actually demonstrated in the organization and must be described in language that it is unique to the organization's work processes, culture, and industry-related issues.

Human capital is worthless if you cannot find the right people in your organization when you need them. A competency inventory makes it possible to do that. This may be a major challenge of the future, since building talent is one thing but finding it on demand when needed is quite another.

Step 9: Establish Individual and Organizational Accountability

Both succession planning and career planning efforts require support from individuals, their immediate supervisors, and senior leaders. Support in this context also means accountability. While planning an IDP may be a simple thing, implementing it may not be. The temptation always exists to focus completely on meeting present work expectations and putting off future development for "free time." Of course, that free time never comes—and people are therefore never developed.

If there is one Achilles heel of all succession planning efforts, it centers on accountability (or the lack of it). Think of it this way: what happens if an individual's IDP is not implemented over a year's time? Are there consequences to individuals, their immediate superiors, and even to senior leaders? In short, what happens when developmental objectives are not met for individuals—or even for whole departments or divisions? How are people held accountable for that?

If the answer is that they are not held accountable—as is, unfortunately, too often the case—then the succession planning program will surely fail. Alternatively, if people are rewarded for achieving their developmental objectives, punished for not doing so, and their immediate supervisors are similarly rewarded or punished for achieving measurable developmental objectives for those reporting to them, then the succession planning program is more likely to be successful. Of course, not all organization leaders are comfortable with rewarding or punishing people. As a result, alternatives may have to be explored, such as holding senior-level meetings in which developmental issues are discussed. Since few senior leaders want to go in front of their peers and report that they did nothing, communicating about development may be one way to hold people accountable for results.

Similarly, individuals can also reward or punish themselves for achieving—or failing to achieve—their own personal career goals and objectives. Developmental objectives may be part of those goals. Not all reward systems must be based on explicit rewards. It is possible to have implicit ones as well, and it is for that reason that workers with the best performance and highest potential are sometimes the toughest when grading themselves. After all, their own standards for themselves may be far higher than what their bosses expect.

Step 10: Evaluate Results

Of course, it is vital to regularly assess the impact of any effort. Evaluating a succession effort allows key stakeholders to make informed decisions about it, and that (in turn) can lead to continuous improvement. Succession programs can, of course, be evaluated in financial terms. Was money saved on external executive searches, for instance? Succession programs can also be evaluated in nonfinancial terms. Were people available in-house, for example, to meet expected or unexpected vacancies as they occurred, and was the time-to-fill metric (how long it takes to find a qualified applicant) reduced through the introduction of the succession program? Was turnover of all employees—or was turnover of high potentials—reduced after the succession program was introduced? Answering these questions may provide valuable information about how well the succession planning program is working, what enhancements might need to be made to it, and how well it is meeting the needs it was intended to meet.

THE CAREER PLANNING MODEL IN RELATION TO THE ORGANIZATION, THE INDIVIDUAL, AND SOCIETY

Medical doctors refer to the side effects of medicine—meaning that a drug intended to cure one illness may impact the user's health in other, usually unpleasant, ways. Career planning programs can also have side effects, though not all are negative. Career planning that influences the individual, the work group, or organization creates by-products that impact other facets of life. The trend is for career development professionals to adopt a holistic approach when helping individuals and organizations meet career planning goals. Figure 2.2 illustrates this concept

Career Development of the Individual Worker	Organizational Career Development	Societal Context of Career Development
1. Individual Self-Assessment	1. Initiate Strategic Corporate Objectives	1. Capitalize on Employee Talent and Civic Responsibility
2. Personal Perspective Interpretation	2. Evaluate Current Workforce	
		2. External Resource/Skill Development Outreach
3. Workplace Environmental Scanning	3. Construct Plan of Action	
4. Current and Future Workplace Opportunities	4. Execute Plan of Action	3. Community/Corporate Partnerships
5. Goal Planning and Achievement	5. Examine, Appraise, and Reengineer	

FIGURE 2.2   Individual, organizational, and societal career systems. *Source*: Knight, S. C. (2004). *Individual, organizational, and societal career systems.* Unpublished manuscript. University Park, PA: Penn State University.

and shows how career planning can affect individuals, organizations, and society. Each component of this model deserves some attention. It is worth noting that, while this model is depicted in a step-by-step (and therefore linear) fashion, the reality is that the process is cyclical as business needs and strategic objectives of organizations change and as individuals change.

Career Planning for Individuals

Career planning for individuals has traditionally been the key focus since the early twentieth century. The model shown in Figure 2.2 explains the process by which an individual addresses career planning issues by first presenting the concept of *individual self-assessment.*

Unfortunately, many individuals do not know exactly "where they are going" in their careers. They tend to select career pathways arbitrarily, hoping to experience positive outcomes. One way to deal with this problem is to adopt a proactive approach by starting with a formal self-assessment of individual skills. Often, this approach could be as simple as completing an interest inventory—or sitting down with a career counselor, mentor, immediate supervisor, or a representative from HR to discuss career interests and potential fits with those existing in the organization. Many other technology-based resources exist to help in this quest for career meaning and are discussed in chapter 6. Regardless of the approach, it is an important step to identify an individual's interests and desires as they relate to work and fit within the confines of situations with family, financial constraints, and individual motivation. These holistic factors play major roles in the second step of the individual career planning process, which addresses *personal perspective and interpretation*.

Individuals are continually trying to interpret how their actions and the subsequent results of those actions will affect them. It is quite common at the outset of the career planning process for individuals to pose such questions as: "How is this [where *this* can mean almost anything happening] going to affect me, my family, or life in general?" Once individuals take responsibility for managing their own career planning activities, they can perform a *workplace environmental scanning process* to evaluate the current state of their organization compared to its mission, corporate goals, strategic methodologies, and policies.

After individuals have addressed what they can or want to do, and understand how it is likely to affect them in their lives, they can scan the workplace to gain a better understanding of how their goals align with those of the organization. To make a successful individual career and succession plan, the abilities and desires of employees must align with the overall functioning of the organization's mission, corporate goals, strategic methodologies, and policies. Individuals must honestly evaluate their own ethics and professional intentions and then compare and contrast them with the organization's approach to business. Additionally, the employee should personally evaluate the strengths and weaknesses of the organizational culture, management of HR functions, the effectiveness of internal communication processes, and how financial issues affect the direction of the organization. Of course, this is not an all-or-nothing proposition. In most cases, differences do exist between individual beliefs and organizational activities. Employees need to understand that, as long as they can be comfortable with the corporate direction, then they have a good reason to maintain their relationship with the organization.

Once individuals have completed the first three steps of this process, they can then begin to assess *present and future workplace opportunities*. The workplace environmental scanning process gives employees a sense of what is currently available as well as what future prospects may surface. When individuals assess opportunities in the workplace that match their interests and developmental goals, an action plan should take shape. That action plan is crucial in driving development, since it requires a description of present career pathways and identified skill gaps (as described in the self-assessment step of the model). Once the preliminary plan is in place, the employee, with the support of the organization, can officially set into motion a *goal planning and achievement process.*

Goal planning and achievement is the point at which employees affect a tangible transformation. In this phase of the process, individuals may participate in developmental experiences such as online courses, internal training programs, or mentoring programs. Individuals who are in the goal planning and achievement phase must understand that there is an ebb and flow to setting professional goals and actually achieving them. Both employer and employee must realize that this is a factor in the individual career planning process and that accountability should be adjusted accordingly. It is important to note that these plans should be discussed and tracked on a regular basis to ensure reasonable progress.

Organizational Career Planning

Individuals must be active participants in monitoring and advancing their professional career plans. This does not, however, alleviate the responsibility of organizational leaders to be fiscally and culturally (organizationally) supportive of employee development. In fact, organizational leaders play a key role in the success or failure of individual goal achievement. The first phase of the organizational career planning model includes *initiating strategic corporate objectives.*

Many organizational leaders spend much time drafting and redrafting corporate objectives to achieve or maintain a competitive advantage. Unsuccessful business leaders tend to create corporate objectives but then fail to implement them, while successful organizational leaders create, implement, and continuously reevaluate where they need to be headed to stay competitive. Initiating objectives is incredibly important in career planning systems because it provides employees with a clear understanding of where the company is going and what they can do to help it succeed. A company that fails to clarify its objectives creates confusion, and it may prohibit individuals from completing phases 3–5 of the individual career planning process, rendering career planning efforts useless.

Step 2 of the organization career planning process is *evaluation of the current workforce* to identify viable candidates for required positions. This phase is crucial in the early stages of implementing a succession plan (as noted in Step 3 of the succession planning model). To complete the evaluation process, organizational leaders typically use competency models and then compare them with individuals' competencies. When the results of all the individual efforts are completed, organizational leaders then possess a comprehensive labor force assessment for use in succession planning. It also facilitates communication with the HR department for effective counseling during the self-assessment phase of an individual career assessment program.

As individuals are expected to create a plan of action and advance toward completing their goals, organizational leaders must also *construct and execute an action plan.* An organization must finalize and implement its mission as it relates to employees and their individual development plans. An effective employer must be a facilitator, assisting individuals with planning and achieving their professional objectives, as well as locating and cultivating internal talent to meet strategic objectives. In the construction plan phase of the organizational career planning effort, employers have the ability—and perhaps the responsibility—to make appropriate matches between competency models and potential candidates. Once such matches have been identified, the employer can leverage the arrangement into action with a succession plan that meets the organization's objectives and is aligned with individuals' professional growth expectations.

It is important to be able to *examine, appraise, and reengineer* the career planning process as needed, a concept that is not new to successful companies. Maintaining an effective and efficient career planning process requires continuous improvement. This phase of the organizational career planning process has a direct impact on building bench strength and realizing corporate strategic objectives. Thus, it renews the career planning process as new strategic objectives are formulated and pursued.

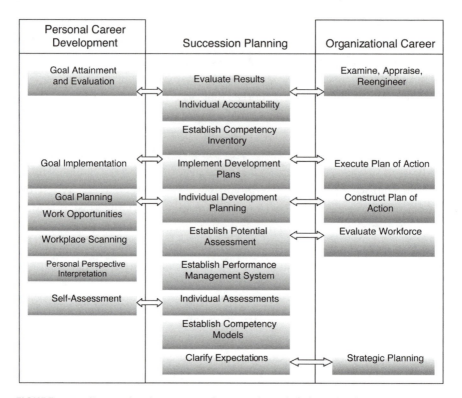

FIGURE 2.3 Career development and succession planning: An integrated model. *Source:* Knight, S. C. (2004). Unpublished manuscript. University Park, PA: Penn State University.

The Societal Context of Career Planning

Societal benefits can result from the effective interaction of individual development and business development. From a societal perspective, communities are developed because they can *capitalize on employee talent and civic responsibility*. The successful integration of career planning within an organization creates employees who are increasing their knowledge and skills. The evolution of skill sets and subsequent talent contributions will yield better overall fiscal performance for the company. This can be beneficial to the communities in which the organization has its operations, since it increases the number of highly trained people available for community leadership outside the workplace. It thus builds social capital. Most communities depend on

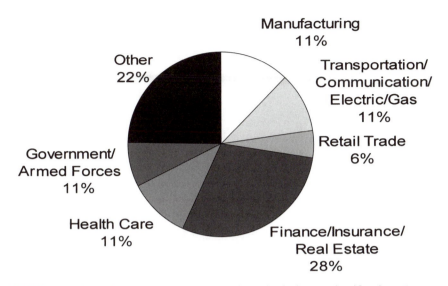

FIGURE 2.4 Distribution of survey respondents by industry classification. *Source*: Rothwell, W., & Wang, W. (2004). *A survey of ISPI members on integrating career planning and succession planning*. Unpublished survey report. University Park, PA: Pennsylvania State University.

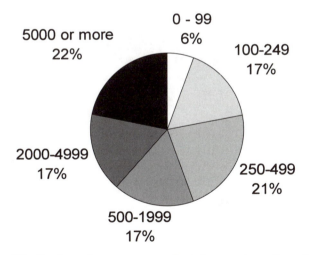

FIGURE 2.5 Distribution of survey respondents by number of employees in the respondents' organizations. *Source*: Rothwell, W., & Wang, W. (2004). *A survey of ISPI members on integrating career planning and succession planning*. Unpublished survey report. University Park, PA: Pennsylvania State University.

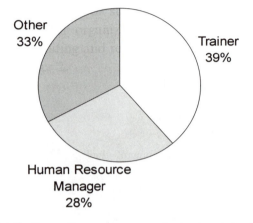

Other
33%

Trainer
39%

Human Resource
Manager
28%

FIGURE 2.6 Distribution of survey respondents by job function. *Source*: Rothwell, W., & Wang, W. (2004). *A survey of ISPI members on integrating career planning and succession planning*. Unpublished survey report. University Park, PA: Pennsylvania State University.

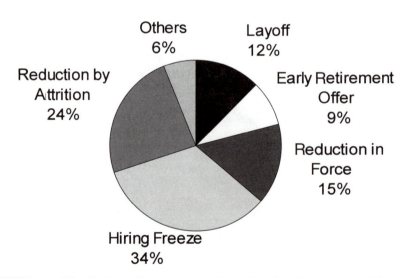

Others
6%

Layoff
12%

Reduction by
Attrition
24%

Early Retirement
Offer
9%

Reduction in
Force
15%

Hiring Freeze
34%

FIGURE 2.7 Distribution of survey respondents based on how many of the organizations have recently experienced some form of large-scale change. *Source*: Rothwell, W., & Wang, W. (2004). *A survey of ISPI members on integrating career planning and succession planning*. Unpublished survey report. University Park, PA: Pennsylvania State University.

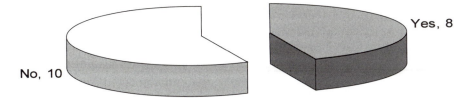

FIGURE 2.8 Distribution of survey respondents based on whether their organizations presently operate both career planning and succession planning programs. *Source*: Rothwell, W., & Wang, W. (2004). *A survey of ISPI members on integrating career planning and succession planning.* Unpublished survey report. University Park, PA: Pennsylvania State University.

volunteers; a more educated populace will provide more value to its population.

A company that is fiscally solvent provides opportunities for expansion of operations, increasing the employment opportunities available to the community and an expanding tax base to support local municipalities. A highly trained workforce (or one that needs further education) also has the potential to create a substantial impact on society through *external resource skill development outreach* and *community and corporate partnerships.*

From an organization's standpoint, seeking outside solutions and training for internal employees creates some synergistic opportunities. Companies that request outside educational training often form sizable, lasting partnerships with community colleges, universities, and technical schools. These partnerships generate substantial financial resources for educational institutions and provide opportunities for synergistic research between businesses and educational institutions. This benefit can go both ways: it is not uncommon for corporate authorities to go into the classrooms of their local schools and colleges to serve as subject matter experts on specific content areas. This interaction builds a partnership for the growth of society and the company, making them bilateral and mutually beneficial. This is a common method of establishing the third phase, community and corporate partnerships, which tends to evolve after some formalized interaction between the community and the organization.

TABLE 2.2   Frequency Distribution of Sample Demographic Data (n = 18)

		Frequency	
Variable		Regular	Relative (%)
Organization industry	Manufacturing	2	11.11
	Transportation/communication/ electric/gas	2	11.11
	Retail trade	1	5.56
	Finance/insurance/real estate	5	27.78
	Health care	2	11.11
	Government/armed forces	2	11.11
	Other	4	22.22
	Total	18	100.00
Organization size	0–99	1	5.56
	100–249	3	16.67
	250–499	4	22.22
	500–1999	3	16.67
	2000–4999	3	16.67
	5000 or more	4	22.22
	Total	18	100.00
Job function	Trainer	7	38.89
	Human Resource Manager	5	27.78
	Other	6	33.33
	Total	18	100.00
Recently experienced organization change	A layoff	4	12.12
	An early retirement offer	3	9.09
	A reduction in force	5	15.15
	A hiring freeze	11	33.33
	Reduction by attrition	8	24.24
	Others	2	6.06
	Total	33	100.00
Presently operate both career planning and succession planning	Yes	8	44.44
	No	10	55.56
	Total	18	100.00

Source: Rothwell, W., & Wang, W. (2004). *A survey of ISPI members on integrating career planning and succession planning.* Unpublished survey report. University Park, PA: The Pennsylvania State University.

THE NEED TO INTEGRATE SUCCESSION PLANNING AND CAREER PLANNING

Quite simply, organizations must maintain a competitive advantage over other businesses to be successful. To do that as efficiently

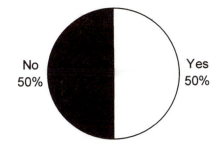

FIGURE 2.9 Whether career planning has become more important to an organization over the last few years. *Source*: Rothwell, W., & Wang, W. (2004). *A survey of ISPI members on integrating career planning and succession planning*. Unpublished survey report. University Park, PA: Pennsylvania State University.

Reasons for Yes answers:

- Anticipated high retirement rate; response to litigation
- Retention, replacement
- War for technology talents
- Realization that senior most officials in the organization did not always get necessary experiences by choice

Reasons for No answers:

- Ongoing tool for promotion and retention
- Anticipated high retirement rate
- Response to litigation
- Procedural system of advancement in place
- Favor less movement

and effectively as possible, companies need to maintain a well-trained and flexible employee base, accurately assess future competency needs compared to the talent on hand, minimize retention problems, and provide clear avenues for employee growth. Decision makers that can understand what talent their organization has on hand, provide strategic direction, and maximize their assets will come out as clear leaders within their respective industrial sectors. To do this, companies must formally support a system that internally develops employees to meet present and future succession needs.

Figure 2.3 visually delineates the relationships among individual, organizational, and career planning and succession planning processes.

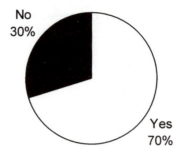

FIGURE 2.10 Whether succession planning has become more important to an organization over the last few years. *Source*: Rothwell, W., & Wang, W. (2004). *A survey of ISPI members on integrating career planning and succession planning.* Unpublished survey report. University Park, PA: Pennsylvania State University.

Reasons for Yes answers:

- Anticipated high retirement rate
- Changing business needs
- Response to litigation
- A large percentage of senior leaders will retire in the next 5 years
- Mergers force selection
- Realization of need to identify potential candidate for senior positions and ensure they get needed experience and development
- There have been many layoffs
  there's a need to identify top leaders

Reasons for No answers:

- Procedural system of advancement in place

While career planning and succession planning programs can stand on their own, integrating them offers valuable benefits. Although there are many ways to implement these efforts, organizational leaders often gravitate to the most successful component first. That sets a precedent for success and builds momentum for change.

THE RESULTS OF A SURVEY ON INTEGRATING CAREER PLANNING AND SUCCESSION PLANNING PROGRAMS

In early 2004, the authors of this book prepared and mailed out a survey to 500 members of the International Society for Performance

TABLE 2.3   Reasons and Importance of Sponsoring a Career or Succession Planning Program

Reasons for Sponsoring a Career Planning Program or a Succession Planning Program	Importance for Career Program *Mean* *(SD)*	Importance for Succession Program *Mean* *(SD)*
A Contribute to implementing the organization's strategic business plans	4.00 (0.75)	4.14 (0.69)
B Cope with effects of downsizing	2.88 (1.36)	1.00 (0.00)
C Cope with the effects of voluntary separation programs	2.33 (1.51)	2.00 (1.73)
D Help individuals realize their career plans within the organization	4.00 (1.31)	3.60 (1.52)
E Improve employee morale	3.71 (1.11)	3.00 (1.00)
F Improve employees' ability to respond to changing environmental demands	3.80 (0.45)	3.67 (0.58)
G Reduce Headcount to essential workers only	2.00 (1.00)	1.00 (0.00)
H Increase the talent pool of promotable employees	4.50 (0.55)	4.43 (0.53)
I Identify "replacement needs" as a means of targeting necessary employee	3.80 (0.84)	3.80 (0.84)
J Decide what workers can be terminated without damage to the organization	1.75 (0.96)	1.75 (0.96)
K Encourage the advancement of diverse groups in future jobs within the organization	4.40 (0.89)	4.33 (0.82)
L Provide increased opportunities for high-potential workers	4.50 (0.58)	4.57 (0.53)
M Tap the potential for intellectual capital in the organization	3.60 (0.89)	3.60 (0.89)

Source: Rothwell, W., & Wang, W. (2004). *A survey of ISPI members on integrating career planning and succession planning.* Unpublished survey report. University Park, PA: Pennsylvania State University.

Improvement (ISPI).* The purpose of the survey was to explore how selected organizations are integrating career planning and succession

---

* The authors acknowledge the leadership of Wei Aleisha Wang in overseeing the survey process.

TABLE 2.4 How Long Respondents' Organizations Have Operated a Career or Succession Planning Program

	Career Program Frequency		Succession Program Frequency	
	Regular	Relative (%)	Regular	Relative (%)
Less than 1 year	0	0.00	0	0.00
More than 1 but less than 2	2	25.00	4	50.00
More than 2 but less than 3	1	12.50	1	12.50
More than 3 but less than 4	1	12.50	0	0.00
More than 4 but less than 5	1	12.50	1	12.50
More than 5 years	3	37.50	2	25.00
Total	8	100.00	8	100.00

Source: Rothwell, W., & Wang, W. (2004). *A survey of ISPI members on integrating career planning and succession planning.* Unpublished survey report. University Park, PA: Pennsylvania State University.

planning programs. Figure 2.4 summarizes the distribution of respondents by industry classification; Figure 2.5 summarizes the distribution of respondents by number of employees working in the respondents' organizations; Figure 2.6 depicts the distribution of respondents by job function; Figure 2.7 depicts the distribution of respondents based on how many of the respondents' organizations have recently experienced some form of large-scale change; and Figure 2.8 depicts the distribution of respondents by whether their organizations presently operate both career planning and succession planning programs. Table 2.2 summarizes the data presented in the figures.

Respondents to the survey answered many questions about the career planning or succession planning programs in their organizations. In Figure 2.9, respondents indicated whether career planning has become a more important issue to their organizations over the last few years. In Figure 2.10, respondents indicated whether succession planning had become more important to their organizations over the last few years. Table 2.3 summarizes the reasons and perceived importance of the organization's career planning and succession planning programs.

Table 2.4 lists how long the respondents' organizations have offered career programs or succession programs. Table 2.5 summarizes what the survey respondents perceive to be the most effective characteristics of

TABLE 2.5 The Most Effective Characteristics of Successful Career and/or Succession Planning Programs

| | Does Organization Have This Characteristic? | | | | | |
| | Career Planning | | Succession Planning | | Importance | |
Characteristics	Yes (%)	No (%)	Yes (%)	No (%)	Mean	SD
A Tied the program to the organizational strategic plans?	50	50	63	38	4.38	0.52
B Tied the program to individual career plans?	100	0	75	25	4.50	0.53
C Tied the program to training programs?	88	13	75	25	4.13	0.83
D Prepared a written purpose statement?	75	25	63	38	3.25	1.28
E Prepared written program goals to indicate what results the program should achieve?	50	50	50	50	3.50	1.20
F Established measurable objectives for program operation?	25	75	50	50	3.75	0.46
G Identified what groups are to be served by the program, in priority order?	50	50	75	25	3.25	1.49
H Established a written policy statement to guide the program?	50	50	50	50	3.88	0.64
I Articulated a written philosophy about the program?	75	25	50	50	3.88	0.83
J Established a program action plan?	38	63	75	25	4.13	0.64
K Established a schedule of program events based on the action plan?	63	38	63	38	3.63	0.74
L Fixed responsibility for organizational oversight of the program?	63	38	63	38	4.75	0.46

TABLE 2.5 *(Continued)*

| | Does Organization Have This Characteristic? | | | | | |
| Characteristics | Career Planning | | Succession Planning | | Importance | |
	Yes (%)	No (%)	Yes (%)	No (%)	Mean	SD
M Fixed responsibility of each participant in the program?	63	38	75	25	4.25	0.46
N Established incentives/rewards for identified successors in the program?	25	75	25	75	2.75	1.04
O Established incentives/rewards for managers with identified successors?	13	88	38	63	2.50	1.20
P Developed a means to budget for a succession planning program?	63	38	75	25	3.38	1.19
Q Devised means to keep records for individuals who are designated as successors?	50	50	75	25	3.63	1.51
R Created workshops to train management employees about the program?	75	25	75	25	4.13	0.64
S Created workshops to train individuals about career planning?	63	38	50	50	4.38	0.74
T Established a means to clarify present position responsibilities?	63	38	63	38	3.88	0.99
U Established a means to clarify future position responsibilities?	50	50	63	38	4.00	0.93
V Established a means to appraise individual performance?	88	13	100	0	4.63	0.52
W Established a means to compare individual skills to the requirements of a future position?	50	50	75	25	4.50	0.53

TABLE 2.5 *(Continued)*

| | | Does Organization Have This Characteristic? | | | | | |
| | | Career Planning | | Succession Planning | | Importance | |
Characteristics		Yes (%)	No (%)	Yes (%)	No (%)	Mean	*SD*
X	Established a way to review organizational talent at least annually?	75	25	88	13	4.75	0.46
Y	Established a way to forecast future talent needs?	50	50	88	13	4.38	0.74
Z	Established a way to plan for meeting succession planning needs through individual development plans?	50	50	75	25	4.13	0.64
AA	Established a means to track development activities to prepare successors for eventual advancement?	63	38	88	13	4.00	0.53
BB	Established a means to evaluate the results of the program?	50	50	63	38	4.63	0.52

Source: Rothwell, W., and Wang, W. (2004). *A survey of ISPI members on integrating career planning and succession planning.* Unpublished survey report. University Park, PA: The Pennsylvania State University.

career planning and succession planning programs. Table 2.6 summarizes possible methods that, according to survey respondents, may be used to "groom" (develop) individuals. The same table also indicates whether the respondents' organizations are using each method and how effective the survey respondents perceive each method to be. Table 2.7 summarizes the chief benefits and chief difficulties of career planning and succession planning programs as perceived by the survey respondents. Table 2.8 explains why organizations that do not sponsor career planning or succession planning programs have chosen not to do so, and this question was answered only by respondents in organizations that do not

TABLE 2.6 Methods to Groom (Develop) Individuals

Column 1	Column 2		Column 3				
Possible Methods by Which to Groom Individuals	Is Your Organization Using This Method to Develop People?		How Effective Do You Feel This Method Is for Developing People to Assume Future Job Responsibilities?				
			Not at All Effective				Very Effective
	Yes (%)	No (%)	1	2	*Mean*	3 4 5	*SD*
A Off-the-job degree programs sponsored by colleges/ universities	75.00	25.00			3.63		0.92
B On-site degree programs colleges/universities	50.00	50.00			3.13		1.25
C Off-the-job sponsored by vendors	75.00	25.00			3.38		0.52
D Off-the-job public seminars sponsored by universities	62.50	37.50			3.25		0.89

E	In-house classroom courses tailor-made for management-level employees	100.00	0.00	4.25	0.71
F	In-house classroom courses purchased from outside sources and modified for in-house use	100.00	0.00	3.75	0.46
G	Unplanned on-the-job training	100.00	0.00	3.63	0.74
H	Planned on-the-job training	87.50	12.50	4.29	0.49
I	Unplanned mentoring programs	62.50	37.50	3.25	1.16
J	Planned mentoring programs	87.50	12.50	3.63	0.92
K	Unplanned job rotation programs	37.50	62.50	3.00	0.76
L	Planned job rotation programs	62.50	37.50	3.71	1.25

Source: Rothwell, W., & Wang, W. (2004). *A survey of ISPI members on integrating career planning and succession planning.* Unpublished survey report. University Park, PA: Pennsylvania State University.

TABLE 2.7 The Chief Benefits and Difficulties That an Organization Has Experienced from Career and Succession Planning Programs

What are the chief benefits that your organization has experienced from a career planning program?
- Motivation
- Better use of T&D
- Increased understanding in workforce of what is needed to achieve goals
- Colleagues have ability to plan careers
- Open communication with management
- Ability to promote from within
- Helps individuals understand their potential
- Provides focus for employee development
- Enhances recruiting, processes, personnel management
- Retain top talent
- Too soon to tell

What are the chief benefits that your organization has experienced from a succession planning program?
- Better decision and fairer decision when naming new leaders
- More exclusionary
- Replace critical roles, develop talent for specific roles
- Better morale
- Improve management accountability for talent management/retention
- More confidence that candidate will be ready to assume biggest jobs
- Showing strong interest in top performance

What are the chief difficulties that your organization has experienced with a career planning program?
- Variation in application and process
- Colleague participation and time constraints
- Fractured among different business units/solos. Data is not shared across entire organization.
- Lack of oversight and formalization
- Mistrust by organization members who think they've seen this before

What are the chief difficulties that your organization has experienced with a succession planning program?
- Time for follow-up
- Jack of truly qualified candidate
- Don't hold to standards set for succession over time
- Fractured among different business units/solos. Data is not shared across entire organization. Often not seen as priority until crisis (like a merger)
- Lack of adequate career planning or post resolved in too small pool from which to draw successors
- Great job planning, but not strong on implementation

Source: Rothwell, W., and Wang, W. (2004). *A survey of ISPI members on integrating career planning and succession planning.* Unpublished survey report. University Park, PA: The Pennsylvania State University.*The responses are given verbatim from the survey.*

TABLE 2.8   The Chief Reason That an Organization Has Chosen Not to Sponsor a Career or Succession Planning Program

Chief Reasons	Regular Frequency	Relative Frequency (%)
We never thought about it	1	10
We don't know how to design one	1	10
We don't know how to implement one	1	10
We don't have enough staff/funds to do it right	5	50
We believe unplanned methods work best	1	10
We rely on so many temporary workers and consultants that career planning or succession planning is really not important	1	10
Total	10	100

Source: Rothwell, W., & Wang, W. (2004). *A survey of ISPI members on integrating career planning and succession planning.* Unpublished survey report. University Park, PA: Pennsylvania State University.

sponsor a career planning or succession planning program. Finally, Table 2.9 summarizes respondents' answers to the survey question: How are decisions made about career paths and successors for positions in your organization? Again, respondents answering that question worked in organizations not having either a career planning or succession planning program.

The test of any research study is always the answer to the simple question "So what?" This study is no different. While the response rate on this survey was disappointingly low, it did shed light on present efforts by some organizations to manage and integrate career planning and succession planning programs. Among the key findings, it is fair to say that:

- The most important reasons for organizations to sponsor career programs are to increase the talent pool of promotable employees, provide increased opportunities for high-potential workers, and encourage the advancement of diverse groups in future jobs within the organization.
- The most important reason for sponsoring succession plans is to achieve the same goals as career programs—that is, increase the talent pool of promotable employees, provide increased oppor-

TABLE 2.9 **How Decisions Are Made About Career Paths and Successors for Positions**

The Methods	Regular Frequency	Relative Frequency(%)
We usually wait until positions are vacant and then scurry around madly to find successors	3	30
We secretly prepare successors	1	10
Whenever a position opens up, we rely on expediency to identify someone to fill it, hoping for the best	6	60
Total	10	100

Source: Rothwell, W., & Wang, W. (2004). *A survey of ISPI members on integrating career planning and succession planning*. Unpublished survey report. University Park, PA: Pennsylvania State University.

tunities for high-potential workers, and encourage the advancement of diverse groups in future jobs within the organization.

- The most important characteristics of successful career and succession planning programs are: fixed responsibility for organizational oversight of the program; a way to review organizational talent at least annually; a means to appraise individual performance; and a means to evaluate program results.
- Survey respondents reflected a bias for using in-house classroom courses as a means to groom individuals but almost equally rate planned on-the-job training.
- "We don't have enough staff/funds to do it right" is the most common reason cited for not sponsoring a career planning or succession planning program by those respondents whose organizations do not have such programs.
- Most survey respondents in organizations not having career or succession planning programs agreed with the statement that "whenever a position opens up, we rely on expediency to identify someone to fill it, hoping for the best." Significantly, the next most common answer was that "we usually wait until positions are vacant and then scurry around madly to find successors."

NOTES

1. Guinn, S. L. (2000). Succession planning without job titles. *Career Development International, 5,* 390.

2. Johnson, J. E., Costa, L. L., Marshall, S. B., Moran, M. J., & Henderson, C. S. (1994). Succession planning: A model for developing nursing leaders. *Nursing Management, 25,* 50–55.

3. Walker, J. W. (1998). Perspectives: Do we need succession planning anymore? *Human Resource Planning, 21,* 9–11.

4. Huang, T.-C. (2001). Succession planning systems and human resource outcomes. *International Journal of Manpower, 22,* 1.

5. Institute of Management and Administration. (2001). What are the biggest threats to employee retention? *Human Resource Department Management Report 9,* 1.

6. Shah, A., Sterrett, C., Chesser, J., & Wilmore, J. (2001). Meeting the need for employee development in the 21st century. *S.A.M. Advanced Management Journal, 66,* 22–28.

7. Rothwell, W. J. (2000). *Effective succession planning: Ensuring leadership continuity and building talent from within.* New York: AMACOM.

8. Getty, C. (1993). Planning successfully for succession planning. *Training and Development, 47,* 31–33.

9. Guinn, S. L. (2000). Succession planning without job titles. *Career Development International 5,* 390–393.

10. Cashman, K. (2001). Succession leadership: Is your organization prepared? *Strategy and Leadership, 29,* 1.

11. Dubois, D. (1993). *Competency-based performance improvement: A strategy for organizational change.* Amherst, MA: HRD Press, 9.

12. Rothwell, W. J. (2002). Succession planning for future success. *Strategic HR Review, 1,* 30–33.

13. Rothwell, W. (2003). Go beyond replacing executives and manage your work and values. In D. Ulrich, L. Carter, M. Goldsmith, J. Bolt, & N. Smallwood (Eds.), *The change champions fieldguide* (pp. 192–204). Waltham, MA: Best Practice Publications.

14. Huang, T.-C. (2001). Succession planning systems and human resource outcomes. *International Journal of Manpower, 22,* 1.

15. Gutteridge, T. G., Leibowitz, Z. B., & Score, J. E. (1993). *Organizational career development: Benchmarks for building a world-class workforce.* San Francisco: Jossey-Bass.

16. Sahl, R. J. (1992). Succession planning drives plant turnaround. *Personnel Management, 71,* 67–70.

17. Walker, J. W. (1998). Perspectives: Do we need succession planning any more? *Human Resource Planning, 21,* 9–11.

18. Parsons, F. (1909). *Choosing a vocation*. Boston: Houghton Mifflin.

19. Phillips, D. J., & Sorenson, J. B. (2003). Competitive position and promotion rates: Commercial television station top management, 1953–1998. *Social Forces, 81,* 819–841.

20. Baron, J. N., Davis-Blake, A., & Bielby, W. T. (1986). The structure of opportunity: How promotion ladders vary within and among organizations. *Administrative Science Quarterly, 31,* 248–273.

21. Doeringer, P. B., & Piore, M. J. (1971). *Internal labor markets and manpower analysis*. Lexinton, MA: D.C. Heath.

22. Pfeffer, J., & Cohen, Y. (1984). Determinants of internal labor markets in organizations. *Administrative Science Organizations, 29,* 550–572.

23. Parsons, F. (1909). *Choosing a vocation*. Boston: Houghton Mifflin.

24. Sears, S. (1982). A definition of career guidance terms: A national vocational guidance perspective. *Vocational Guidance Quarterly, 31,* 137–143.

25. Spokane, A. R. (1991). *Career intervention*. Englewood Cliffs, NJ: Prentice Hall, 22.

26. Liptak, J. J. (2000). *Treatment planning in career counseling*. Pacific Grove, CA: Brooks/Cole.

27. Seibert, K. W., Hall, D. T., & Kram, K. E. (1995). Strengthening the weak link in strategic executive development: Integrating individual development and global business strategy. *Human Resource Management, 34,* 549–567.

28. Rothwell, W. J., & Sredl, H. J. (2000). *The ASTD reference guide to workplace learning and performance* (3rd ed.). Amherst: HRD Press, 400.

29. Shah, A., Sterrett, C., Chesser, J., & Wilmore, J. (2001). Meeting the need for employee development in the 21st century. *S.A.M. Advanced Management Journal, 66,* 22–28.

30. Dubois, D., & Rothwell, W. J. (2004). Competency based or a traditional approach to training? *Training and Development, 4,* 46-57.

31. Jackson, T., & Vitberg, A. (1987, February). Career development, pt. 1: Careers and entrepreneurship. *Personnel,* 12–17.

II

FOUNDATIONS FOR INTEGRATING CAREER AND SUCCESSION PLANNING

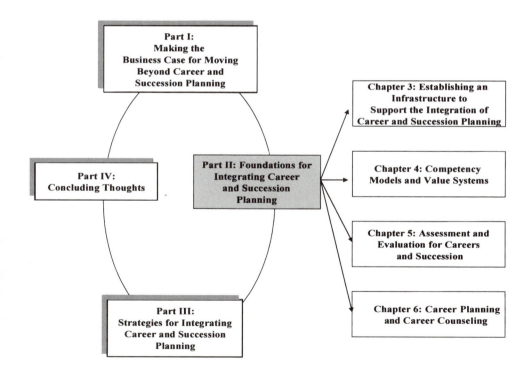

ESTABLISHING AN INFRASTRUCTURE TO SUPPORT THE INTEGRATION OF CAREER AND SUCCESSION PLANNING

The previous chapter examined the current state of your organization and provided a baseline for why career and succession planning should be done to maintain or enhance a strategic process proven to return financial rewards. This chapter takes the integration of career and succession planning to the next level. It is not hard to make a case to show how it can positively impact your business or even why it should be done in the first place. The data are obvious and evident.

Crucial to the success of quality succession and career planning programs is the understanding that they are not to be used as crisis management strategies, since they require financial resources, employee support, and time. To help further this point and shed some light on the how-to portion of the integration of career and succession planning, three real-world case studies are presented to allow the reader to focus on the following points:

1. What level of integration has each organization achieved with its career planning and succession planning programs?

2. What key success and failure factors appear to be associated with integrating career and succession planning in each case?

3. What key factors have contributed to the success and failure of each organization in integrating career and succession planning?

4. What solutions might an organization's leaders implement to achieve or maintain a goal of effectively integrating career and succession planning?

5. What future issues should each organization consider to improve the likelihood of success in integrating career and succession planning programs?

The ability to answer these questions will prepare the reader as the rest of the chapter explains how to assess the needs of an organization, clarify programmatic goals and alignment, gain and retain management and employee support, and finally understand the dynamics of corporate culture.

Quality succession planning and career planning programs are not crisis management strategies. They cannot be immediately implemented to mitigate present or pending staffing crises. They are long-term strategies, often requiring significant, long-lasting, and profound corporate culture change. They require careful strategic planning, necessitating a cooperative effort between stakeholders. Further, a comprehensive career planning and succession planning effort must become institutionalized, ingrained in the organization. They do not work well as stand-alone ventures that are poorly aligned with business needs. It must be clear to employees that participating in career planning benefits them individually. It must be clear to executives that succession planning benefits the organization. Integrating career planning and succession planning brings about a marriage of self interests and organizational interests. Without that integration, both efforts may well be doomed to failure.

Financial resources, employee support, and time are crucial to success. This chapter examines key issues needed to support the integration of career planning and succession planning programs. The chapter opens with three brief case studies of real organizations at various stages of implementing career planning programs. After that, the case studies are analyzed for their common themes and solutions are recommended to the problems apparent in the cases. This chapter also covers how to assess needs for the programs, clarify roles in the programs, gain and preserve stakeholder support, ensure alignment among career plans, succession plans and strategic plans, and the impact of career planning and succession planning programs on corporate culture.

CASE STUDIES

The following three case studies are based on real organizations involved in establishing and implementing career planning and succession planning programs. While reading these case studies, you should be contemplating the following questions:

- What level of integration has each organization achieved with its career planning and succession planning programs?
- What key success and failure factors appear to be associated with integrating career planning and succession planning in each case?
- What key factors have contributed to the success and failure of each organization in integrating career planning and succession planning?
- What solutions might an organization's leaders implement to achieve or maintain a goal of effectively integrating career planning and succession planning?
- What future issues should each organization consider to improve the likelihood of success in integrating career planning and succession planning programs?

Case Study 1

The first organization provides extensive computer technical support worldwide for various software and hardware products created by many Fortune 500 companies. The organization currently employs over 300 individuals and has been doing business for just over five years. To date, the company has been economically profitable and has averaged growth rates of over 20 percent per year. Many employees have been quite satisfied with the work environment; the CEO has been very involved with the progress of the organization from a bottom-up approach. Specifically, the CEO has made an effort to be highly visible and available to every employee of the organization. Corporate mission meetings and updates have been provided to all employees at least twice per year and have proven to be very popular.

Over the past year, the organization has faced several key challenges. First, the company's leaders are seeking ways to combat the outsourcing of technical assistance centers (their core business) to India, China, and Singapore. People in the organization have grown increasingly nervous as the news media have publicized the popularity of outsourcing. The company's margins have shrunk consistently over the last four quarters.

Second, the organization is witnessing a rise in attrition—from about 7 percent over the past four years to just over 18 percent this year alone. Exit interviews indicate that three issues seem to be the causes of rising attrition. These issues are low pay, lack of upward mobility potential, and few training opportunities.

Company leaders have traditionally believed that company-provided training should focus on current business needs related to technical assistance support. Many employees were required to attend training sessions that addressed customer service skills, technical troubleshooting, and conflict resolution tactics to help them assist angry customers. Supplemental income is not available for individuals wishing to pursue formalized educational programs. Internal training typically consists of two- to three-day sessions periodically spread throughout the year and is scheduled by topic according to feedback received from customers. Although the company has focused heavily on training about some topics for extended periods to improve in identified areas, managers have recently noticed that employee absenteeism goes up when mandatory training is conducted.

Since the organization only employs a few hundred people, internal movement has been fairly slow. Promotions are perceived to be made arbitrarily. Many employees do not know where they fit into the organization's future, especially given today's competitive market forces. Executives felt that they had a well-established succession system, since they were able to predict potential movements for high-performing employees with relative accuracy. This year, the company has lost about

20 percent of its workforce due to attrition. The CEO has deemed the succession planning system inadequate. She wants to find another solution to make it a viable avenue for developing employees and building bench strength.

Low base pay is the third issue that seems to be causing increased attrition. Financial data suggest that employees are not earning what an average worker should be earning who possesses a similar educational background and experience in the organization's geographic area. This is a thorny issue, since the recruitment process has been very slow and turnover continues to skyrocket. Because company margins are so tight, executives contend that the company cannot support a large influx of work-hour expenditures. The CEO is arranging an evaluation of the organization's career planning and succession planning processes so that the company can meet employee needs while also achieving the organization's strategic objectives.

Case Study 2

The second organization is one of the largest defense-related companies in the world. It employs 140,000 people worldwide and is growing rapidly due to numerous government contracts it has acquired over the last year. This case study will evaluate one of its most profitable divisions, which currently employs over 10,000 people, and must hire an additional 4,000 over the next year. This company has ample financial resources available to develop employees. The CEO has intense expectations of all employees to continue to develop professionally while working for the organization. A large training structure is already incorporated into the organization's culture. Employees are able to freely select courses to meet their career interests and satisfy their professional and organizational goals. The company also has on-site career counselors in its HR department. Numerous self-assessment tools are available. Additionally, interactive computer-based and live professional development seminars are available to all employees. Competency models have been identified to support lateral and upward movement in the organization. The organization has also made all job descriptions and competency models available to every employee through a technological portal system. More than half of the company's employees participate in the company's liberal postsecondary training.

Explosive staffing growth has given rise to difficulties in integrating new hires. At the same time, staff use of the company's portal system to access competency charts for internal positions has decreased dramatically. So has attendance at training sessions, even though the organization expends significant financial resources to make its career planning centers cutting edge. The president of this unit wants his senior-level staff to come up with solutions to these problems. He believes that the company has a comprehensive and effective career planning program, well-designed competency models, and effective ways to integrate career planning and succession planning through the use of hiring managers and self-assessment approaches. However, with an increasing attrition rate of senior staff members, and a new personnel increase of more than 40 percent this year, many challenges remain to achieve success.

Case Study 3

The third organization is a financial services provider of some of the largest mutual funds and equities in the world. The company currently employs over 22,000 individuals in multiple domestic (U.S.-based) locations. The organization has been proactive in career planning, succession planning, and integrating efforts. In fact, new hires are explicitly informed that the corporate culture demands that all employees be committed to professional development and seek promotion.

Efforts to integrate career planning and succession planning in this company are extensive. Company leaders have built an on-site corporate university that supplies employees with access to the latest technology and to training sessions. Competency models have been developed throughout the organization, and development is tied to building competencies and to helping individuals achieve their career goals. Data are regularly compared to determine if competency achievement is consistent with internal career goals identified by supervisors and employees. Stakeholders offer recommendations and periodic reevaluation to determine the most appropriate ways to develop talent.

The CEO has set the expectation that every member of management will proactively assist workers in their developmental efforts. That expectation is closely aligned to company goals of keeping attrition rates low, building future bench strength, and realizing the potential of prospective leaders. Company managers make it a point to promote from within and emphasize to employees that, if they want to advance, they must develop their competencies to qualify for the next level on the chain of command. Employees indicate that they know exactly where they can go within the organization, and they know how to get there because they are familiar with the available developmental activities.

This company's leaders believe that developing employees provides a competitive advantage over other organizations in their business sector. This company leads their industry in retention rates, recruitment of potential candidates, and overall employee job satisfaction. The CEO is currently defining key factors to their success and pinpointing business issues expected to be the focus of future plans.

Summary of the Cases

The case studies above illustrate organizations at different stages of integrating career planning and succession planning. Several key issues must be addressed to ensure that the integration process is successful. Understanding the needs of the organization is a good place to start when deciding how, when, and how much an integrated career planning and succession planning program is appropriate.

In addition to these cases, and to give readers a sense of real-world issues, the authors conducted in-depth interviews with two HR practitioners—one in a health care organization and another in a non-profit organization—that had attempted to integrate the career planning and succession planning efforts of these organizations. These cases are presented in the boxes that follow. Pause for a moment to read the cases and think about some of the issues they may raise.

ASSESSING THE NEED

Accurately defining strategic objectives and expected outcomes can be extremely difficult. It is possible to pursue career planning and succession planning actively and systematically, align those efforts with the organization's strategic objectives, and integrate those efforts. To those ends, however, the organization's leaders must establish a supportive

An Interview with an HR Professional in a Health-Care Organization About Issues in Integrating Career and Succession Planning[*]

Part I: The Respondents' Job Requirements

Question 1:   What are your work requirements? Describe your work duties.

Answer: My job is to develop leaders in industry. I focus on middle managers, frontline supervisors, and senior managers. I teach courses such as conflict resolution, time management, 360 degree feedback, leading others, and manager style profiles. My focus is on soft skills. I work to get the commitment of people to go above and beyond the call of duty. I help the employee to see a future . . . reasons why he or she should work harder and be committed. I help individuals understand they are all part of the company's ownership. I demonstrate how the leadership and career development group adds value to the organization, and how training adds value and fosters employee satisfaction. I quantify my services and have to help components of the organization's success. I do ask questions to help identify the impact of what I do. Examples of such questions may include: How was your training helpful to your line of business? Did it result in a production increase? Less turnover? I must tie production increases to training. I obtain testimony of line business managers about the added value of my efforts. I work to help them achieve their goals. I also work to help retain the workforce. Exactly 34 percent of my organization's workforce is fifty years of age or older. In 2003, one-third of my organization's workforce was eligible for retirement. How do we replace the valuable experience leaving? And how do we do that today? Tomorrow? In five years? In ten years? We must prepare people for advancement, too.

Part II: Describing the Organization's Career Planning and Succession Planning Program

Question 2:   Would you please spend a few minutes describing the career planning *program* that your organization operates? Please describe, as completely as you can, who it was established to serve, what it is designed or intended to do, when people typically use it, where (geographically) people use it the most, why it was established,

* The interviewer was Tiffani D. Payne.

how it works for participants, and what benefits your organization has derived from it.

Answer: First, we offer a course called Taking Control of Your Career to all employees on all levels. It is offered in two half-day sessions. We cover such topics as assessing work values, competency skills, and employee values; finding work that matters to you—life's work; Employee Development Action Plan; work on resumes and networking; and giving employees the resources internally that they need to develop.

Second, we conduct individual development planning (IDP). That involves one-on-one interviews between employees and their managers. Employees choose to sign up for this program and can contact the career development group themselves.

Third, I am a certified coach and offer coaching sessions—Career Coach Institute. I completed twenty-seven quizzes, successfully passed a seventy-five-question exam, twelve online coaching sessions, 12 hours one-on-one IDP with employees, and time with my personal coach.

Fourth, we offer a mentoring program.

Fifth, we operate a HiPo—The Bold Program (Business Operation Leadership Development). We interview and select high-potential employees to participate. Once someone is accepted, he or she takes a real live work project and, working on a team, the hi-po employee tackles issues in the workplace. It is an action learning project that can last nine to twelve months.

Sixth, we offer tuition reimbursement—an education assistance program. Participants must exhibit a proficient level of performance to qualify for reimbursement with management support.

Seventh and finally, we offer a virtual university that has training and development as well as a number of things employees can do for personal development.

Question 3: Would you please spend a few minutes describing the succession planning *program* that your organization operates? Please describe, as completely as you can, who it was established to serve, what it is designed or intended to do, when people typically use it, where (geographically) people use it the most, why it was established, how it works for participants, and what benefits your organization has derived from it.

Answer: When anyone leaves a current position, someone else should be ready and able to step up to the plate. So we have a communication strategy, we identify expected vacancies, and use selection tools. We are certified from Development Dimensions International (DDI) for our Targeted Selection Interviewing program and help people make right and informed hiring decisions. We do look at current and future competencies. We help to develop employees before the need arises. We focus on soft skills throughout the organization. We keep a database of internal resumes, the classes that employees have taken, and how many hours of training an employee has taken per year. We identify gaps. That means we identify proficiency levels and skills for every competency for every employee. If a person is not at the proper level, we use IDP to bring that person up to a level of proficiency for the competency. We evaluate where they are—how big the developmental gap is. We develop an individual development plan to help them succeed. We rely on mentoring and coaching to help close developmental gaps. The organization's senior staff identifies talent needs for the next five years.

Part III: Integrating the Organization's Career Planning and Succession Planning Programs

Question 4:   What efforts, if any, has your organization made to integrate the career planning program and the succession planning program, and how well did those efforts work? In other words, what efforts has your organization made to get the two programs to work together in any way? Or are they separately administered, and (if so) what has your organization experienced as a result of this separation?

Answer: In trying to integrate career and succession programs, we try to understand the organization's long-term goals and objectives. We also look at workforce trends—including workforce predictions for the region, state, and nation. We identify workforce needs and disseminate that information to senior management, working with them and other stakeholders to develop succession plans for necessary positions.

Question 5:   If you were giving someone in another organization advice on integrating career planning and succession planning, what would that advice be? Please try to be specific in your answers and explain why you would give that advice.

Answer: Career development should be an integral part of succession planning. Both should be based on regular contact with line of business managers. Senior managers should be part of an internal board of directors to oversee the programs.

Question 6:   What other comments, if any, do you have to make about integrating career planning and succession planning in an organization?

Answer: Every organization has three major assets: physical (brick and mortar), financial (function in black, good ROI), and human. The human asset is the most important. By focusing on human assets, leaders are able to get the other two assets to fall in line. Organizations that integrate career development and succession planning have automatically taken care of all three assets.

infrastructure and provide the resources. Of greatest importance, perhaps, is assessing the need.

The key to understanding organizational need is a thorough examination of corporate objectives, current workforce, and product output, aimed at identifying organizational goals and competency deficiencies.[1] A rigorous needs assessment examines what is happening, what should be and what will be happening, and then pinpoints talent or staffing deficiencies for action. Consider several important questions:

- Where does the business stand in comparison to competitors?
- What is the company particularly good at producing or providing?
- What competencies does the organization possess in human and physical capital?
- What areas need the most attention to meet strategic objectives?

The answers to these questions can provide key stakeholders with much useful information so they can develop strategic planning efforts to address career planning and succession planning needs. According to Scherrer, there is a clear link between effective oversight of key corporate personnel and the economic viability of the organization.[2] Further, leaders who proactively participate in key decision-making activities tend to lead more financially solvent organizations.[3]

An Interview with an HR Professional in a Nonprofit Organization About Issues in Integrating Career and Succession Planning*

Part I: The Respondents' Job Requirements

Question 1: What are your work requirements? Describe your work duties.

Answer: My job is to help to establish personal professional development plans for employees based on their job descriptions, skills, competencies, and personal career objectives. I work with the employee to determine courses he or she should take to perform the job optimally and foster personal growth. For the succession planning piece, I identify and prepare the future leadership by taking shared ownership of the career development of employees. I act as the corporate core HR liaison in matters primarily concerning career development. I develop overall company strategy, policies, and processes for my organization's career development and for potential future executives.

Part II: Describing the Organization's Career Planning and Succession Planning Programs

Question 2: Would you please spend a few minutes describing the career planning *program* that your organization operates? Please describe, as completely as you can, who it was established to serve, what it is designed or intended to do, when people typically use it, where (geographically) people use it the most, why it was established, how it works for participants, and what benefits your organization has derived from it.

Answer: We regularly post course offerings that range from Preventing Sexual Harassment to Stepping up to Supervisor. All employees are allowed to take courses, provided they have management support. Some high-level courses require senior management approval.

We have a Professional Development Plan program in which an interview is conducted with the employee seeking a career path within the organization. We outline a course of action that includes objectives for the career, the nature of the desired career, the courses

*This interview was conducted by Tiffani D. Payne.

needed for professional development, and evaluation tools. Employees choose to sign up for this program at any time, provided they are not on probation or suspension and are in good standing with the organization.

We also have a mentoring program where we assign an employee with an executive from a different but complementary line of business for professional coaching. Each mentor must participate in a coaching series of courses.

Question 3:   Would you please spend a few minutes describing the succession planning *program* that your organization operates? Please describe, as completely as you can, who it was established to serve, what it is designed or intended to do, when people typically use it, where (geographically) people use it the most, why it was established, how it works for participants, and what benefits your organization has derived from it.

Answer: We track employees' progress and identify high-potential individuals. Of course, we work with top management to identify these employees. We also work with top managers to identify potential vacancies of key positions. We monitor the high-potential employees' performance by requesting performance assessments and keep their personnel files in a separate administration system.

We act as career counselors for high-potential employees and support them in identifying and fulfilling their specific education/training/development requirements. We meet each of these employees in person at least once every two years.

Part III: Integrating the Organization's Career Planning and Succession Planning Programs

Question 4:   What efforts, if any, has your organization made to integrate the career planning program and the succession planning program, and how well did those efforts work? In other words, what efforts has your organization made to get the two programs to work together in any way? Or are they separately administered, and (if so) what has your organization experienced as a result of this separation?

Answer: Our career planning program and our succession planning program simply work hand in hand. Through our professional development program, we identify high-potential employees and track their progress career and personal growth.

Question 5:   If you were giving someone in another organization advice on integrating career planning and succession planning, what would that advice be? Please try to be specific in your answers and explain why you would give that advice.

Answer: I would tell anyone that you cannot have a successful succession planning program without a professional development program. I would also tell them that you cannot have successful professional development and succession planning programs without the support of senior managers. Therefore, it is their job to show evidence of the value that these two programs offer to their organization. One other important piece of advice: develop programs that have built-in evaluation and measurement mechanisms.

CLARIFYING PROGRAMMATIC GOALS AND ALIGNMENT

Once a needs assessment is completed and reviewed by senior executives (and other key stakeholders, such as board of directors members, as appropriate), the key objectives must be established as organizational policy. In most organizations, high-level policy makers tend to focus on long-term objectives, requiring additional training for employees and identification of star performers.[4] Defining objectives for the program is the first step. Much remains to be done after that step, however.

It is crucial to recognize the impact that program objectives may have. Achieving alignment among the objectives of the career planning program, the succession program, and the organization's strategy is key to success. Only when that happens can executive support become clearly focused, resources identified and brought to bear to achieve results, and human resource efforts brought in line to support the objectives. Once the program objectives are clear and have been aligned, informing employees with an effectively crafted media strategy—that is, a planned series of messages over time—is crucial to building awareness.

Effectively communicating a corporate message or strategic plan to an organization can be challenging in its own right. While some employees are skeptical of new initiatives, skilled and committed leaders can transform disbelievers into supporters. That is especially important to the subsequent success of career planning and succession planning programs. Employees will become interested if they know that they will benefit from developing their competencies in organized career planning programs.

Clarifying and aligning programmatic goals to meet defined objectives continues the process of gaining acceptance and support from employees. Some executive-level personnel hesitate to share their strategic vision with employees, fearing negative repercussions if information leaks to competitors.[5] However, the notion that making employees fully aware of business strategy can hurt an organization has been dispelled.

GAINING AND RETAINING MANAGEMENT AND EMPLOYEE SUPPORT

Employees who feel that they have a say in their organizations tend to be more committed to achieving corporate objectives.[6] Further, buy-in and subsequent implementation of an effort cannot take place if implementers (employees) do not enjoy ownership in the process.[7] This can also lead to a greater sense of trust by employees when a final strategic plan is communicated throughout the entire organization.[8]

It was noted in 1982 by Mowday, Porter, and Steers that three factors must exist for individuals to be classified as supporters of an initiative:

- A resilient belief in the processes, mission, and approaches established by the organization
- A desire to put forth the effort to contribute to the mission of the organization
- An inherent pride and sense of loyalty to the company

Follow these guidelines to build and maintain support for an integrated career planning and succession planning process:

- Make sure that employees have a say—and that their say is acted on—in planning professional development efforts.
- Craft communication to employees that is clear and appropriate to the audience, relating to their needs rather than to those of management.

- Credit those who contributed to creating the program to show broad-based support.
- Demonstrate the benefits that will be experienced by those participating in developing themselves professionally.
- Indicate that developmental opportunities and succession pathways are not limited to a chosen few in the organization and that they are available to all to share and succeed.
- Set a clear expectation of corporate culture: what it was, what it now is, and what it is to be in the future.

CORPORATE CULTURE

Values, defined as fundamental beliefs about right and wrong ways of doing things, are fundamental to the growth of any corporate culture.[9] The culture of an organization can be defined as a compilation of the knowledge gathered through employees' work and life experiences.[10] Company leaders that wish to overhaul the career planning and succession planning programs of their organization must first consider the existing corporate culture. This consideration is crucial to determining where the organization can modify its processes without causing substantial disruption in production. Key to avoiding disruptions in production is a thorough understanding of the workforce and its capabilities. The following questions can assist in reaching this understanding:

- What message is being communicated to the organization? Is it consistent with previous goals and missions, or is it a completely new process?
- If this is a new process, are employees willing and able to make a change to better the organization and themselves? (If not, modifying the intended system may be necessary.)
- Are changes in the career planning program and the succession planning program pertinent, clear, and achievable?
- Have the benefits of integrating the career planning and the succession planning programs been compellingly communicated to employees?

- What resources are required to achieve this change or reinforcement in corporate culture, and will they be provided?

The answers to these questions can be used to shape decisions about ways of implementing career planning and succession planning programs and ensuring their integration. Corporate culture is not changed suddenly or painlessly. On the contrary, corporate culture is a product of organizational experience, and key to changing culture is giving the organizations' members new and successful experiences so that they see new, effective ways to achieve career goals.

NOTES

1. Brown, J. (2002). Training needs assessment: A must for developing an effective training program. *Public Personnel Management, 31,* 569–579.

2. Scherrer, P. S. (2003). Directors' responsibilities and participation in the strategic decision making process. *Corporate Governance, 3,* 86–91.

3. Judge, W. Q., & Zeithaml, C. P. (1992). Institutional and strategic choice perspectives on board involvement in the strategic decision process. *Academy of Management Journal, 35,* 766–794.

4. Sherrer, Philip S. (2003). Directors' responsibilities and participation in the strategic decision making process. *Corporate Governance, 3,* 86–91.

5. Guffey, R. W., & Nienhaus, B. J. (2002). Determinants of employee support for the strategic plan of a business unit. *S.A.M. Advanced Management Journal, 67,* 23–30.

6. Foltz, R. G. (1985). Communication and Contemporary Organizations. In C. Reuss & D. Silvis (Eds.), *Communication in contemporary organizations: Inside Organizational Communication* (2nd ed., pp. 3–14). New York: Longman.

7. Frost, C. (1986). Participative ownership: A competitive necessity. *New Management, 3,* 44–49.

8. Giles, W. D. (1991). Making strategy work. *Long Range Planning, 24,* 75–91.

9. Mowday, R. T., Porter, L. C., & Steers, R. M. (1982). *Employee–organizational linkages: The psychology of commitment, Absenteeism, and turnover.* New York: Academic Press.

10. Sarros, J. (2002). The heart and soul of leadership: The personal journey. In C. Baker & R. Coy (Eds.), *The heart and soul of leadership* (pp. 6–22). Sydney: McGraw-Hill.

FOUR

COMPETENCY MODELS AND VALUE SYSTEMS

Thinking systemically is a key component of performance. Ensuring that succession plans and career development are integrated requires awareness of corporate culture and how systems thinking is used throughout an organization. Systems thinking is a way of analyzing an event by looking beyond the closest elements in an event to include people and processes related to an event that are located downstream of the immediate relationships. Systems thinking is seeing the forest and the trees. Companies that are creating an infrastructure to align succession plans and career development programs apply systems thinking by aligning the organization's growth through the individual's career plan. This chapter uses systems thinking by linking an organization's competency model to an individual's value system. In this chapter you will learn:

- How competency models are constructed
- How value systems are used to guide behaviors
- How to align succession planning and organizational development
- How to integrate competency models and value systems

Clear expectations are the foundation for performance. Competency models and value systems are critical to establishing an organization's succession plan and an employee's career plan. Linking them has the potential to create a synergistic program that is employee centered and performance driven. Research on competency modeling shows that examining a person's intent while performing a job is crucial to understanding the full competency picture. This chapter describes how competency models and value systems can be designed and developed into succession and career planning practices.

A *competency model*, while a much misunderstood term, is a way to describe work-related behaviors that are required components for achieving work results. Competency models speak to results and the kind of person needed to achieve them. A *value system* is an implicit way of behaving that reflects priorities and worth within an organization. Values are associated with ethics, morality, and beliefs and attitudes about right and wrong. Competency models and value systems are linked by the common element of motives as determining variables for success. For competency models to improve performance, managers must be aware of behaviors or outputs that result in below-average, average, and above-average performance. Ideally, managers describe the behaviors or outputs required for exemplary (outstanding) job performance, implicitly revealing the value systems and motives inherent to the competency model and the organization.

COMPETENCY MODELING

Competency models should be developed with the best performance in mind since they provide the foundation for all aspects of human resource management—including recruitment, selection, appraisal, career paths, reward systems, training and development, and more. Levels of performance are governed by individuals' approaches to work as well as their knowledge, skills, and abilities. Three levels of competency are used for describing work:

1. *Job competencies:* Behaviors that are commonly demonstrated in performing the job and are demonstrated by all performers of a job.

2. *Performance competencies:* Behaviors that are critical to the successful performance of a job and are demonstrated by the highest-level of performers in a job.
3. *Succession competencies:* Behaviors that are common to all jobs in an organization and are strengthened and expanded through increased learning and leadership experiences.

When general models of managerial competency were first published in the early 1980s, the pace of workplace change was not as great as it is today. When competency models were first introduced, behaviors that resulted in superior (exemplary) performance were assumed to be relatively enduring. Models were researched and designed based on job (work) outputs. The outputs associated with a job were then used to identify behaviors required for successful performance. This process, while still valid, is more difficult in today's business world because markets are more fluid, products and services are constantly changing, and the workforce is increasingly mobile and contingent.

Competency models may be created for job categories (such as supervisor), departments (such as HR), or occupations (such as accountant). They may also be defined for hierarchical levels on the organization chart—such as all jobs on each level. Special competency models, called *metacompetency models*, may be focused on issues that cut across job categories or departments—such as leadership.

Due to the traditionally high costs associated with developing a valid, reliable, and legally defensible competency model, such models are typically found in high value-added jobs and senior-level leadership positions. However, advances in software and training in competency modeling methodology have broadened the potential application of competency identification to all positions within an organization. The following list outlines typical steps involved in creating a competency model, though various schools of competency modeling methodology exist and may be used instead.

1. *Identify job outputs and standards.* For each job, identify the expected outputs and performance measures. It is critical to clearly establish what does not meet, what meets, and what

exceeds expectations. It is recommended to use both numeric and description measurement forms for each output.

2. *Identify job performers to include in the study.* It is very important to include exemplary and fully sufficient performers in the study. Because this model will be used to create base performance levels, those included in the study should have intermediate to expert competency levels.

3. *Collect data.* Historically, the most rigorous models have been built through behavioral event interviews (BEIs). Other methods include surveys, expert panels, and job analysis. The method used will be determined by the size of the group studied and available resources. Data collectors should not know who is categorized into the performance categories.

4. *Analyze data.* Data are analyed and organized into common performance-oriented themes. Performance themes of each person in the study will be identified and, if exemplary and sufficient performers are chosen well, the differences will be apparent.

5. *Establish job competencies.* From the common themes, draft competencies will be developed. Draft competencies should include a comprehensive set of behaviors demonstrated in all aspects of the job, a definition of the competency, and a ranking of how important the competency is to the total performance of the job.

6. *Competencies feedback review.* A review and feedback report is distributed to study participants. From feedback, revisions can be made to any aspect of the competency list, definition, and ranking. Following the feedback, a competency profile for the job is established.

7. *Implement competencies.* Job competencies are used for selection, interviewing, evaluating performance, establishing a training program, succession planning, and career planning.

How change is introduced and implemented in a workplace reflects the corporate culture and the value system of the organization. The increasing speed of workplace change has necessitated competency models that are more dynamic. To integrate the speed of change in the workplace, competency models in some organizations are currently being updated every 18 to 36 months, reflecting their link to the organization's strategic business planning horizon. Dynamic competency models are recognized as a way to keep up with changing business needs.[1] Recognizing changing competency requirements and reacting in ways that enable employees to acquire new performance behaviors is a challenge for today's organizations. Aligning value systems with competency models can be extremely useful.

VALUE SYSTEMS

Corporate corruption cases such as those of Andersen, Enron, WorldCom, and Tyco have increased concern for ethics and morality in corporate governance. Combining value systems with competency models can be beneficial to an organization and its employees. Value systems are crucial to decision making and provide the common ground from which leaders approach challenges. While competency models represent a hierarchy of specific job performance behaviors, value systems represent a framework for individual behaviors that transcend any single job and are linked to an overall career plan and to ethical dilemmas that may be unique to the work, organization, or industry.

To clarify, *values* are ways of thinking about intangible and tangible areas of life that place worth on activities and possessions. *Intangible values* cannot be quantified through accounting and inventory processes; they are mind-sets that reinforce behaviors such as respect for each other, honesty, inclusiveness, integrity, and accountability. *Tangible values* are possessions that can be appraised for their monetary worth. We choose careers, develop relationships, make purchases, get involved in community groups, and engage each other based on our values. Knowing what people value helps us to understand the motivations behind what they do, why they do it, and how they do it. A *value system* is a set of intangible values that guide behavior. Table 4.1 presents a framework for assessing and ranking personal values.

Documenting value systems can clarify behaviors. Research on organizational behavior reveals that less than 10 percent of organizations around the world have clearly identified value statements, and that, for value statements to have an impact on behavior, they should be limited to three or four values.[2] People turn to their values when making difficult

TABLE 4.1 Values System Identification Tool

Value	Assessment (1 = Low; 10 High)	Value System Rank
Accountability		
Achievement		
Communications		
Inclusion		
Openness		
Professionalism		
Respect for others		
Respect for self		
Timeliness		

decisions. For value systems to be effective, they must be ranked and prioritized. Clearly defined and prioritized values lend insight to any decision-making process and help to solve ethical problems with which individuals may be faced.

Value systems are not codes of ethics. *Codes of ethics* are standards to which employees and group members should adhere. They are developed for professional organizations, trade associations, and civic groups so that members can demonstrate common conduct. They provide a basis for nonmembers to develop expectations about group behavior.

Value systems help employees prioritize behaviors in ways that reinforce codes of ethics. Put simply, a value system is the reason why we acknowledge a code of ethics. While a code of ethics reflects an existing set of principles for members of an organization, value systems bring people together to achieve common objectives.

ALIGNING CAREER PLANNING AND SUCCESSION PLANNING PROGRAMS

It is a truism that business is changing at every level. Strategic transformation is seen in marketing new business lines, global customers, client types, and services provided. Operational transformation is seen in new information technology applications, organizational structures, ways of measuring and reporting, and ways of improving productivity. New approaches to operational management require leaders to help all employees understand why the company is in the business it is in and how

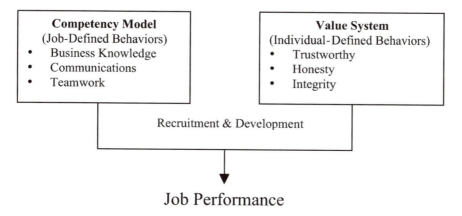

FIGURE 4.1   Competency-values flow chart.

company programs and processes will help the organization achieve its goals. Connecting competency models and value systems is a new approach that recognizes the importance of documenting and screening people's internal motives and the values governing their work behavior. Competencies and values are used together to show employees how their personal aspirations are reflected in behaviors supporting job performance (Figure 4.1).

Succession planning programs ensure a continuous supply of organizational leaders and can provide managers and employees alike with a growth map. To create such programs, organizational leaders must link each individual job to strategy, performance measures, and succession competencies so employees can recognize what is necessary to progress to higher-level responsibility or higher-level management. Studies on human resource planning in government agencies in Australia, Canada, New Zealand, and the United Kingdom have identified the following six best practices as critical to coordinating succession planning with organizational transformation.

Best Practice 1: Receive Active Support from Senior Leadership

Effective succession planning programs enjoy the active support and commitment of the organization's top leaders. Senior leaders in succession planning activities must offer support by providing hands-on, regular, and active participation. They promote from within for a critical number of positions. And they supply sufficient funding and staff resources to encourage succession planning.

Best Practice 2: Link HR Programs to Future Strategic Staffing Needs

Succession planning programs should focus on present and future staffing needs to develop so-called *talent pools* of high-potential candidates. These programs help build bench strength over time.

Best Practice 3: Identify High Potential Talent on Multiple Levels, Early in Career

Succession planning programs must be developed for entry, mid-level, and senior-level positions and people. They must be designed to strengthen essential competencies that are key to success in high-level work assignments. In other words, participants should be involved in building competencies suitable to reach at least the next level.

Best Practice 4: Emphasize Developmental Assignments to Complement Formal Training

Succession planning programs should push participants to build their competencies. One way to do that is to place them in new or unfamiliar roles. That helps them acquire new competencies and broadens their experience.

Best Practice 5: Address Specific HR Planning Challenges Such as Diversity, Leadership Development, and Retention

Succession planning programs should be used to address long-term HR initiatives and coordinate an organization's workforce vision for the future. Increased recognition of the benefits of a diverse workforce supports programs targeted at developing minorities (and other protected groups) through organized and active efforts such as leadership programs, coaching or mentoring programs, training and development programs, and on-the-job or off-the-job developmental assignments.

Best Practice 6: Further Integrate Change Efforts

Succession planning programs can provide a focal point for efforts to integrate the organization's capacities to perform, change, and transform. Encouraging employees to continually grow and expand creates an organization-wide mind-set for change and performance. It builds a corporate culture in which development is expected and is established as an accountability for individuals and for their immediate supervisors alike.

Today's employees know that their personal development depends on organizational success. Succession plans allow the organization to plan for future talent needs. Career plans enable employees to chart their careers. An organization's investment in retaining and developing high-potential employees should pay for itself because it creates a valuable internal pool of proven talent and thereby slashes unproductive breaking-in periods and long cycle times to recruit qualified people to fill important vacancies. Succession planning begins with well-built job descriptions that go beyond job duties, responsibilities, and minimum requirements to include job outputs, competencies, and behaviors. This information clarifies performance expectations for individuals and enables managers to operate consistently. By expanding the information presented in a job description, organizational leaders can integrate competencies into a succession planning program. While some leaders will be recruited, selected, and developed from within the organization, others will always need to be brought in from the outside at various points in their careers to infuse the organization with new ideas and new approaches. Balancing leaders' experience by combining in-house developed leaders (who have a long-term cultural understanding of the organization) with those who have gained knowledge from outside of the organization is a strategic HR decision. An organization's value system determines the weight it places on each side of this equation.

Career planning programs can be presented as individually driven programs that parallel succession planning programs. They can help individuals clarify what they want to do in the future, portray training and development as means to the end of qualifying for higher-level responsibility, and take initiative to achieve their own career objectives. Just as effective succession planning programs begin with support at the top, successful career planning programs start with individuals making values-based, honest assessments of their career visions. Sample questions to pose for such an assessment may include any of the following:

- What are my personal characteristics that are reflected in the way I live my life?
- How would I list the most important aspects of my work?
- At the end of the day, on what do I place the greatest value?

Once individual value systems are documented, their present job competencies can be identified. It is also possible to pinpoint gaps between present and future competencies and individual values (see Table 4.2).

INTEGRATING COMPETENCY MODELS AND VALUE SYSTEMS

The following nine points should provide some useful guidance in aligning value systems and competency models.

Point 1: Start with Values

Competency models are strongest when individual values are demonstrated as job behaviors. Organizational value statements should be reflected in job descriptions. They may be listed in separate documents or described as work behaviors.

Point 2: Incorporate Competencies

Job competencies drive performance; competencies are driven by values. At their best, clearly described competencies explain behaviors

TABLE 4.2. Competency/Values Gap Analysis

Analysis Area	Myself	Job/Organization	Gap
Personal values			
Performance competencies			
Short-term goals			
Long-term goals/strategies			

that are essential to work performance. Each succession plan should have clearly described competencies, the values that they reflect, and the progression of competency level to leadership level in the organization. Codes of conduct are also increasingly helpful as are the rating systems based on them, since no one wants to promote individuals who do not adhere to, and embody, the organization's value system and who cannot cope with the ethical challenges they will encounter in their work.

Point 3: Involve Employees in Discussions

Just as job performers are at the heart of competency model data, they are also at the heart of value system data. Proper alignment depends on employee involvement in formulating, implementing, and evaluating programs. Before any competency model/value system program can be implemented, it should be reviewed—and verified—by employees.

Point 4: Include Senior-Level Leadership to Promote Involvement

Effective career and succession planning programs require the active involvement of senior leaders. Senior leaders should be engaged in clearly communicating the importance of individual value alignment with competencies. They should also be role models for the values that the organization wishes to project.

Point 5: Identify Strategic Goals and Measures

Include key performance indicators at the organizational level that managers can use during performance reviews and employee development planning sessions. Competencies must be measurable, and they should be integrated in performance management systems as well.

Point 6: Establish Global and Local Linkages

Involve international HR input as early as possible to make sure that the program has global impact and local relevancy.

Point 7: Establish a Tracking and Correction Mechanism

Job competencies are dynamic. They should be the focus of continuous assessment of job outputs and performance measures. A system that tracks how competencies are changing, and the correlating change in values, is crucial.

Point 8: Reinforce the Reason Why the Program Is Taking Place

Establish a communication system to provide program updates and changes. Use that to explain to employees what strategic links exist among competencies, values, succession plans, career plans, and strategic business objectives.

Point 9: Explain How the Program Will Be Reflected in Organizational Operations

Provide new operational processes to be used during performance reviews, job evaluations, recruiting, and the selection process (as well as any other appropriate processes). Communicate these processes—and provide testimonies of success—in regular messages to employees and managers alike.

NOTES

1. Argyris, C., & Schön, D. (1996). *Organizational learning II.* Reading, MA: Addison-Wesley.

2. Blanchard, K., & Stoner, J. (2004, Winter). *The vision thing: Without it you'll never be a world class organization.* [Online]. Available: http://leaderto-leader.org/leaderbooks/l2l/winter2004blanchardandstoner.html.

FIVE

ASSESSMENT AND EVALUATION FOR CAREER AND SUCCESSION PLANNING PROGRAMS

Assessing, evaluating, and planning processes require data. Competency models provide behavioral data that are used to assess and evaluate a person's job performance and development needs. Financial data are the primary form for measuring organizational performance, and underneath the financial data are the intangible data, which include customer feedback, employee retention, and workforce capabilities. Coordinating measurement for career and succession plans requires organizations to use measurement systems and tools to collect meaningful data that are used for both career and succession programs. In this chapter you will learn:

- How to assess individual and succession plans
- How to integrate mission-driven career and succession plans
- How to align personal and organizational feedback
- How to coordinate measurement tools

Historically, career planning programs have been used to help individuals discover their goals in an organizational (or personal) context and then coach individuals through developing and implementing a long-term career plan. An individual's vision, dreams, and feedback on competencies have provided a focus and foundation for assessing career plans to ground them in reality. An organization's strategic plan, competency models, performance management systems, potential assessment methods, and individual development planning have provided a focus for succession planning. Each program relies on developmental strategies to help individuals build their competencies. Performance feedback helps individuals keep their career objectives grounded in reality, and performance feedback also helps an organization's leaders keep the succession plan grounded in present business needs (Figure 5.1).

Ideally, what people learn to develop along their career paths builds upon what they learn to perform in their jobs. Organizational leaders who can integrate career planning and succession planning programs create parallel systems that can synergize with each other. Career planning and succession planning programs both rely on performance feedback. Understanding how assessment and evaluation are used in career planning and succession planning programs is crucial to implementing, and integrating, both programs effectively.

FIGURE 5.1 Performance feedback alignment.

USING INDIVIDUAL PERFORMANCE MANAGEMENT SYSTEMS
IN CAREER AND SUCCESSION PLANNING

Individual performance reviews are common to almost every organization. Effective performance management begins with identifying job expectations. Workers must know what the goals are if they are to achieve them. While managers are responsible for explaining to workers what is required for job success, individuals are becoming increasingly responsible for determining measurable work outputs and descriptions of how their performance will be assessed. Knowing what is expected in a job is the first step to success. People must know what results they are expected to achieve in their current work. To realize career objectives, they must know what is expected for other work. To realize succession plans, organizational leaders must clarify what competencies and work results are expected in other jobs and at other levels of responsibility in the organization.

Jobs with competency models have clearly defined output expectations, but for those jobs with no competency model (or output objectives), identifying measurable job expectations is the first step in aligning assessment and evaluation. As a process, performance management identifies, documents, measures, communicates, and develops individual contributions to an organization. (In some organizations, group contributions are also assessed—as in team evaluation.) This process creates a shared understanding between managers and employees about where the organization is going, how it is doing in getting there, and what must happen for goals to be reached.

Through assessment and evaluation, managers charged with responsibility for performance management develop guidelines for their employees to use in achieving the results desired from their current jobs and in planning for surmounting barriers to those results. Assessment and evaluation help employees complete difficult tasks, reduce cycle time in completing projects, provide specific issues to address, and involve multiple measurement points to connect employee contributions to strategic business objectives. While assessment and evaluation are both used for performance measurement, each is used differently.

Assessment provides a basis for mentoring and development feedback. Evaluation provides a basis for coaching and training feedback.

Managers assess an employee's performance to help the employee grow from one level to the next. A manager evaluates an employee's performance to help the employee perform better in a current job. Put simply, assessment is a development measurement process; evaluation is a training measurement process (Figure 5.2).

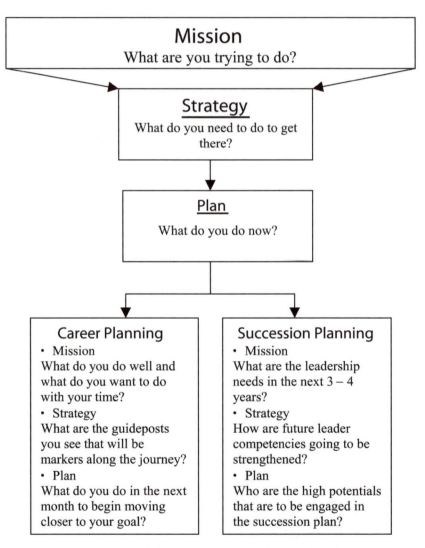

FIGURE 5.2   Mission-driven career and succession plan.

TABLE 5.1   Assessment and Evaluation in Career and Succession Planning

	Assessment	Evaluation
Step 1	What are the employee's career goals?	What are the job outputs (quality and quantity expectations)?
Step 2	What are the career experiences that are relevant to promotional growth?	What has the employee delivered within the current job?
Step 3	Weigh the importance of past experience.	Weigh the importance of past experience.
Step 4	What are the critical indicators for achieving career goals?	What are the critical indicators for achieving job performance?
Step 5	Against what quality and quantity standards are these goals measured?	Against what quality and quantity standards are these goals measured?
Step 6	Reflect and assess performance.	Reflect and evaluate performance.
Step 7	Plan for next experience.	Plan for improvement or increased responsibility.

The closer a person's career plan is to his or her personal strengths, the stronger the synergy between the person and the organization's succession plan. When people develop career objectives based on what they do well—that is, they leverage their talents or individual strengths—their performance often naturally leads them to higher levels in an organization. Feedback and reflection by individuals and their managers is the process that gives synergy to, and helps to integrate, career planning and succession planning. The steps in this dialogue are presented in Table 5.1.

COORDINATED MEASUREMENT: ALIGNING ASSESSMENT AND EVALUATION FOR CAREER AND SUCCESSION PLANNING

A balanced approach to assessing and evaluating potential is the key to aligning career plans and succession plans. In discussing the so-called balanced scorecard approach, Robert Kaplan and David Norton indicate that a successful measurement system includes measures across four areas: financial, customer, organizational processes, and learning and growth.[1] Balancing areas of measurement makes for more accurate and broadly applicable results. Effective organizational leaders know that multiple measurement points are crucial to identifying strengths and weaknesses in supply chains, work processes, decision systems, employee skills, and customer expectations. Such an approach involves using quantitative and qualitative variables to evaluate how well work is being performed. *Quantitative measures* examine factors such as time to complete, cost figures, error rates, quality rankings, net revenue, and profitability. *Qualitative measures* look at professional conduct, critical thinking, innovation, openness, and customer concern. While a balanced approach to measuring performance uses multiple layers of data taken from different stages of work, customer expectations are ultimately what must be met (or exceeded). This section describes how coordinated measurement systems fit within the performance management process and link career and succession programs (Figure 5.3).

Effective performance improvement in career planning and succession planning efforts requires attention to six key issues:

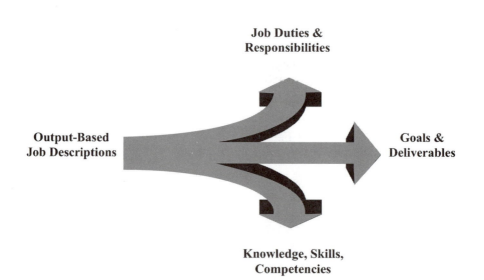

Job Duties & Responsibilities

Output-Based Job Descriptions

Goals & Deliverables

Knowledge, Skills, Competencies

Individual Output-Based Performance Assessment
Aligning organizational goals to individual contributions

FIGURE 5.3 Assessment through outputs.

1. *An ongoing system of planning, coaching, and reviewing.* These stages reflect the cycle of people management and continuously occur in an individual's career planning process and an organization's succession planning process.
2. *Links to specific business objectives.* An individual's career position determines his or her immediate performance goals and career objectives. The depth of available capabilities determines an organization's succession plan goals.
3. *Measures are balanced between quantitative objectives and behavioral competencies.* Assessing potential is a function of "hard" and "soft" measures that are weighted by a person's immediate career position.
4. *Managerial support at all levels.* Succession plans are most effective when senior leaders know the criteria being used to assess potential and contribute to developing that potential.
5. *Links to other systems and clear communication on goals.* Career plans should be linked to life plans that encompass a person's family, desired work and life balance, and spirituality. Each system supports (or strains) a career plan. A succession plan should be linked to an organization's reward system, recruitment and selection methods, and learning programs.
6. *Multiple sources for input into performance reviews.* Multiple sources of competency assessment should be used to help individuals reflect on where they are now (current competencies) and what competencies will be needed for them to realize their career objectives or else assume more responsibility. A succession plan can be based on input from senior leaders, current managers, and other stakeholders.

The characteristics of performance management described above provide a framework for building a system to assess and evaluate present performance and future potential. Proper measurement of performance, competencies, and potential is critical to successful career planning and succession planning. Performance ratings, output measures, and final evaluations are important because each gives feedback to individuals and provides documentation for the organization.

Performance measurement can also be organized into six processes that are found within all performance systems. The following measurement steps provide a broad framework for assessing a person's performance possibilities.

1. *Review capabilities.* Assessing and evaluating present capabilities is the first step in the measurement process. This *capability audit* results in an understanding of current strengths and weaknesses in career planning and succession planning.

2. *Clarify measurement starting points and goals.* How and where capabilities are to be measured should be clearly marked as a starting point. Career and succession goals should then be identified and worked toward.

3. *Weigh results.* With an understanding of their capabilities and potential, individuals can identify what competencies should be given priority in achieving career objectives and qualifying for advancement according to succession objectives. In developing a succession plan, capability and leadership development areas should be weighed against short- and long-term business strategy.

4. *Identify specific measures.* It is important to list the individual measures used to evaluate job performance. This current list can be built upon with previous individual measurement points so that a pattern of accomplishment can be identified. If this pattern reinforces a career plan, then measurement areas can be deepened to grow higher levels of capability. In succession planning, measurement points may reinforce core competencies found in the existing senior leadership ranks. A succession plan's measures should reinforce organizational goals by furnishing individuals with targets for performance as they carry out their work.

5. *Develop standards.* Effective measures have gradations. Providing a standard for evaluating capabilities logically follows identifying measurement points. General standards of measurement can be grouped into three levels: exceeds, meets, and does not meet expectations. Of course, depending on the nature of the work, these measures may be made more specific—and thus less likely to be subjective judgments. These standards are

only useful if each level has a definition or guideline for achieving the standard.

6. *Track performance.* As the outputs of work are delivered, performance measures should be documented and tracked. Tracking results and correcting deficiency areas advances a person along his or her career path by providing points of reference. Tracking individual performance in a succession plan provides organizational leaders with data to assess workforce capability and leadership preparation.

The six characteristics of performance management and the six steps in measuring performance create a process that links global performance processes to local appraisal processes. That can result in an organization-wide understanding of how individual appraisal contributes to organization development.

Decision makers assess potential by reviewing past accomplishments and by comparing individuals to the competencies needed in other departments or levels of the organization's hierarchy. Outputs and deliverables are the critical points that individuals and employers alike are interested in. In career planning, recognizing accomplishments and organizing them into groups of strengths and weaknesses highlights areas to build current job assignments around and areas requiring further training and development. In succession planning, decision makers examine the outputs of high-potential workers as a starting point for developing their abilities by assigning them future job responsibilities and providing feedback that will contribute to their development.

MEASUREMENT TOOLS

To measure and sustain success, decision makers must focus on outcomes that are meaningful to the individual (for career planning) and the customer (for succession planning). It is crucial to set appropriate performance goals. A common method for assessing performance potential is through the acronym SMART. SMART defines effective measures as meeting the following criteria:

- *Specific.* In specifying potential, for instance, measures must answer questions such as: "A person is capable at what?" "...under what circumstances?" "...how much?"
- *Measurable.* Effective assessment points reflect a combination of four areas: speed or time, cost, quality or customer expectations, and positive yield (the impact to be delivered for customers, shareholders, or the organization).
- *Assertive.* Assertive potential measures reflect challenges that have been attempted (whether overcome or not). Assertive measurement points reflect confidence and inspire workers.
- *Relevant.* Measurement areas must be directly related to performance challenges. They should address the needs of the user or customer.
- *Timely.* Performance measures answer the question "By when?" and are free of arbitrary constraints (such as the quarter, fiscal year, or academic year).

Measuring performance and potential has come a long way. Growing awareness exists of the need for multiple measures. New forms of measurement have been developed, and adapted to, unique work environments. Tools for measuring financial results, delivery time, processes efficiency, product quality, customer satisfaction, and employee involvement are being redesigned and made available online so that feedback is real-time, all the time.

Four tools for assessing performance and potential are presented below. Each tool is used to measure performance and potential under specific work environments and demands:

- Team Stakeholder Diagram (see Figure 5.4)
- Results Pyramid (see Figure 5.5)
- Mapping Work Process (see Figure 5.6)
- Role-Results Matrix (see Figure 5.7)

Six Sigma is an example of a performance measurement methodology that can provide common ground for assessing and evaluating present performance and future potential. While the Six Sigma system was originally designed to achieve virtual perfection in production

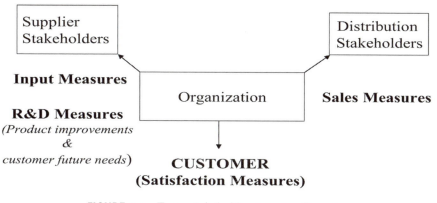

FIGURE 5.4 Team stakeholder measure diagram.

processes, it is now recognized as a universal approach to achieve output perfection through process improvement. The Six Sigma vision, philosophy, and measurement tools can be applied to assessing and evaluating individual potential in career plans and in succession plans. As a vision, the Six Sigma guidepost is a goal of flawless products and services delivered to the customer. As a philosophy, the goal of this process is virtual perfection by attempting to achieve 3.4 defects per million opportunities. The mind-set of the Six Sigma approach is directed to coordinating and perfecting work processes and instilling a work culture of continuous improvement. This mind-set can facilitate synergy in both career planning and succession planning.

The Six Sigma process involves setting goals, collecting data, assessing performance, correcting errors, and improving products and

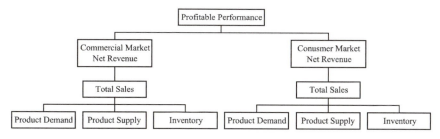

FIGURE 5.5 Results Pyramid.

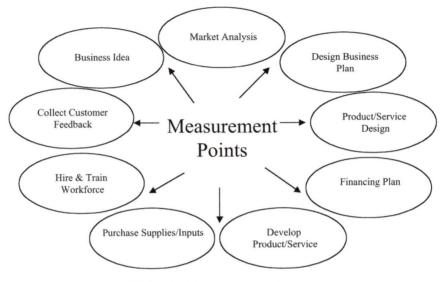

FIGURE 5.6 Mapping the work process.

services. It provides a framework for thinking about performance that seeks answers to the following questions:

- What does the customer want?
- How are the customer's wants delivered?
- How do I know how well I'm doing at fulfilling the customer's needs?
- How do I improve?
- How do I build in continuous improvement?

Formally, a Six Sigma process uses the DMAIC model for improvement:

- *Define* the problem
- *Measure* results at multiple process points
- *Analyze* data for root causes
- *Improve* the process through corrective actions
- *Control* for process improvement through monitoring, documenting, and responding output reports.

Role-Results	New Product Design	Shipped Products	Profitable Sales
Production team	Cost estimates	Delivered products	Cost-saving ideas
Marketing team	•Focus groups •Product ideas •Competitive analysis		•Sales •Orders
Human resources team	Competency assessment of existing employees	Trained employees	More productive employees

FIGURE 5.7 Role-results matrix.

At the core of a Six Sigma process is a focus on the customer and accountability for the product or service. The primary role of assessing and evaluating data collected in a Six Sigma process parallels the role of performance data collected on an individual or an organization's entire workforce used in career planning and succession planning. The success of Six Sigma, career plans, and succession plans hinges on the accuracy of competency and capability data obtained during performance assessment and evaluation processes. Six Sigma is the most rigorous approach to assessing and evaluating work processes and their results. Through this process, assessment and evaluation of competencies can be used in strategic HR planning and for addressing issues in employee retention, job rotation, and workforce development programming.

Assessing and evaluating capability and potential is critical to career and succession planning, as well as meeting current performance goals. Pfeffer clarifies:

> Leaders who have successfully built high-performing workplaces make sure to measure the practices that constitute high-commitment management. *The way to do this is by tracking and weighing financial measures against measures of customer satisfaction and retention, employee attitudes and retention, new product and new business development, or readiness for change.* Some of these indicators are more difficult to measure than past

financial performance, but sophisticated leaders recognize that measurement systems focus organizational attention, and that the adage "what gets measured gets done" is accurate.[2]

NOTES

1. Kaplan & Norton, 1996.
2. Pfeffer, J. (1998, Spring). The real keys to high performance. [On-line] Available: http://www.pfdf.org/leaderbooks/l2l/spring98/pfeffer.html.

BIBLIOGRAPHY

Herzingler, R. (1997, Winter). *Full discloser: A strategy for performance.* [On-line]. Available: http://www.pfdf.org/leaderbooks/l2l/winter97/herzlinger.html.
Pfeffer, J. (1998, Spring). *The real keys to high performance.* [On-line] Available: http://www.pfdf.org/leaderbooks/l2l/spring98/pfeffer.html.
Smith, D. K. (2000, Winter). *Better than plan: Managing beyond the budget.* [On-Line] Available: http://www.pfdf.org/leaderbooks/l2l/winter2000/smith.html.

SIX

CAREER PLANNING AND CAREER COUNSELING

How many organizations do you know that claim to have a comprehensive career planning and/or career counseling center, but if you look you will find that it consists of nothing more than a "resource" library of dusty, outdated books from the 1980s? Career planning and career counseling should go hand-in-hand within any organization to be truly effective. While either process can be, and in many cases is, performed without the other, this is merely a "performance" rather than a complete production.

Career counseling and planning must be utilized to reap the synergistic properties of both processes. This chapter specifically addresses the following:

1. The continual evolution of employee development technology
2. Multiple methodologies for implementation of career planning and career counseling to employees
3. Alternative methods of employee development
4. Precautionary measures needed to be realized in this form of development

Employee development has surged to the forefront of concerns for HR departments. Many organizations have established career centers to enhance employees' professional growth. Many factors can inhibit an individual worker from initiating or completing developmental activities outside of the workplace, such as work load responsibilities, family issues, financial concerns, and in some instances health issues. Hall and Associates claim that maximizing employees' opportunities to learn and increase their professional experiences on the job leads to the most effective development.[1] Further, a number of career planning centers have calculated that economic reality necessitates that organizations and employees change according to corporate strategic objectives.[2]

To clarify the meaning of the term *employee development*, Rothwell and Sredl define it as "development, when sponsored by an organization for its workers...focused on identifying, assuring, and helping evoke new insights through planned learning. It gives individuals opportunities to grow; it gives organizations employees who are capable of working smarter rather than harder because they have a burgeoning storehouse of creativity, experience, and knowledge from which to draw as they do their work."[3] Career planning activities assisted by technology are becoming extremely common due to rapidly changing worker and employer roles.

THE EVOLUTION OF EMPLOYEE DEVELOPMENT TECHNOLOGY

Computer-based career planning (CBCP) systems began in 1966 when International Business Machines (IBM) produced their initial cathode ray tube.[4] The use of a phone or cable line terminal directly linked to a mainframe system allowed individuals to use a multiple-choice career assessment system and writing process to evaluate career interests. More than 12 CBCP systems were created during the next five years.[5]

The next step in CBCP was with the development of the Computerized Vocational Information System (CVIS) by JoAnn Harris-Bowlsbey. With the co-leadership of Jack Rayman, CVIS led to the eventual creation of DISCOVER, which was primarily focused on providing individuals completing their formal education with tools to make informed career decisions. Many career development planning software products have been created throughout the 1990s and until the present. The evolution of CBCP systems added flexible career assessment components to address specific individual needs.[6] To maintain high-quality employee development activities, organizational leaders must ensure that the content is kept accurate and current. In addition to formalized commercial products, many organizations have developed customized career development products.

EMPLOYEE MANAGEMENT IN THE TWENTY-FIRST CENTURY

Organizations such as Intel, Motorola, and Chevron have committed to creating stronger work environments by creating career centers designed to support employees with career development training, career counseling, and technological assessments aimed at clearly defining career aspirations.[7] Many organizational leaders take the position that, while they will supply the technology and resources to assist employees in developing career plans, individual workers bear responsibility for the process.

Individual career planning can benefit both employees and employers. Proactive career planning efforts have several benefits. They can match competencies to job functions, create resources (a talent pool) for effective succession planning efforts, and maintain employee satisfaction levels by providing employee learning and development opportunities.

Integrated career solutions for organizations are likely to continue due to more readily available technological solutions for career development, videoconferencing technology, e-mail, and other relevant internal materials.[8] These tools reinforce the notion that technology will provide the means for employee development activities through many media. Today's organizational leaders cannot ignore the endless possibilities of technology-based systems that can be mass customized to meet the unique needs of their businesses.

The Impact of the Internet

Technology—and especially the Internet—has redefined approaches to career education delivery through reducing costs, increasing availability, and leveraging on-site solutions.[9] The Internet has dramatically changed how education is delivered, since it makes learning experiences available at any time and location to anyone with a computer. Traditional educational institutions are gradually changing into on-site "virtual" institutions that can make many blended career development tools available. These tools can address individual development needs through learning technologies such as CD tutorials, interactive training seminars, and inter- and intranet learning environments supplemented by online chat environments.[10] The conversion of traditional learning models to technology-based approaches is growing at about 30 percent annually, combining technical and softer skills development to create well-rounded employees.[11]

Technology-Based Employee Development Training

Many companies today should make greater use of available technology to help them realize their employees' potential. Numerous ways exist to use technology to develop employees. Four principal approaches have evolved over the last 10 years: client/server systems, computer- and Web-based training, distance learning, and e-learning.

Technological advances have also fostered the development of virtual universities, which have become very popular because they offer the flexibility of conducting development activities that are convenient for learners, employers, and training providers. As businesses branch out to become more internationally involved due to economic strategy and necessity, "just-in-time" training is becoming crucial to remaining competitive.

Client/Server Systems

The client/server training system became popular early in the 1990s. While computer-based training (CBT) and Web-based training (WBT) are the newest advancements in technology-based training systems, many smaller organizations are still using client/server instruction to support career development. Client/server systems operate by using a central server to store software applications in which computers from other sites (clients) transfer information back and forth on an Intranet. In 1994, 70 percent of Fortune 1000 companies were using client/server technologies as a means of offering career planning opportunities to employees.[12]

Most client/server systems require other methods of learning to supplement the technology. The training activities on client/server applications are limited because large amounts of information cannot be stored in the computer network; incorporating large amounts of multimedia within a training package on a client/server system can reduce the overall effectiveness and performance of the training. Client/server training can still be an effective tool for small businesses with specific learning objectives that do not require much computing power. As an introductory computer-based training program, the client/server approach has proven to be successful. As the Internet and high bandwidth–capable computer networks developed, technology-based employee development systems took a leap forward. Multimedia enhancements and online simulation-based programs allowed the creation of computer and Web-based training systems.

COMPUTER-BASED AND WEB-BASED TRAINING

CBT and WBT have become incredibly common in business. This training primarily focuses on completing specific learning/development objectives. CBT instruction typically originates from a CD-ROM and tends to be presented in a self-study format. WBT tends to focus on non-subjective learning initiatives designed to transfer knowledge on formalized work processes and procedures.[13]

CBT/WBT Utilization in Business Organizations

As intranet technologies become more easily configurable and manageable, large companies are leveraging this methodology to train, develop, and prepare for internal succession efforts and career goal achievement. Digital Equipment Corporation has created an intranet career development site that focuses on helping employees create individual performance plans and development goals that are directly related to their business strategy through the creation of more than 1,000 training courses.[14] Driscoll indicates that a report from International

Data Corporation forecast that this market would exceed $6 billion by 2002, representing a compound annual growth rate of almost 95 percent from 1997 to 2002.[15]

Additional Benefits of CBT/WBT

While WBT allows individuals to complete training at their own pace, success in these programs hinges on participants' abilities to engage in self-directed learning and develop metacognitive skills for the Web. Some experts assert that Web-based training should be considered one method of competency development that compliments other required training methodologies. It is important to note that, while WBT and CBT have obvious benefits for employee development, they are not the only approaches to training. Multiple approaches and learning styles must be taken into account when developing employees with computer-based tools.

An important benefit of WBT is the reduction in training costs. WBT has been shown to cost only half as much as traditional classroom training, as there are fewer limitations on space, time, and travel expenses.[16] WBT also assists employers in maintaining records of training progress.

Technology offers additional benefits that can streamline human resource functions. Many organizations devoted vast amounts of staff time before the assistance of computer technology to aid in the accumulation, data processing, and planning of employee development progression. Organizations using computers in training have minimized the employee hours spent in planning, compiling, and analyzing data. These benefits serve as a financial incentive for businesses to implement technology-assisted career planning approaches that use training to build individual competencies.

DISTANCE LEARNING

Distance learning (DL) is more interactive than CBT or WBT. DL relies heavily on technology and can be valuable for making development opportunities available. DL takes many forms, including videoconferencing, Internet chat rooms, virtual universities, and teleconferencing. These delivery methods can be combined with traditional print workbooks, educational videos, and assorted printed training documents.

The Purpose of Distance Learning

DL as an instructional methodology focuses on building job-specific competencies required to achieve organizational goals. Personalized DL reduces the time needed by learners to acquire skills and progress to competence; it also provides efficient methods for reviewing pertinent material to maximize on-the-job training.[17]

The Application of Distance Learning

DL facilitates consistent training for employees working in domestic or multinational organizations. Many organizations are seizing competitive advantage by pursuing business opportunities around the globe. DL provides the training needed for a decentralized workforce that engages in work 24/7. Additionally, this method of providing employee development allows participants to engage in personal interaction and can encourage problem-solving discussions.

Virtual Universities

DL allows individuals to study many areas to increase their marketability to prepare for future employment opportunities. This approach is growing in popularity at large universities and is regarded as an alternative to on-site education for workers. Virtual universities offer individuals the flexibility of completing their courses when convenient for them and their employers. Many online certificate and degree programs are available to individuals wanting to take advantage of formally accredited programs to enhance their skills. That is particularly appealing to individuals who are constrained by time and geography, as many adult learners are.

E-LEARNING

Leading companies worldwide are implementing e-learning initiatives to develop their workforces.[18] E-learning, as a method of training, refers to the manipulation of information provided through many electronic formats to enhance desired learning outcomes for participants.

The Intent of E-Learning

While distance learning primarily focuses on developing job-specific skills, e-learning provides similar training while also making available a vast employee development and planning component through the Internet. One key benefit of e-learning the ease with which participants may access the training. Learners facing training obstacles due to their geographic location or technology limitations can receive equally focused training from a larger pool of trained individuals.[19] That is especially important when an employer provides only limited on-the-job time for employee development. The ability to access and continually utilize services while away from work serves to enhance the potential of the individual (who may then better serve the employer). E-learning through the Internet also provides a sense of anonymity for those people who fear researching career-oriented information because they worry about repercussions from their employers. The ability to remain anonymous may also have a positive impact on those learners who are hesitant to "expose" their skill gaps, as they have a greater tendency to avail themselves of these services.[20] Since e-learning is accessible from work or home, this training tool provides a sense of learner empowerment, since they can manage when, where, and what they learn.[21]

Employee Development through the World Wide Web

Internet Web sites linked to career development topics have been commonplace since 2000. More are added daily.[22] Table 6.1 lists Web sites offering tools and assessments that can be used with career planning programs.

Computer-Assisted Career Guidance Systems

The new wave of technology-based systems, provided primarily over the Internet, is known as computer-assisted career guidance (CACG) systems. These systems are often promoted to organizations on a

TABLE 6.1   Internet-Based Career Development Web Sites

Career development Web sites	http://www.careerexperience.com/index.html/
	http://www.rileyguide.com/
	http://www.careermag.com/careermag/
	http://www.petersons.com/
	http://www.careerbuilder.com/
	http://www.jobbankusa.com/
	http://www.careerdevelopment-resources.net/
	http://www.jobstar.org/tools/career/spec-car.cfm
	http://www.monster.com/
	http://www.employment911.com/
Career development Web sites for workers with disabilities	http://www.business-disability.com/
	http://www.disability.gov/
	http://www.eop.com/
	http://janweb.icdi.wvu.edu/
Career development Web sites for diverse populations	http://www.diversityworking.com/home/
	http://www.culturaldiversitysite. com/Minority-Job-Bank.html
	http://www.newsjobs.com/
Career development Web sites for job-specific searches	http://www.coolworks.com/
	http://www.hrsjobs.com/
	http://federaljobs.net/
Career and wage specific information Web sites	http://www.doleta.gov/programs/onet/
	http://www.wageweb.com/
	http://www.salary.com/salary/layoutscripts/ sall_display.asp
Professional career development organization Web sites	http://ncda.org/
	http://www.astd.org/

Source: Kingh, S. C. (2004). Internet-based career development Web sites. Unpublished manuscript. University Park, PA: Penn State University.

fee-per-use or contractual basis.[23] CACG systems enhance what employers offer in career services to their employees. To make this method of career training more successful, many fee-based groups are also utilizing autonomous Web sites as supplemental tools to their services.[24] Offer and Sampson indicate that a comprehensive, effective computer-based guidance system must be integrated with various tools that may include formalized career-related assessments for diagnostic identification of needs, a plan to address identified skill gaps, and instruments to develop learners based on testing and planning results.[25] While subscription-based CACG systems may not appeal to cost-sensitive managers, the evidence is overwhelming that e-learning investments can substantially reduce training costs.

CACG systems that have been implemented in many large organizations have unique purposes. A CACG is not a training application; rather, it is a diagnostic tool that clarifies and prioritizes developmental areas. Moreover, CACG systems facilitate gap analysis by permitting ways to compare employees' education and skills to the competencies required for present or future positions. Training intervention should be based on the results of CACG rather than the reverse. If this assessment and training is done properly, the training costs can be sharply reduced.

The initial costs of incorporating a fully functional and all-encompassing employee development technology center can be cost-prohibitive for some companies. Therefore, technology-based employee development activities vary widely among organizations. Many small organizations continue to use client/server technology to their advantage.

Employers with the appropriate financial resources or technology have embraced distance learning and e-learning as modes of career development. Distance learning has marked differences from client/server, WBT, and CBT, as it relies on human interaction to be a successful learning and development tool. E-learning has become very popular as a tool to reach many individuals, due to its ability to serve workers on a global basis through the Internet. The Internet has also allowed individuals to tap career development Web sites to assist in their development. Additionally, e-learning provides access to current, pertinent information, allowing employees to make informed decisions concerning their career planning.

ALTERNATIVE EMPLOYEE DEVELOPMENT TECHNOLOGIES

Corporations have seized the opportunity to put technology to work in many ways to meet employee needs. "Personalized" career-planning resources are being used in many organizations today. They include internal job postings for open positions, work performance data, and even competency-based, and computerized training that allow employees to assess their skills with particular job classifications.

There are essential components to Warner and Keagey's technological career development solution in which businesses competitively
generate career planning systems that are fully integrated in an effort to
be more effective and cost-efficient.[26] Technology is also being "pushed"
further to provide the next generation of employee development tools.
One such emerging technology is a tool that learns about an employee
and custom designs training to facilitate their development.

EMPLOYEE DEVELOPMENT TECHNOLOGY CAUTIONS

While ample evidence exists to support the benefits of technology-
based training, some issues must be addressed to ensure peak effectiveness. One issue to consider is that good instructional design and delivery
remain of crucial importance in achieving effective learner outcomes.
They are especially important for self-paced activities with little human
interaction. Poorly designed courses can create frustration.

Another issue that must be addressed is the need for multisensory
environments that provide for human interaction. These environments
assist in collaboration and provide a feedback method that allows
learners to improve their skills. Further, recognition of learners' cognitive and perceptual abilities is significant when planning to implement a
career development system. Individuals lacking the ability to make informed career-related decisions may require special attention to make
their planning meaningful.

While good instructional design and delivery are always important,
along with due consideration of the targeted learner audience, other
issues must also be addressed. Securing sufficient financial resources to
design and implement a computer-based career system is another issue.
Developing and using technology can be costly. To combat soaring
technology costs, many smaller businesses have created learning con-
sortia to pool available technology for use by several organizations.

The Need for Effective Instructional Design

One important factor in successful online teaching and learning
is how the information is designed and delivered. Synchronous and

asynchronous training must be properly planned to meet the needs of the audience, and the materials must be appropriate to the targeted learners.[27] Poorly developed e-learning courses are the result of poor planning and lead to ineffective and inefficient training.[28] To simulate the traditional classroom and create successful technology-based employee development programs, learners must be the primary concern.

Multisensory Environments

An ideal learning environment engages the audience in interactive discussion and activities, provides evaluation as necessary, and offers methods for workplace simulation to encourage learning transfer back to the workplace.[29] To make courses as realistic as possible, as well as pertinent to employees' career goals, training must be tailored to the unique needs of the targeted learners—as best those needs can be determined.

The Human Connection

Learning must be interactive if it is to be effective.[30] Additionally, programs that blend training methodologies and technology within the classroom environment can be much more specific, competent, and calculated. Human contact can help to create an interactive environment, which can be achieved through use of face-to-face meetings, teleconferencing, chat rooms, and in some cases the traditional classroom.

Cognitive and Perceptual Capabilities

Understanding the adult learning process can be difficult but is essential to creating meaningful training and development. The ways by which individuals acquire knowledge can change over time, so age-specific training procedures are sometimes necessary.[31] In general, individuals with low initiative or basic skill sets should receive targeted assistance to maximize their learning and developmental potential.[32] Addressing the special needs of specific worker groups is crucial.

Technology Troubles

The start-up costs of creating a computer-based employee development program can be overwhelming. To maintain a cutting-edge development program that uses online components, companies need high bandwidth capacity. Each organization should have clearly defined goals for their career development system and use available technology as effectively as possible. Formulating technology and training partnerships with other trade organizations and postsecondary educational institutions is often a viable solution.[33]

Organizational Collaboration and Ethical Issues

Ethical issues can surface when several institutions share computer-based employee development program. As with any activity that takes place over the Internet, security should always be a concern. Ethical concerns should be at the forefront of an organization's plans when developing online components for a comprehensive career development system.

CONCLUSION

A career planning program is key to employee retention. After all, employees have evolved in that they want further training and a clearer understanding of competencies required for present and future jobs. Employers who choose not to incorporate a career program may risk higher rates of turnover and worker dissatisfaction. Combining technology and human interaction can usually address the needs of all employees. The partnering of organizations and academic programs has emerged as a way to leverage financial resources for career planning and training.[34]

NOTES

1. Hall, D. T., & Associates (1986). *Career development in organizations.* San Francisco: Jossey-Bass.

2. Harris-Bowlsbey, J., & Sampson Jr., J. P. (2001). Computer-based career planning systems: Dreams and realities. *Career Development Quarterly, 49,* 250–260.

3. Rothwell, W. J., & Sredl, H. J. (1992). *Professional human resource development roles and competencies* (2nd ed.). Amherst, MA: HRD Press, 400.

4. Harris-Bowlsbey, J., & Sampson Jr., J. P. (2001). Computer-based career planning systems: Dreams and realities. *Career Development Quarterly, 49,* 250–260.

5. Myers, R. (1970). Computer-aided counseling: Some issues of adoption and use. In D. E. Super (Ed.), *Computer-assisted counseling* (pp. 109–117). New York: Teachers College Press.

6. Sampson, J. P., Jr., Reardon, R. C., Reed, C., Rudd, E., Lumsden, J., Epstein, S., Folsom, B., et al. (1998). A differential feature-cost analysis of seventeen computer-assisted career guidance systems (8th ed., Technical Report No. 10). Tallahassee: Florida State University, Center for the Study of Technology in Counseling and Career Development [On-line]. Available: http://www.career.fsu.edu/techcenter/trl0.html.

7. Caudron, S. (1995, September). HR revamps career itineraries. *Business Credit, 97,* 20–23.

8. Harris-Bowlsbey, J., & Sampson Jr., J. P. (2001). Computer–based career planning systems: Dreams and realities. *Career Development Quarterly, 49,* 250–260.

9. McMorrow, J. (1999, September). Future trends in human resources. *HR Focus, 76,* 7–9.

10. Shah, A., Sterrett, C., Chesser, J., & Wilmore, J. (2001). Meeting the need for employee development in the 21st century. *S.A.M. Advanced Management Journal, 66,* 22–28.

11. St-Amour, D. (2000, Fall). Technology: A vital tool to teach professional development skills. *Canadian Manager, 25,* 13, 15.

12. Haber, L. (1994, May 2). The first step to success. *Computer Reseller, 576,* SS49.

13. Driscoll, M. (1999). Web-based training in the workplace. *Adult Learning, 10,* 21–25.

14. Smith, B. (1997, October). Career development: Compliments of . . . your employer? *Management Review, 86,* 25–27.

15. Driscoll, M. (1999). Web-based training in the workplace. *Adult Learning, 10,* 21–25.

16. Shah, A., Sterrett, C., Chesser, J., & Wilmore, J. (2001). Meeting the need for employee development in the 21st century. *S.A.M. Advanced Management Journal, 66,* 22–28.

17. Ibid.

18. Oliver, R. W. (2001). The return of human capital. *Journal of Business Strategy, 22,* 7–10.

19. Offer, M., & Sampson, J. P. (1999). Quality in the content and use of information and communication technology in guidance. *British Journal of Guidance and Counseling, 27,* 501–516.

20. Krumboltz, J. D., & Winzelberg, A. (1997). Technology applied to learning and group support for career-related concerns. *Career Planning and Adult Development Journal, 13,* 101–110; Offer, M., & Watts, A. G. (1997). *The Internet and careers work.* NICEC Briefing. Cambridge, UK: National Institute for Careers Education and Counseling; Sampson, J. P., Jr. (1998a). The Internet as a potential force for a social change. In C. C. Lee & G. R. Walz (Eds.), *Social action: A mandate for counselors* (pp. 213–225). Greensboro, NC: University of North Carolina, ERIC Clearinghouse on Counseling and Student Services.

21. Alutto, J. A. (1999, January). Just in time management education in the 21st century. *HR Magazine, 44,* 56.

22. Bleuer, J. C., & Walz, G. R. (1998). ERIC/CASS virtual libraries: Online resources for parents, teachers, and counselors. In J. M. Allen (Ed.), *School counseling: New perspectives and practices* (pp. 177–185). Greensboro, NC: ERIC/CASS, University of North Carolina; Offer, M. (1997). *Supporting career guidance in the information society: A review of the use of computer-assisted guidance and the Internet in Europe.* [Report without identification number]. Dublin, Ireland: National Centre for Guidance in Education; Offer, M., & Watts, A. G. (1997). *The Internet and careers work.* NICEC Briefing. Cambridge, UK: National Institute for Careers Education and Counseling; Smith, M. (1997). The benefits of integrating Internet technologies into career services. *Australian Journal of Career Development, 6,* 11–13; Wolfinger, A. (1998). *The quick Internet guide to career and college information.* Indianapolis, IN: JIST Works; Woods, J. F., & Ollis, H. (1996). Labor market, job information proliferates on-line. *Workforce Journal, 5,* 32–44; Woods, J. F., Ollis, H., & Kaplan, R. (1996). *To spin a web: Job, career, and labor market on the Internet* (Occasional paper no. 08). Washington, DC: National Occupational Information Coordinating Committee.

23. Sampson, J. P., Jr. (1999). Integrating Internet-based distance guidance with services provided in career centers. *Career Development Quarterly, 47* (3), 243–254.

24. Sampson, J. P., Jr. (1997, October). *Enhancing the use of career information with computer-assisted career guidance systems.* Plenary paper presented at the symposium, The Present and Future of Computer-Assisted Career Guidance Systems in Japan, Japan Institute of Labor, Tokyo.

25. Offer, M., & Sampson, J. P. (1999). Quality in the content and use of information and communication technology in guidance. *British Journal of Guidance and Counseling, 27,* 501–516.

26. Warner, J. & Keagey, J. (1997). Creating a virtual career development center. *HR Focus, 74* (10), 11–12.

27. Lau, R. S. M. (2000, December). Issues and outlook of e-learning. *South Dakota Business Review, 59* (2), 1, 4+.

28. Oliver, R. W. (2001). The return of human capital. *Journal of Business Strategy, 22,* 7–10.

29. Ibid.

30. Motti, J. N. (2000, January 3). Learn at a distance. *Informationweek, 767,* 75.

31. Mead, S. L., & Fisk, A. D. (1998). Measuring skill acquisition and retention with an ATM simulator: The need for age-specific training. *Human Factors, 40,* 516–523.

32. Sampson, J. P., Jr., Peterson, G. W., Reardon, R. C., & Lenz, J. G. (2000). Using readiness assessment to improve career services: A cognitive information-processing approach. *Career Development Quarterly, 49,* 146–174.

33. Shah, A., Sterrett, C., Chesser, J., & Wilmore, J. (2001). Meeting the need for employee development in the 21st century. *S.A.M. Advanced Management Journal, 66,* 22–28.

34. Ibid.

III

STRATEGIES FOR INTEGRATING CAREER AND SUCCESSION PLANNING

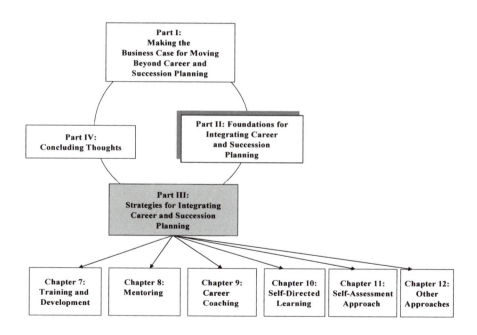

SEVEN

TRAINING AND DEVELOPMENT

This is the nuts-and-bolts chapter that deals with the how-to of career development. We cut to the chase with these questions:

- Does your organization have an active career development function that serves your employees?
- Do you believe that your organization pays proper attention to your employees' career development?
- Are career development issues addressed strategically or tactically?
- Does your organization maintain an up-to-date career management strategy?
- Is workforce transition a key function of your HR department, or does your HR department still serve as just a transactional function?

In previous chapters, we discussed competencies, assessments, and evaluation of career development and succession planning. Think of the following four chapters as your tool kit that holds the ideas, methods, and resources to actualize an effective career development and succession planning program within your organization. More questions and challenges develop:

- What tools—if any—are used effectively by your organization's career development professionals?
- What is career planning, organizational career development, and career management?
- EVERYONE into the talent pool?

The answers are hardly simple!

Many retirements are soon expected in all U.S. economic sectors. That is one reason why many organizational leaders are scrambling to put succession planning programs in place. Another reason is to use succession planning programs as a retention strategy to address the high percentage in the workforce of *new age* or *free agent* workers, who feel limited loyalty to one organization. To remain ahead of the low supply and high demand for high-potential employees, organizational leaders must be proactive. They must establish and implement long-term talent plans that are integrated with strategic business plans.

Career planning and succession planning are both efforts intended to address gaps between what is and what should be. Career planning focuses on individual goals compared to existing roles and competencies. Succession planning may focus on meeting the future talent needs of the organization at all levels. Integrating them brings together individual interests and organizational needs. However, to achieve this integration, HR efforts must be aligned with the goals of these programs. Examples of HR efforts, which may encourage or discourage individuals from taking action to develop themselves and thereby to help build bench strength, include any or all of the following:

- Workforce planning
- Recruitment and hiring
- Employee promotion, transfer, rotational, and other movement policies

- Employee orientation and socialization efforts that are intended to help individuals become enculturated to the organization
- Training employees
- Performance management
- Coaching and feedback approaches
- Employee development
- Other relevant HR policies and practices, including reward policies[1]

This chapter focuses on the role of training in narrowing developmental gaps to meet career planning and succession planning program needs. Training is singled out for special attention precisely because it is often the first thing that managers—and employees—think of when they think about how to narrow developmental gaps between existing and needed competencies. While it is not the only way to do that, and may not even be the most effective way, it still warrants attention simply because it is the first thing that people think of.

THE FUTURE OF WORK

In the mid-1990s, Hall and Associates noted that what "work" will really be is unpredictable in the future. To begin planning for a career, individuals must invest time and effort to explore the future of what work really is—and what it will become.[2] In 1999, the World Future Society published 93 ways our lives will change by 2025 through advances made by "cyber society." Based on current trends, Cornish anticipates changes in the concept of "work" in Table 7.1.[3]

"Work" is now a new paradigm: it is not about what a person is or should be, or what that person does, but is about who he or she is and can become.[4] To stay current and thus remain employable, individuals must continuously acquire and build competencies through self-directed, lifelong learning. Many acute economic and business changes are causing dramatic shifts in how career planning and succession planning are conceptualized and implemented. Zheng and Kleiner address environmental stimuli and career development:[5]

TABLE 7.1 The Concept of Work

Future Work Developments	Anticipations
Permanent mass unemployment is a serious possibility for the near future.	The world is not running out of work for people to do. Developing programs that will successfully move the unemployed into doing the jobs that need doing is one of the great challenges of the future.
	Computer networks should make it easy to locate the exact sort of specialist or product that you want. In the past, poor communications often made it impractical or even impossible for people with highly specialized skills or knowledge to find enough customers to earn a living, but electronic databanks should solve that problem.
Jobs will become more specialized than ever.	The result could be a "golden age" for highly specialized consultants. Hiring such an expert for a quick consultation will be easy due to electronic credit systems.
	Employers look for workers with leading-edge skills, but the leading edge can soon become the laggard edge.
Skills and knowledge will become obsolete faster than ever.	The half-life of an engineer's knowledge—as little as three years in some fields—will rapidly shrink. Constant retraining is essential to keep people from becoming increasingly less qualified for their jobs.
	A fast-changing society poses major dangers for people who have difficulty adjusting to new situations, but it is a wonderland for entrepreneurs—those imaginative and energetic self-starters who can recognize emerging needs and create ways to fill them.
The cyber society will put a high premium on entrepreneurship.	Entrepreneurs have developed thousands of new occupations. Some of the biggest companies in the world today (Intel and Microsoft, for example) are based on products that could hardly have been imagined a few decades ago.

Source: Cornish, E. (1999). Ways our lives will change by the year 2025. From *The cyber future.* Bethesda, MD: World Future Society. Used by permission. From the World Future Society.

Specialized versus Generalized Career Planning

Internet and database technology have allowed free agents and skilled specialists (consultants and trainers) to market their services around the world and develop a unique customer base. Meanwhile, organizations often need specialized expertise to contribute solutions to a unique project or design and deliver training on exotic work. In this case, the free agent consultant and the organization match perfectly. However, if specialists fail to remain at the leading edge of their professions, demand for their services will quickly disappear.

The Shrinking Globe

There is no geographic isolation anymore. The "shrinking globe" is forcing managers and workers alike to learn about and deal with the rules of other cultures.

Computers Everywhere

Computers are now performing many jobs formerly done by people. The presence of computers in virtually every job necessitates specific technological competencies. Technology competence is becoming fused with competence in every line of work.

Inadequate Educational Systems

The traditional education system, in which students receive an education and use it for the rest of their lives, is no longer sufficient. In today's world, workers must constantly upgrade and update their skills. Training and retraining are required for almost all jobs in the future.

Newfound Loyalties

Employers' commitment to workers is now temporary, lasting only as long as work is to be done. Likewise, workers no longer expect a traditional employment contract. Instead, workers make a commitment to their own crafts or skill repertoires. Workers must learn—as part of a continuing growth pattern—to pick up new skills to be less vulnerable to risk.

THE ESSENTIAL LINK: HUMAN CAPITAL TO CAREER DEVELOPMENT

One key concept in linking career development with human capital is the belief that human capital represents the chief competitive difference between organizations. Naturally, all assets are critical to organizational success, but to build and operate a solid, loyal, and valued workforce, a career development program must be strategically linked to human capital management. If organizational leaders do not support the concept that human capital adds value to the company, any career development program will be practically useless. An active career program aids in attracting and retaining talented people and can uncover hidden talent within the workforce.

When employees are surveyed on what they view as important benefits, training and opportunities to develop in their profession are always in the top three. It is important to note that inadequate career opportunities can lead to a disconnect between training, which is a means of building competencies, and promotional opportunities. In such instances, employee turnover rates may increase as trained and fully developed high performers flee to competitors.[6]

Human capital management activities may differ slightly by enterprise, but they generally include planning, acquiring, maintaining or supporting, developing, and retaining employees.[7] As discussed in Chapter 1, the U.S. General Accounting Office presents four "human capital cornerstones" in its model of strategic human capital management:[8]

- Leadership
- Strategic human capital planning
- Acquiring, developing, and retaining talent
- Results-oriented organizational cultures

Table 7.2 outlines important cornerstones in acquiring, developing, and retaining talent.

TABLE 7.2 Human Capital Cornerstones—Acquiring, Developing, and Retaining Talent (Explanation of levels 1, 2, 3 appear in table 7.3)

Critical Success Factors	Level 1	Level 2	Level 3
Targeted invest-ments in people	Organization leaders approach human capital expenditures (e.g., professional development and knowledge management, recruiting program, pay and benefits, performance incentives, and enabling technol-ogy) as costs that should be minimized rather than as investments that should be managed to maximize value while minimizing risk. Funding decisions may be ad hoc, without clearly de-fined objectives or adequate con-sideration of their implications for the workforce.	Human capital expenditures are regarded as investments in people and in the organization's capacity to perform its mission. Investment strate-gies for acquiring, developing, and retaining staff are evaluated and developed in light of modern capital management practices.	Organization strategies for investing in human capital are fully integrated with needs identified through its strategic and annual planning. The goals and expectations for those investments are transparent and clearly defined, and their rationale is consistent across the range of human capital programs. The efficiency of the investments is continuously monitored and the effectiveness is periodically evaluated.
Human capital approaches tailored to meet organizational needs	Managers believe that meaningful improvements in human capital management are not feasible.	Standardizations and by-the-book human capital management are yielding to flexible and innovative approaches.	Organization tailors its human capital strategies to meet specific mission needs. It is taking all appropriate administrative actions available.

TABLE 7.2 *(Continued)*

Critical Success Factors	Level 1	Level 2	Level 3
	The range of tools and flexibilities available to the organization under current laws and regulations has yet to be explored. Organization may have self-imposed constraints in place that are excessively process-oriented or based on obsolete perceptions or laws, rules, or regulations.	Managers have identified the tools and flexibilities available to them and are using many of these to modernize their human capital approaches to help meet current and emerging needs. Organization is looking both within and outside itself for model principles and practices and is pursing opportunities to test new and more results-oriented approaches.	It is exploring opportunities to enhance its competitiveness as an employer and eliminate barriers to effective human capital management. If needed, this includes producing a compelling business case to support select initiatives.

Source: Adapted from U.S. General Accounting Office. (2002, March). *A Model of Strategic Human Capital Management.* GAO-02-373SP. Washington, DC: Author.

Associated with each cornerstone are critical success factors. These factors are critical to organizational success. Each factor is divided into three levels of organization performance evaluation (see Table 7.3).[9] The two critical success factors for acquiring, developing, and retaining talent are targeted investments in people and human capital approaches tailored to meet organizational needs.[10]

WHAT'S IN A NAME?

The concept of the career has evolved over the past 50 years and will continue to change as technology reinvents and redefines the

TABLE 7.3   Three Levels of Evaluation

Level 1	• Approach is largely compliance-based • Organization has yet to realize the value of managing human capital strategically to achieve results • Existing human capital approaches have yet to be assessed in light of current and emerging organizational needs
Level 2	• Organization recognizes that people are a critical asset and must be managed strategically • New human capital policies, programs, and practices are being designed and implemented to support mission accomplishment
Level 3	• Organization's human capital approaches contribute to improved organization performance • Human capital considerations are fully integrated into strategic planning and day-to-day operations • Organizations continuously seeking ways to further improve its people management to achieve results

Source: Adapted from U.S. General Accounting Office. (2002, March). *A Model of Strategic Human Capital Management.* GAO-02-373SP. Washington, DC: Author.

business world. The traditional organizational career has been replaced by free agent workers who pursue boundaryless careers in boundaryless organizations.[11] In the context of this book, career development is addressed as one of the three major human resource development functions, along with training and development and organization development. Traditionally, the term *career* represented the logical progression of an employee from one position (typically entry level) to positions of greater importance, responsibility, and authority along with corresponding increases in pay, respect, and status.[12] Historically, careers were guided by paternalistic leaders in organizations. Individuals had minimal input regarding their future with the organization. In the "new age" of business, competition became extreme, levels of customer expectations increased, reorganization became standard, and sufficient quantities of qualified, skilled workers had to be trained and prepared for a new technology-based work environment (see Table 7.4).

For the purposes of this volume, the terminology presented by Gutteridge in his model of organizational career development will be used to define *career planning, career development,* and *career management* (see Figure 7.1).[13]

TABLE 7.4 The Career in a Changing World

Key Survey Findings	Results from Findings
Career information digital divide	People without computer skills and Internet access could be at a disadvantage in pursuing job and career opportunities.
	Americans who have limited incomes and lower levels of education, as well as members of some minority groups, will have less access to job and career information.
Adults in the United States express need for career assistance	9% of adults in the labor force reported needing assistance with career planning, in making career plans or in selecting, changing or getting a job. Young adults and nonwhites are more likely to report needing help in the job market.
	69% of respondents state that they would try to get more information about the job and career options open to them than they got the first time.
	39% would seek assistance from a counselor; 35% from informal sources (family, friends, neighbors, relatives, associates)
Job change is viewed by many as a positive experience	61% of employed adults expect to stay at their current job over the next three-year period.
	17% expect to change jobs voluntarily.
	Career transitions are often voluntary and are positive for the individual making them.
Adults appreciate the need for lifelong learning	70% of employed adults report receiving some type of career assistance from their employer.
	53% of adults say they will need more training or education to maintain or increase their earning power.
Adults are not clear on the effects of globalization on their job	38% said they didn't believe that globalization would affect their job.

Source: National Career Development Association. (2000, June). *Career connecting in a changing context: A summary of the key findings of the 1999 national survey of working America.* Retrieved January 8, 2004, from http://ncda.org/pdf/gallupwhitepaper.pdf. Reprinted with permission of the National Career Development Association.

- *Career planning:* A deliberate process for (1) becoming aware of self, opportunities, constraints, choices, and consequences; (2) identifying career-related goals; and (3) programming work, education, and related developmental experiences to provide the direction, timing, and sequence of steps to attain a specific career goal.

- *Organizational career development:* The outcomes emanating from the interaction of individual career planning and institutional (organizational) career management processes.
- *Career management:* An ongoing process of preparing, implementing, and monitoring career plans undertaken by the individual alone or in concert with the organization's career system.[14]

Each warrants elaboration.

Career Planning

Career planning is a process in which individuals study—formally or informally—what factors affect their world of work. As this process is based on individual efforts, results vary from formal approaches that involve professional career counselors and diagnostic instruments to informal job searches that are carried out by electronic or print want ads. According to Hall and associates, key components of career planning are as follows:

- Discovering one's self, opportunities, constraints, choices, and consequences
- Identifying career-related goals

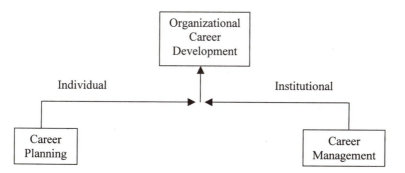

FIGURE 7.1   A working model of organizational career development. *Source:* Gutteridge, T. G. (1986). Organizational career development systems: The State of the practice. In D. T. Hall & Associates (eds.), *Career Development in Organizations,* San Francisco: Jossey-Bass, 1986, 54. Copyright © 1986. This material is used by permission of John Wiley & Sons, Inc.

- Assembling work, education, networks, personal talents, and similar work/life experiences to develop a logical strategy or plan to achieve a specific career goal[15]

Various career planning models are available. The University of Waterloo, Canada, provides an excellent model through its online *Career Development eManual*. The e-manual is organized into six steps to illustrate career movement from the bottom step, self-assessment, up to the top step, life/work planning (see Figure 7.2).[16]

Career Development

Career development is the collaboration of an organization and its employees to ensure that the right people with the right knowledge, skills, and abilities are in the right places at the right times to produce the

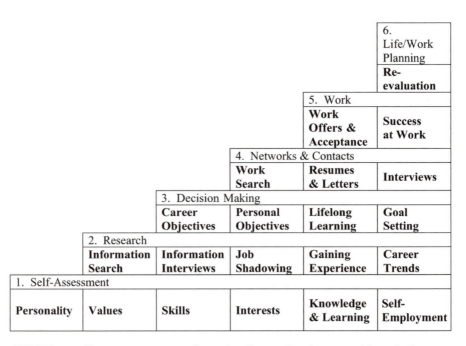

				6. Life/Work Planning
				Re-evaluation
		5. Work		
		Work Offers & Acceptance	**Success at Work**	
	4. Networks & Contacts			
	Work Search	**Resumes & Letters**	**Interviews**	
3. Decision Making				
Career Objectives	**Personal Objectives**	**Lifelong Learning**	**Goal Setting**	
2. Research				
Information Search	**Information Interviews**	**Job Shadowing**	**Gaining Experience**	**Career Trends**
1. Self-Assessment				
Personality	**Values**	**Skills**	**Interests**	**Knowledge & Learning**	**Self-Employment**

FIGURE 7.2 Six steps to success from the *Career Development eManual. Source: Career Development eManual* (Waterloo, Canada: University of Waterloo). Retrieved from http://www.cdm.uwaterloo.ca/steps.asp. Used with permission from Career Services, University of Waterloo.

right goods or services. It is a challenge for an organization to stay competitive (or "right sized") while keeping its workforce sufficiently developed to achieve and sustain peak performance. Career development activities consist of interaction between an employee and a representative of the organization such as a supervisor, manager, or career advisor from the HR department. Although career development is the point at which the employee and the organization link for mutual planning, the role of career development is often interpreted differently by the employee and organizational leaders.

Traditionally, employees have understood career development to mean their roadmap to advancing through the ranks of one organization. Today's employees base their loyalty to one organization on how much intrinsic motivation or psychological reward they find in their work. For that reason, robust career development programs often help to retain employees because they enhance intrinsic motivation.

To the employee's immediate supervisor, career development means motivation and retention.[17] While an employee plans how to move up in the organization, his or her immediate supervisor is attempting to motivate the employee to be as productive as possible—and to remain on the job for as long as possible. The supervisor may take on the role of a coach or mentor, providing developmental "stretch" opportunities for the employee to excel and giving the employee visibility with even more senior-level managers.

Middle management tends to view career development from a completely different perspective, the systems view. Middle managers are interested in integrating career development and the human resource system. The more tightly career development is linked to human capital strategy, the more efficient the services rendered by the career development function will be.[18]

Top management may regard career development as a component of the organization's succession planning process. For succession planning to work, talented employees must be identified, developed, and prepared for advancement. If employees do not wish to advance—and growing numbers of employees remain in the same positions because they wish to balance work and life—then they must be pinpointed so that organizational resources are not squandered on those who do not want to prepare for higher-level responsibility.

Human resources is a logical place to position career development efforts, since their missions are closely aligned. An organization's mechanisms for measuring and forecasting workforce strength, recruiting, selecting, training, developing, appraising, promoting, and rewarding employees rely on HR.[19] However, organizations that maintain a performance unit may host the career development function there to capitalize on the synergy of organizational and human development activities.[20]

Career Management

Career management encompasses an organization's overall strategic focus on the workforce: staffing, managing onboard talent, employee retention, nonstandard staffing arrangements, and organization succession planning. The ultimate goal of career management is to ensure that an organization's human capital needs are met at all times and at all levels.

TRAINING AND DEVELOPMENT

Ideally, everyone hired by an organization would have participated in a program such as Canada's Blueprint for Life[21] or other individual development program so each employee's individual career paths would already be established. Meanwhile, the organization's human resource department would sponsor a fully functioning career resource center stocked with educational information and catalogs as well as materials describing the organization and how to progress successfully in it. The resource center would be staffed with a diverse group consisting of certified career counselors, paraprofessional career assistance advisors, and support staff. All supervisors and managers would be successful, and trained, performance coaches and mentors who encourage employees to pursue self-directed learning. Continuous performance appraisals would be welcomed by employees as a valuable source of personal and work-related feedback and regarded by supervisors and managers as fundamentally important to what they do. The organization would maintain, and continuously update, all aspects of its succession planning program.

Unfortunately, few organizations actually function this way. New hires often come to work with no idea where their careers may take them and can find no time to write an individual development plan as they fight daily fires. Those with workforce or career development responsibilities may be called career counselors but may never have received training to do it, let alone hold professional counseling certification. Supervisors and managers often claim they have better things to do than provide performance feedback to their employees. Succession planning is put off for rainy days (that never come), with the result that catastrophic losses or sudden death of incumbents in key positions may devastate the organization—and lead to plummeting stock prices.

Individual career planning is best addressed by certified career counselors, psychologists,[22] companies,[23] and colleges;[24] this section focuses on the role of training in narrowing the development gaps at the career development level. Specifically, we will address the roles and competencies of the positions responsible for career development.

CAREER ADVISOR

If the individual who performs actual career development functions is not formally trained and properly certified as a practicing counselor, the title "career advisor" is appropriate (rather than "career counselor"). The distinction may seem minor, but in a litigious society, it can protect the organization.

The National Career Development Association (NCDA) is explicit in its assertion that "career development professionals must only perform activities for which they 'possess or have access to the necessary skills and resources for giving the kind of help that is needed.' "[25] As the NCDA is the primary organization for establishing ethical standards for the career counseling field, its Career Counseling Competencies and Performance Indicators are published in Appendix 2. According to NCDA standards, "to work as a professional engaged in career counseling, the individual must demonstrate minimum competencies in 11 designated areas":[26]

- Career development theory
- Individual and group counseling skills
- Individual/group assessment

- Information/resources
- Program promotion, management, and implementation
- Coaching, consultation, and performance improvement
- Diverse populations
- Supervision
- Ethical/legal issues
- Research/evaluation
- Technology

These competencies were developed to serve as guidelines for those interested in career development occupations. They are intended for persons training at the master's degree level or higher with a specialty in career counseling.[27] Because the NCDA encourages the use of these competency statements by organizations wishing to establish career development training guidelines, we strongly recommend the adoption of these competencies for career advisors. Of course, there may be a need to adapt these general competencies to the unique corporate cultural environments of organizations using them.

WORKFORCE PLANNING

Another HR responsibility in which the career development function is involved is workforce planning. It is the process of identifying and addressing gaps between an organization's current workforce and its future human capital needs. One key question the career development function must answer is, "What type of career development and training does the organization provide to employees to maintain a highly skilled workforce?"

Since the competencies for success needed by employees are growing in number and changing rapidly, an organization's training program must be flexible if it is to be successful in training and retraining the organization's workforce. The continuous development of all employees is required to keep up with changes in organizational mission, strategic objectives, changing technology, and dynamically shifting work content. Continuous employee development also attracts, and helps to retain, younger workers for whom self-development is a top priority.

What follows are a few career development strategies to consider when developing a workforce:

- Individual development planning (IDP) (Chapter 10)
- Online learning (Chapter 6)
- Tuition reimbursement programs
- Mentoring programs (Chapter 8)
- Coaching programs (Chapter 9)
- Executive coaching
- Leadership development programs

An active retention strategy can keep high-performing and high-potential employees. Career development professionals must understand what attracts and keeps employees in an organization. Some examples of retention strategies are:

- Bonuses
- Incentive awards
- Promotions
- Work/life (family) programs
- Employee empowerment
- Improved communications
- Feedback

A particularly useful strategy is to take a hard look at the organization's exit interview approach. Traditional approaches, carried out on the last day, may lead to social desirability bias as workers give understandable, but false, reasons for leaving so that they can preserve good references. At the same time, it is also useful to ask why employees stay, focusing attention on the unique features of the organization that encourage some people to remain.

THE TRAINING DEPARTMENT AND SUCCESSION PLANNING

Succession planning has the role of ensuring that the organization has the right people in the right places at the right times. A succession planning team can monitor an organization's talent pool to ensure that it is continuously "stocked." Training is one means by which to build the competencies that individuals need to qualify for higher-level, or different, work responsibilities. Training is thus a means to the end of building bench strength and an active ingredient in building a talent pool.

Training Management Staff

An organization's training function should be responsible for ensuring that those responsible for succession planning understand the succession process. Rothwell provides sample outlines for training about succession planning and such related issues as competency identification and modeling, employee performance management, employee potential assessment, and individual development planning.[28]

There are various developmental opportunities that the training function may provide. These opportunities may be delivered to supervisors and/or members of the talent pool to build their competencies and prepare them for promotions. Typical developmental strategies that can help individuals narrow gaps between the competencies they presently possess and those they need to qualify for promotion may include any or all of the following (as well as many others):

- Coaching and mentoring (Chapters 8 and 9)
- Action learning (providing work assignments in which candidates expand their knowledge, skills, and abilities)
- Job rotation (moving candidates through a series of positions for periods of time to prepare them for more challenging assignments)
- Special job assignments (opportunities for individuals to achieve stretch goals)
- University-based programs (paid for by the organization)

Training for the Talent Pool

Depending on an organization's policy about revealing an individual's status as a possible successor or as a member of a talent pool, training may—or may not—be required. If the organization chooses to share an individual's succession status, there are three general ways to provide additional training: (1) direct training, (2) training integrated with other issues, and (3) training tied to career development.[29]

After training and career development strategies are put into action, it is important to establish processes to monitor and assess a succession program. Organizations recognized for their best practices in succession recommend the following:

- Keeping the monitoring and assessing process simple
- Using and leveraging technology to support the process
- Aligning succession planning with overall business strategy
- Securing and preserving senior-level support for, and participation in, the process.[30]

NOTES

1. Slavenski, L., & Buckner, M. (1988). *Career development programs in the workplace*. Columbus, OH: Center on Education and Training for Employment, Ohio State University. ERIC Document Reproduction Service No. ED303681.

2. Hall, D. T., & Associates (Eds.). (1996). *The career is dead: Long live the career*. San Francisco: Jossey-Bass.

3. Cornish, E. (1999). *The cyber future: 93 ways our lives will change by the year 2025*. Bethesda, MD: World Future Society.

4. Foord Kirk, J. (2003, December). *The new paradigm of work*. Retrieved from http://thestar.workopolis.com/servlet/Content/torontostar/20031209/paradigm?section=TORSTAR.

5. Zheng, Y., & Kleiner, B. (2001). Developments concerning career development and transition. *Management Research News, 24,* 33.

6. Pfau, B., & Kay, I. (2002, August). Playing the training game and losing. *HR Magazine,* 49–51.

7. Fitz-enz, J. (2000). *The ROI of human capital: Measuring the economic value of employee performance*. New York: AMACOM, p. 92.

8. U.S. General Accounting Office. (2002). *A model of strategic human capital management* (GAO-02-373SP). Washington, DC: Author.

9. Ibid.

10. Ibid.

11. Arthur, M. B., & Rousseau, D. M. (1996). *The boundaryless career: A new employment principle for a new organizational era*. New York: Oxford University Press.

12. Pink, D. H. (2001). *Free agent nation: How America's new independent workers are transforming the way we live.* New York: Warner Books.

13. Gutteridge, T. G. (1986). Organizational career development systems: The state of the practice. In D. T. Hall & Associates (Eds.), *Career development in organizations* (p. 54). San Francisco: Jossey-Bass.

14. Ibid.

15. Hall, D. T., & Associates (Eds.). (1986). *Career development in organizations.* San Francisco: Jossey-Bass.

16. University of Waterloo (n.d.). *Career development emanual.* Retrieved from http://www.cdm.uwaterloo.ca/.

17. Knowdell, R. L. (1996). *Building a career development program: Nine steps for effective implementation.* Palo Alta, CA: Davies-Black, 17.

18. Ibid.

19. Greenhaus, J. H., Callanan, G. A., & Godshalk, V. M. (2000). *Career management.* Orlando, FL: Dryden Press, 402.

20. Poister, T. H. (2002, July). *Transforming PENNDOT: A case study in the continuing drive for excellence.* Alpharetta, GA: Author, 37. In 2000, the Pennsylvania Department of Transportation (PENNDOT) consolidated three operations into a single bureau, the Center for Performance Excellence (CPE). The training and career development systems functions were moved from the Bureau of Personnel (now the Bureau of Human Resources) into the Knowledge and Assessment Division of CPE.

21. The Blueprint for Life/Work Designs is a not-for-profit consortium led by the National Life/Work Centre, Human Resources Development Canada and the Canada Career Information Partnership as well as hundreds of public and private sector agencies throughout Canada. The Blueprint provides a common career language and features a map of specific competencies (personal management, learning and work exploration, and life/work building) with performance indicators all categorized by learning stages starting at the elementary school level through adulthood. The Blueprint for Life Web site is http://blueprint4life.ca.

22. Dr. Barbara Moses is a North American leader in career self-management and author of *What next? The complete guide to taking control of your working life.* New York: DK Publishing.

23. Career Systems International is a division of Beverly Kay (another leader in career development) & Associates, Inc., www.careersystemsintl.com.

24. *Career Development eManual* developed by the University of Waterloo, Waterloo, Canada at http://www.cdm.uwaterloo.ca/steps.asp.

25. National Career Development Association (1994, April). *Ethical responsibilities.* Retrieved from http://www.ncda.org/pdf/counselingcompetencies.pdf.

26. Ibid.

27. Ibid.

28. Rothwell, W. J. (2001). *Effective succession planning: Ensuring leadership continuity and building talent from within* (2nd ed.). New York: AMACOM.

29. Ibid., p. 163.

30. American Productivity and Quality Center. (2001). *Succession management: Identifying and cultivating tomorrow's leaders*. Houston, TX: Author, 9.

EIGHT

MENTORING

Have you ever wondered:

- What is mentoring—really?
- How does a mentor function—really?
- Could I be a mentor—really?

It is a fact now that executives of any size and type of organization must install a mentoring process so that soon-to-be retirees can mentor younger protégés in developing interpersonal relationships, enhancing career advancement opportunities, and assuming organizational roles. This chapter details one of the most efficient, proactive, and cost-efficient armaments in your arsenal to fight the talent war—the mentoring process.

Mentoring (a concept from Homer's *Odyssey*, actually) is a frequently misunderstood concept that is often confused with coaching. In this chapter, we sort out mentoring misconceptions and help you on your mentoring way to:

- Enhance professional leadership skills within your organization
- Increase employee job satisfaction
- Transfer institutional knowledge or organizational expertise

We also provide nine questions to help you determine if a mentoring program will really benefit your employees. Mentoring has many benefits for mentors, protégés, and the organization. These are just a few of the items in this chapter's tool kit, which is crammed with ideas, methods, and resources to establish and operate an effective mentoring program within your organization.

M entoring is a means by which to narrow gaps between what should be and what is. Individuals may use it to devise or verify career goals and objectives. Hence, mentoring can become an important component of a career planning program. Organizational leaders may also use it to help narrow gaps between present work requirements and present performance, or present performance and future competencies required. In that respect, then, mentoring may contribute to implementing a succession plan by helping individuals build the requisite competencies needed for performing successfully at present and qualifying for advancement in the future.

What special terms are used when discussing mentoring? What types of mentoring exist? What is the difference between formal and informal mentoring? What are the benefits of mentoring? What are the roles and responsibilities of mentors? What are the roles and responsibilities of a protégé? What is the difference between mentoring and coaching? How does mentoring contribute to career planning and succession planning? This chapter addresses these questions and, by doing so, provides readers with an important starting point for using mentoring as a tool by which to build competencies to help individuals achieve their career goals and organizational leaders build bench strength in succession programs.

A MENTORING CASE STUDY: LEADERS FOR TOMORROW

The U.S. Department of Transportation's Leaders for Tomorrow is a formal mentoring program that provides workforce development for emerging midlevel leaders.[1] The program adds value to the organization by (a) enhancing professional leadership skills within the organization, (b) increasing employee job satisfaction, and (c) transferring institutional knowledge and corporate expertise. The mentoring program also establishes a pipeline of trained professionals who are prepared to handle organizational challenges and equipped to meet future goals of the U.S. Department of Transportation.

The program is designed to propel its participants to heightened learning levels and develop the organization. The program's objectives are to: (a) build skills and develop management through training, (b) develop career plans, and (c) provide networking opportunities for individuals. A manager, supervisor, or executive in a specific federal grade level serves as the mentor and is paired with a protégé, an employee at a lower grade level, for the primary purpose of transferring knowledge and providing hands-on developmental experiences and classroom training. Continuing communication between the mentor-protégé pairs occurs to facilitate achievement of mutually agreed on outcomes. In this partnership, both individuals share in the growth and professional career development of one another.[2]

This case sheds light on an example of a mentoring program (described further in Appendix 3). It explains why organizational leaders may establish and implement such programs. Table 8.1 can help an

TABLE 8.1   Determining Need for a Mentoring Program

Questions to help determine if a mentoring program will benefit your organization's employees	Yes	No
Are employees limited in ability to advance to a new level or take on a new project?		
Do employees wish to sharpen their technical skills?		
Do employees wish to sharpen their interpersonal skills?		
Do employees need to acquire skills to manage people, handle negotiations, resolve human resource conflicts, or interact with clients?		
Are employees being considered for promotion?		
Are employees asking for professional development?		
Are employees asking for a career management program?		
Are employees interested in shifting their career focus to a new specialty area?		
Do new employees need to have a clear understanding of the organization's culture, policies, and procedures?		

Source: Gregg, C. (1999, November). Someone to look up to. *Journal of Accountancy*, 91.

organization's leaders determine if their organizations might benefit from a mentoring program.

SPECIAL TERMS

The term *mentor* has evolved to mean "one who hands down knowledge and wisdom gathered through years of experience."[3] Depending on the context in which the term is used, it can have different meanings associated with learning. In an educational context, mentoring programs are popular with students at both secondary and postsecondary levels (as career exploration programs involving work-site mentors).[4] Community mentoring typically addresses literacy, schools, children, crime, neighborhood renewal, or learning skills. From a business perspective, a mentor is a "senior-experienced employee who serves as a role model to provide direction, support and feedback to younger employees, usually for interpersonal development and career planning."[5]

Regardless of the context or business endeavor, a mentoring relationship allows protégés to receive guidance in "developing the skills, networks, and organizational savvy necessary to survive in turbulent times."[6]

One who performs the mentoring service is known as the mentor, while the one who directly benefits from the mentoring service is known by several names: *mentoree, mentee,* or *protégé.* While any of these terms are perfectly acceptable, we use *protégé* to describe one who receives mentoring.

TYPES OF MENTORING

There are numerous categories of mentoring:[7]

- *Face-to-face mentoring:* The most common form of mentoring; occurs one-on-one and in person in a formal setting (office) or informal setting (coffee shop).
- *Electronic mentoring:* E-mentoring is the merging of traditional one-on-one mentoring with the digital age and is rapidly becoming a mentoring method of choice. With time becoming a

scarce commodity, e-mentoring through e-mail, Internet chat rooms, electronic bulletin boards, or instant messaging systems provide opportunities for virtual meetings when face-to-face sessions may not be possible. "Blended" mentoring relationships combine face-to-face and online sessions. E-mentoring provides the protégé with many mentors from whom to choose.[8]

- *Team or group mentoring:* An even-numbered group (usually four or six) of employees sit as protégés to a mentor who is viewed as a learning leader. Protégés may be from the same unit/ department or may be a cross-functional group. Protégés are encouraged to establish relationships with each other to enhance reinforcement.
- *Tri-mentoring:* A take-off of the train-the-trainer concept; protégés receive mentoring while being trained to become mentors.[9]
- *Research mentoring:* Protégés receive special mentoring in ongoing research strategies; this may be conducted in a research group or cluster.
- *Reverse mentoring:* Infusing corporate strategy with the savvy of newer, younger employees to provide fresh perspectives on new products, services, and younger markets.[10]
- *Informal and Formal Mentoring:* This is discussed in the following section.

INFORMAL AND FORMAL MENTORING

Informal mentoring is the most common, occurring when two people establish a developmental alliance without assistance or guidance from an organization. Informal mentoring may be conducted by anyone who is considered a high performer and is knowledgeable in the subject matter. This is traditionally viewed as spontaneous, exclusive, and reliant upon the "chemistry" between mentor and protégé.

Unless the mentoring arrangement is designated as *supervisory*, a mentor is typically not the protégé's supervisor or even in the protégé's chain of command. Often, a mentor will encourage a protégé to strive to achieve stretch goals or support experimentation, which implies the chance of mistakes (in the name of learning). "Overcoming authority/

power obstacles to learning can only happen through a partnership relationship."[11]

Informal mentoring is generally recognized as the stronger personal mentoring of the two approaches. Spontaneity, longevity, comprehensiveness, and "chemistry" reveal that the roles assumed by the informal mentor can vary greatly in both number and specificity. While extremely useful, informal mentoring is generally less suited to achieving organization-wide objectives.

Formal mentoring involves a deliberate pairing of protégé and mentor by an organization, to develop specific skills and competencies. The organization provides a standardized, but flexible, support structure to ensure that both mentor and protégé have a clear purpose and support to achieve the goals of their relationship. Assisted formal mentoring takes full advantage of the benefits of formal mentoring, while maintaining the flexibility of tailoring mentoring objectives to meet the specific needs and goals of the protégé. Table 8.2 clarifies the distinctions between formal and informal mentoring.

TABLE 8.2   Characteristics of Informal and Formal Mentoring

Informal Mentoring	Formal Mentoring
Spontaneous by the participants	Planned by the organization
No defined end; may result in lifetime relationships	Designated end time; 4 months to 2 years, more or less
Comprehensive or universal impact	Tailored for intentional impact in a specific area
Relationship between mentor and protégé evolves	Mentor and protégé are matched pairings
Special chemistry usually exists between mentor and protégé	Usually a signed commitment agreement exits between mentor and protégé
Generally no organizational support is available	Mentoring supported by the organization
Post hoc evaluation	Monitored evaluation
Voluntary	Voluntary; participation may be part of performance evaluation

Source: A plan to implement assisted mentoring (1995). Retrieved from http://www.au.af.mil/au/ awc/awcgate/mentor/mentor.htm.

THE BENEFITS OF A MENTORING PROGRAM

Research results show that people who have been mentored report greater satisfaction and career success than nonmentored individuals. Two thirds of top corporate officers interviewed for one study reported having had at least one mentor who significantly helped them in their careers. Of 25 successful women executives interviewed in a different study, all were found to have had at least one mentor.[12]

Benefits for Mentors

- Personal satisfaction from fostering the professional development of a protégé
- Gratification of passing a legacy to the next generation of employees
- Development of new professional contacts
- Exposure to new ideas, technologies, and perspectives
- Enhanced reputation
- Sense of accomplishment
- Personal growth
- Increased knowledge and experience
- Broadened perspective
- Job enrichment

Benefits for Protégés

- Acquisition of new technical, interpersonal or management skills
- Professional development and career direction
- Increased personal confidence in the work setting
- Key information on the culture and inner workings of the organization (that could not be gained in a training class)
- Development of a relationship with a role model and sounding board to give feedback on ideas and career plans
- Development of new professional contacts
- Exposure to new ideas, technologies, and perspectives; greater connectivity with all parts of the organization
- Organizational support; increased performance

- Greater understanding of their role in accomplishing the organization's mission

Benefits for the Organization

- Across-the-board development of employee talent in a variety of skills
- Motivated employees.
- Effective communication of the history, culture, mission, and goals of the organization
- Creation of a workplace environment conducive to greater productivity
- Improvement of management's counseling skills
- Increased interaction between staff across functions and levels to:

  Cross-fertilize work efforts to generate new ideas and skills
  Maximize exposure to new knowledge areas, perspectives and ideas

- Increased organizational communication and understanding
- Better integration of new employees into the workplace; employee retention; reduced turnover
- Cost effectiveness, as participants receive new skills and knowledge without the cost of structured training classes
- Bridging the gap between classroom learning and real-world applications

THE ROLES AND RESPONSIBILITIES OF A MENTOR

Mentor Roles

The following is a list of the roles a mentor must perform in an effective mentor/protégé relationship:[13]

- A mentor is a role model who helps facilitate and foster the development of a protégé through teaching, counseling, and championing.
- A mentor teaches technical skills, culture, and politics of the organization.

- A mentor coaches via comments, support, encouragement, and even criticism about the skills, talents, behavior, and career of the protégé.
- A mentor counsels with advice on how to confront difficult situations at work, ways to advance, and approaches to improving professional skills.
- A mentor champions the protégé by showcasing the protégé's talents through introductions to senior management, and offering opportunities to carry out new assignments and "be seen."

Responsibilities of the Mentor

- *Serve as a role model* by presenting a polished, professional image.
- *Be a resource person* by providing general information on the organization, such as its code of conduct, professional training opportunities, phone numbers, names, etc.
- *Listen actively* by being open, flexible, and understanding, while keeping conversations confidential.
- *Counsel* by establishing a trusting, open relationship, and helping identify strategies for achieving the protégé's career goals and objectives.
- *Motivate* by providing encouragement, support, positive feedback, and incentives.
- *Guide* by empowering, offering suggestions and options, but allowing the protégé to make final decisions.
- *Offer insight* by explaining the written and unwritten rules of the organization, helping the protégé see the big organizational picture.
- *Be honest* by communicating openly, asking for feedback, and acknowledging protégés' suggestions.

The balance of these roles and responsibilities will differ from one mentoring relationship to another. What is important is that the mentor displays a positive interest in helping the protégé grow and develop. Critical mentoring skills include:

- Being a good listener and knowing how to give effective feedback
- Knowing how to help with goal setting and planning

- Knowing when and when not to give advice
- Having the ability to instill confidence and motivate people

THE ROLES AND RESPONSIBILITIES OF A PROTÉGÉ

A protégé must be committed to learning, take responsibility for his or her career development, and agree to work with a mentor. The protégé's roles include making an estimate of current skills and competencies, participating in any style preference and needs assessments, and working with the prospective mentor to create a "learning contract" to reach agreed-upon goals. The protégé must commit to follow through on their action plans, including readdressing things that do not appear to be working well.[14]

Responsibilities of the Protégé

- *Initiate:* Be proactive; schedule meetings; actively seek out a mentor (in the case of an informal mentorship).
- *Participate:* Be eager to learn; take advantage of information and suggestions offered; contemplate career goals and objectives; interact with the mentor to achieve desired goals.
- *Listen:* Actively listen; be open to constructive criticism and positive feedback; consider all suggestions and options with an open mind; respect the mentor's confidence and trust.
- *Be responsible:* Always be considerate and respectful of the mentor's time; express appreciation for assistance; make only positive or neutral comments about the mentor to others.

It Takes Two to Make a Successful Mentoring Relationship: The Nine Commandments

1. *Be proactive:* Don't wait for your mentor or protégé to contact you.
2. *Negotiate a commitment:* Agree to have regular contact at predefined intervals.

3. *Establish rapport:* Learn as much as you can about one another.
4. *Be confident:* Each of you has something important to offer the other.
5. *Communicate:* Share your knowledge and experience openly.
6. *Be a good listener:* Hear what your mentor or protégé is saying to you.
7. *Be responsive:* Act on what you have planned.
8. *Be accessible:* Have an open-door or open-phone policy.
9. *Take responsibility:* It takes two to create a successful mentoring relationship.[15]

DIFFERENTIATING BETWEEN MENTORING AND COACHING

Workforce and career developers should understand the difference between mentoring and coaching. Some maintain that there is a fine line between the two, while others claim that there is a world of difference between mentoring and coaching. Matt Starcevich, founder of the Center for Coaching and Mentoring, conducted an online survey in 1998 to determine what actual protégés had to say about the matter. An abstract of his survey appears in Appendix 4. Literature supports the view that there is a difference between mentoring and coaching. A coach focuses on performance on the job, while a mentor focuses on the growth of the individual.[16] "Coaching is also more closely aligned with on-the-job training (OJT) than mentoring. A coach will often assist employees with the transfer of training and coaching into practice. A mentor is unlikely to get involved in OJT or skills-related training."[17] Table 8.3 clarifies the differences between coaching and mentoring.

MENTOR COMPETENCIES

Listed below are eight competency dimensions identified by the National Asian Pacific Bar Association as important for mentors. This is an excellent tool for evaluating potential mentors.[18]

Potential mentors should read each competency description below and check all the statements that apply. Use the Comments section to provide further explanation.

TABLE 8.3   Differences Between Coaching and Mentoring

	Coaching	Mentoring
Scope	Raising job performance expectations	Organizational, career, or personal transitions
Focus	Task-centered; links individual effectiveness to organizational performance	Possibility-centered; options, exploration, not necessarily linked to organizational performance
Purpose	Develop and select options for behavior modification for improved organizational performance	Address individuals' identity in the context of the bigger picture—both inside and outside of the organization

Source: How can we provide mentoring for future supervisors? (n.d.) *Workforce Management.* Retrieved from http://www.workforce.com/archive/article/22/13/28_printer.php.

Approachability

Easy to approach and talk with; spends extra effort to put others at ease; sensitive to and patient with others; builds rapport.

Potential mentor check characteristics that apply:

Listen to others   Comments:
Make others comfortable
Respond appropriately to
    others
Build rapport
Assist others when approached

Compassion

Genuinely cares about people; is concerned about their work and nonwork problems; is ready to help; demonstrates a social conscience; shows real empathy.

Potential mentor check characteristics that apply:

Express concern for others   Comments:
Seek to understand others'
    issues and concerns

Care for others
Demonstrate responsiveness
Show empathy

Motivating Others

Motivates staff and team; invites input and shares ownership; fosters an exciting and enjoyable work environment.
Potential mentor check characteristics that apply:

Understand motivation and   Comments:
    recognition
Acknowledge others
Regularly reinforce
    performance
Generate enthusiasm and
    commitment
Foster a motivating environment

Listening

Practices attentive and active listening; has the patience to hear people out; can accurately restate the opinions of others.
Potential mentor check characteristics that apply:

Acknowledge different views   Comments:
Display active listening skills
Solicit others' views
Willing to adopt others' ideas
Create opportunities for
    listening

Organizational Agility

Knowledgeable about how organizations function; knows how to get things done through formal channels and informal network;

understands the origin and reasoning behind key policies, practices, and procedures.

Potential mentor check characteristics that apply:

Know the basic organizational   Comments:
   structure
Use the organizational
   structure
Know the climate and culture
Use organization dynamics to
   obtain goals
Understand the evolving
   business

Valuing Diversity

Respects and appreciates different perspectives that may arise from background, culture, nationality, race, age, gender, styles, physical attributes, values, lifestyles, or interests.

Potential mentor check characteristics that apply:

Value differences   Comments:
Act positively on diversity
Solicit different ideas
Include diverse ideas
Champion diversity

Personal Disclosure

Willingly shares thoughts about personal strengths, weaknesses, and limitations; freely and publicly admits mistakes and shortcomings; is open about personal beliefs and feelings; is an open book to those around him/her regularly.

Potential mentor check characteristics that apply:

Share information about self   Comments:
   when asked

Open about personal beliefs
   and feelings
Share negative personal
   information
Encourage others to share
   personal information
Facilitate a sharing environment

Perspective

Looks toward the broadest view of an issue/challenge; has broad-ranging personal and business interests and pursuits; sees farther into the future than most; can easily pose credible alternative scenarios for planning things globally.

Potential mentor check characteristics that apply:

Use past experiences   Comments:
Interpret trends and events
Integrate patterns and
   observations
Use "what if" thinking
Envision new possibilities
Adapted with permission of the National Asian Pacific Bar Association

HOW MENTORING CONTRIBUTES TO CAREER DEVELOPMENT AND SUCCESSION PLANNING

One of the most efficient, proactive, and cost-effective ways to fight the "talent war" is through the mentoring process. It is becoming imperative for executives to take immediate action to install a mentoring process so that soon-to-be retirees can mentor younger protégés in developing interpersonal relationships, enhancing career advancement opportunities, and assuming organizational structural roles.

Mentor, protégé, and organization benefit from mentoring programs. The mentor gains a feeling of accomplishment and satisfaction by passing knowledge and abilities on to younger employees, while the protégé moves into an improved position for greater mobility, promotion, and increased levels of responsibility. The biggest beneficiary of mentoring is the organization. Hunt and Cook write, "mentors can facilitate the promotion of women and other underrepresented groups into management, helping to create a more diverse leadership team. Mentoring serves as an efficient way of transferring company values down through the ranks, and facilitates learning within the organization. Behavioral changes occur faster when a protégé is modeling behavior after that of a qualified and experienced mentor. Most important, mentoring transfers knowledge from senior employees to their younger successors."[19]

Installing a mentoring program is relatively easy, and can be accomplished at virtually no cost other than employee time. Many mentoring models are available online that can be tailored by in-house workforce or human resource specialists to fit an organization's structure and culture. "Prior to moving forward with a mentoring program, an organization should determine whether its employees are willing and able to participate in their own career development. To determine the effectiveness of the program, management must set measurable goals. If a mentoring program is to have a sustained positive impact on an organization, it must be constantly evaluated, adjusted, and administered for the long term,"[20] according to Hunt and Cook.

Once complete buy-in to a mentoring program is achieved, long-term strategy and goals must be established. A mentoring manual must be prepared, or purchased and customized. Trainers must be prepared to introduce formal mentoring to both mentors and protégés. The mentoring program must be marketed to selected, qualified employees. After candidates have had sufficient time to discuss and decide whether to participate in the mentoring program, leadership must select candidates and take great care in choosing and monitoring formal mentoring dyads. After the dyads are formed, mentor and protégé should immediately identify and agree on goals and outcomes, and the life span of the mentoring process. Organizations can also benefit from encouraging and supporting informal mentoring.

In summarizing the preparation of proteges, Hunt and Cook state, "staffing and continuity are critical for organizational success. With the looming shortage of senior workers and the inherent potential loss of intellectual assets, mentoring can help to guarantee the permanence of core competencies within an organization. Now is the time to invest in the future of employees, and consequently, the future of the organiza-tion. Mentoring is a venture worth undertaking."[21]

NOTES

1. Excerpted from Leaders for Tomorrow, the U.S. Department of Transportation's midlevel mentoring program. The complete description of the program appears in Appendix 3.

2. U.S. Department of Transportation mentoring overview. (n.d.). *Leaders for tomorrow*. Retrieved from http://dothr.ost.dot.gov/HR_Programs/DOTMEN_1/dotmen_1.htm.

3. Lanser, E. G. (2000, May/June). Reaping the benefits of mentorship. *Healthcare Executive, 15*, 18.

4. Naylor, M. (1997). *Work-based learning* (ERIC Digest No. 187). Columbus, OH: ERIC Clearinghouse on Adult, Career, and Vocational Education. ERIC Document Reproduction Service No. 411417.

5. Lockwood, N. R. (2003, November). *The role of age in mentoring relationships*. Retrieved from http://www.shrm.org/research/researchtranslations/pdf/03mentoring.pdf.

6. Restifo, V. & Yoder, L. (2004). *Partnership: Making the most of mentoring*. University of Chicago Hospitals. Retrieved from http://nsweb.nursing-spectrum.com/ce/ce190.htm.

7. How mentoring works. (n.d.). *Realm*. Retrieved from http://realm.net/mentor/howment/index.html.

8. An excellent example of a mentoring program that takes place exclusively over the Internet is CanadaInfoNet. This service offers an online mentoring program that connects newcomers and potential newcomers to Canada with experienced professional, business and trades people in Canada. This Web site also provides an interactive forum to share a wide range of occupation-related knowledge for immigrants.

9. At Ryerson University, Toronto, Canada, the first of a three-year tri-mentoring program is being piloted to ESL (English as a second language) students. The program assists non-Anglophone, first-generation or recent immigrant students during their transition into postsecondary education at Ryerson and into the world of work through student mentoring partnerships. First-year students are paired with third-year student mentors. In their second year, students receive leadership and career development training. In their third year, students have the opportunity to be a mentor to a first-year student. Students in their final year are paired with alumni or continuing education student mentors working in their field of study.

10. Gregg, C. (1999, November). Someone to look up to: How mentoring will position your firm or company for tomorrow. *Journal of Accountancy, 188,*

91. For example, a company with a product geared toward young adults may rely on reverse mentoring from employees who are recent college graduates and closely match the firm's targeted demographics. Acting as a "focus group," these individuals participate in meetings with more senior employees to provide firsthand knowledge of the trends and buying habits of younger consumers.

11. Bell, C. R. (2000, February). The mentor as partner. *Training and Development, 54,* 54.

12. *A plan to implement assisted mentoring.* (1995, May). Retrieved from http://www.au.af.mil/au/awc/awcgate/mentor/mentor.htm.

13. *NIST pilot mentoring program.* (n.d.). Retrieved from http://www.nist.gov/admin/diversity/handbook02.htm#Benefits%20of%20Mentoring%20Relationships.

14. *A plan to implement assisted mentoring.* (1995, May). Retrieved from http://www.au.af.mil/au/awc/awcgate/mentor/mentor.htm.

15. *Pharmacy mentoring program information.* (n.d.). Retrieved from http://www.hhs.gov/pharmacy/mentguid.html#RESPONSIBILITIES.

16. Starcevich, M. M. (2004, January 15). *Coach, mentor: Is there a difference?* Retrieved from http://www.coachingandmentoring.com/Articles/mentoring.html.

17. McKeown, J. L. (n.d.). *The complete guide to mentoring and coaching.* San Anselmo, CA: Author, 29.

18. *Mentor selection competencies.* (n.d.). National Asian Pacific Bar Association. Retrieved from http://www.napaba.org/uploads/napaba/InHouse Mentor.pdf.

19. Hunt, A., & Cook, E. (2002, June). Managing growth: Preparing protégés for succession. *Businessleader.com, 13.* No. 12, Raleigh, NC. Retrieved from http://www.businessleader.com/bl/jun02/proteges.html.

20. Ibid.

21. Ibid.

NINE

CAREER COACHING

Do you know that there are at least thirty different coaching models, plus scores more of occupational coaches? You can easily understand, then, why there is no specific agreed-upon definition of a coach or coaching. The best universally accepted definition of the concept comes from the French origin of the word *coach*: a vehicle to move people from one place to another.

Simply put, the coaching function helps employees improve their performance from one level to a higher level. And that is accomplished through:

- Building trust between the coach and the employee
- Sharing information and knowledge
- Discussing options
- Planning actions
- Reviewing results

This chapter is yet another compartment of your tool kit jammed with ideas, methods, and resources to establish and operate an effective coaching program within your organization.

WHICH COACH IS WHICH?

Executive coach and *personal coach* are familiar terms, but many other coaching models exist. The following list of 30 different coaching models was developed by the late Thomas Leonard, founder of Coach-Ville LLC, the premier community for independent coaches:[1]

Traditional or basic coaching	Paradigm coaching
Intermediate coaching	Solution coaching
Advanced coaching	Spiritual coaching
Integrity coaching	Zen coaching
Block removal coaching	Leap coaching
Personal evolution coaching	Grace coaching
Innovation coaching	Paradox coaching
Attraction coaching	Shift coaching
3-D coaching	Recovery coaching
Linear coaching	Laser coaching
Personal foundation coaching	Strategic coaching
Extreme self-care coaching	Performance coaching
Bigger thinking coaching	Turnaround coaching
Vision coaching	Quality of life coaching
Distinction coaching	Acceptance coaching

Coaching by occupation is becoming increasingly popular. There are parent coaches, career coaches, wellness coaches, chemotherapy coaches, cop coaches, rock-and-roll band coaches, irresistible attraction coaches, book marketing coaches, chronic care coaches, money coaches, Generation X coaches, Web coaches, stockbroker coaches, health care professional coaches, and attorney coaches.[2] This chapter examines one specific coaching model: career coaching.

TERMINOLOGY

The word *coach* is translated from French as "a vehicle to transport people from one place to another." Today's coach moves a person from one point to another by enhancing a skill, boosting performance, or changing the way the person thinks. Coaches help people grow, assisting them in seeing beyond what and where they are today to what they can become tomorrow. A great coach helps ordinary people do extraordinary things.[3]

Career coaching helps workers achieve specific goals to improve their careers.[4] Popularized in the late 1980s and early 1990s, career coaching evolved as a practice to help midcareer[5] employees plan for the future.[6] In turbulent corporate environments, midcareer employees turned to their supervisors or managers for help.[7] As subordinates' outputs, attitudes, and professional development were ultimately the responsibility of the supervisor, many supervisors became effective coaches.[8] The teamwork approach between supervisor/manager and employee was considered the best means to create motivated and productive employees.[9]

As career coaching is used in varied work settings, it combines the concepts of career counseling, organizational consulting, and employee development (see Table 9.1).[10]

SOURCES OF CAREER COACHES

Career management is the process through which employees take responsibility for developing their abilities and expanding their contribution to an organization. Since career management can improve employee satisfaction, it makes sense for organizations to provide career coaching.[11]

Career coaching programs may be developed in-house. IBM and Ernst & Young developed the very first in-house coaching programs in corporate America, and have begun to openly share their positive outcomes, which can be seen in revenue, market share, productivity, recruiting, and retention. Many organizations are interested in learning how to put such programs together, obtain buy-in from management, and account for results. A recent national survey indicates widespread interest in developing corporate coaching programs.[12]

Hiring a Career Coach

Career coaches may be hired as independent contractors by an organization, or contracted directly by employees to help them create and carry out plans related to their lives and career directions. A career coach

TABLE 9.1 Characteristics of Career Coaches, Career Counselors, and Career Development Facilitators

Career Coach	Career Counselor	Career Development Facilitator
Not required to hold professional license; formal degree not required	Professional license required; master's degree in counseling	Professional license not required; formal degree not required
Several proprietary schools such as Coach U and Corporate Coach U provide training	Formally trained in career interventions	Some formal training possible
Does not delve into person's past	Seeks to achieve self-understanding by workers	Information provider (labor market info, ethical and legal issues, employability skills, etc.)
Uses assessment instruments to aid in awareness function	Uses assessment instruments to aid in awareness function	Uses assessment instruments to aid in awareness function
Less restricted by professional boundaries; may assume informal role in providing assistance	Personal interactions are more structured; face-to-face meetings in office environment	Facilitate career development of people in virtually every setting including job centers, schools and other businesses
Takes on a participatory role	Takes on a facilitative role	Takes on an informative role
Interaction may be longer term (3 months to 5 years)	Short-term approach	Provides information when needed
No nationally recognized profession organization to issue certification and other professional guidelines	Council for Accreditation of Counseling and Related Educational Programs; American Counseling Association; National Career Development Association	National Career Development Association; National Employment Counseling Association; National Association of Workplace Development Professionals all promote professional standards.

Source: Chung, Y. B., and Gfroerer, M. C. (2003). Career coaching: Practice, training, professional, and ethical issues. *Career Development Quarterly, 52,* 142–143. Reprinted with permission of the National Career Development Association.

may be hired by an unemployed individual who is seeking guidance toward suitable fields, assistance in job searches, or help with resolving career challenges. Because clients pay for these services, they can expect career coaches to work for them, supporting their best interests.[13]

Contracted coaches' strategies vary, but they usually do one or more of the following:[14]

- Conduct personal coaching sessions with individuals and groups to help clarify life and career goals
- Administer and interpret tests and inventories to assess clients' interests and abilities and identify career options
- Provide information on career planning and occupations
- Help improve decision-making skills
- Help develop individualized career plans
- Teach job-hunting strategies and skills and help develop résumés
- Teach human relations skills that can resolve potential personal conflicts on the job
- Help integrate work with other roles in life
- Provide support for people going through job stress, job loss, or career transition

If an individual is privately seeking a career coach, it is best to do this when his or her career is relatively stable. Sound career decisions cannot be made in a crisis, or when survival is the chief motivator. Career coaching can assist individuals with creating a vision of where they want to go with their working life, and guide them in developing a strategy to get there.[15]

How to Find a Coach

Most states do not require licenses, certifications, or credentials to work in the career development field. As a consumer, it is important to determine what approaches will best address specific needs. Online resources include these:[16]

- The International Association of Career Professionals
- The National Career Development Association
- International Board for Career Management Certification

Obviously, reviewing credentials is important, but credentials only measure a coach's education and expertise; they do not tell much about the coach's personal style. It is best to interview three or more coaches before making a decision.[17] Career coaches should provide detailed explanations of services, fees, time commitments, and copies of their ethical guidelines. The consumer should beware of services that require large up-front fees with promises of better jobs, higher salaries, or speedy results.[18] It is also important to ask for references from other clients, and make certain that services may be ended at any time (and billed accordingly). In the end, the best career coaching relationships are built on competence as well as the chemistry between coach and client.[19]

CAREER COACHING WITHIN THE ORGANIZATION

Helping employees develop skills and increase knowledge strengthens an organization: employees feel valuable and tend to be more efficient when they can perform more job functions. Managers or supervisors who do not encourage career development may lose productive employees when positions are eliminated or people become dissatisfied. It is crucial for managers to assume a coaching role, accepting a few additional responsibilities.[20]

White identifies the following steps in career coaching:[21]

- *Build a trusting and productive working relationship.* It may take time, but listening and building rapport can establish solid communication channels.
- *Share information and insights.* Be honest when coaching. Instead of ignoring employee concerns, find the needed information or admit to not knowing the answer.
- *Identify options.* Once an open relationship is established, work together to clarify the employee's plans and maximize their talents. Build on each other's ideas.
- *Plan actions.* After a coaching session, let the employee review the options discussed earlier, and consider how they can be implemented.

- *Review results.* Review results with employees frequently to acknowledge accomplishments and to modify or build upon individual career plans.

Managers can provide career coaching in several ways:[22]

- Identify employee weaknesses or areas in which employees require professional growth.
- Communicate direction, needs, and expectations of the organization.
- Provide information about job and career development opportunities, and refer employees to available resources.
- Guide employees in selecting appropriate goals (based on what they want to do).
- Coach employees on steps for achieving goals, help identify on-the-job learning opportunities, and assign projects accordingly.

From a career development and succession planning perspective, career coaching can be very effective. To preserve a solid workforce, supervisors or managers must provide career coaching services to help valued employees successfully navigate through the organization. The investment in time and effort will pay off with long-term benefits of employee satisfaction, effectiveness, and productivity.[23]

NOTES

1. CoachVille, LLC. Retrieved from http://www.coachville.com/coachingmodels/models/models.html.

2. Coach, U. (2002). *An incredible variety of coaching niches.* Retrieved from http://www.coachinc.com/CoachInc/Media/Story%20Angles%20for%20Coaching/default.asp?s=1.

3. Goldsmith, M., Lyons, L., & Freas, A. (Eds.). (2000). *Coaching for leadership: How the world's greatest coaches help leaders learn* (p. xii). San Francisco: Jossey-Bass Pfeiffer.

4. Hube, K. (1996, December). A coach may be the guardian angel you need to rev up your career. *Money, 25,* 43.

5. Greenhaus, J. H., & Callanan, G. A. (1994). *Career management* (2nd ed.). Fort Worth, TX: Dryden Press. Greenhaus and Callanan define midcareer as the typical age range of 40 to 55.

6. Chung, Y. B., & Gfroerer, M. C. (2003, December). Career coaching: Practice, training, professional, and ethical issues. *Career Development Quarterly, 52,* 141.

7. Durity, A. R. (Ed.). (1991, January). Career coaching comes out of the closet. *Personnel, 68,* 4.

8. Ibid.

9. Chung, Y. B., & Gfroerer, M. C. (2003, December). Career coaching: Practice, training, professional, and ethical issues. *Career Development Quarterly, 52,* 144.

10. Ibid., p. 141.

11. Sturman, G. M. (1990, November). The supervisor as career "coach." *Supervisory Management, 35,* 6.

12. Coach U. (2002). *An incredible variety of coaching niches.* Retrieved from http://www.coachinc.com/CoachInc/Media/Story%20Angles%20for%20 Coaching/default.asp?s=1.

13. King, D. (2001). *How to find a good career coach: Tips for making the right choice.* Retrieved from http://www.careerfirm.com/tips.htm.

14. Ibid.

15. Ibid.

16. Ibid.

17. Ibid.

18. Ibid.

19. Ibid.

20. Tyler, K. (1997, June). Prepare managers to become career coaches. *HR Magazine, 42,* 99.

21. Durity, A. R. (Ed.). (1991, January). Career coaching comes out of the closet. *Personnel, 68,* 4.

22. Tyler, K. (1997, June). Prepare managers to become career coaches. *HR Magazine, 42,* 101.

23. Sturman, G. M. (1990, November). The supervisor as career "coach." *Supervisory Management, 35,* 6.

TEN

SELF-DIRECTED LEARNING

This is the digital age, a new economy that is powered by technology, fueled by information, and driven by knowledge. It is an age with the slogan "knowing means growing." In the digital age, it is becoming impossible to train, educate, or keep employees current by using the tried and true methods of an earlier time.

This chapter addresses the thinking, acting, and reacting modus operandi of the digital age, which requires specific skills:

- Literacy in technical knowledge
- Effective communication skills
- Inventive analytical and logical thinking
- A much higher order of productivity

To survive in the digital age, it is incumbent upon every human level of the organization to employ a desire to know as the fuel for lifelong learning. In this chapter, we discuss the traits one must develop to become a self-directed learner:

- Ability to set one's own personal goals related to learning
- Plan for the achievement of those goals

- Independently manage time and effort whenever and wherever one chooses
- Independently assess the quality of learning that results from the learning experience

If you are in a leadership role in any organization, one of your primary responsibilities is to help provide avenues—intranet, Internet, other up-to-date resources—to help employees meet their self-directed learning needs and interests. If you are not yet in a leadership role, develop a self-directed learning style now. This chapter explains why.

It (self-directed learning) is really the only way for most healthcare practitioners to stay current. For example, I can't even tell you how many new medications come on the market each year. As their educator/trainer, there is no way...none...that I could provide education to each and every staff member about these types of change/advances. Some however embrace SDL (self-directed learning) more than others—those individuals are in every field. I believe that one of my primary roles is helping to provide avenues (intranet, Internet, up-to-date resources, etc.) for them to meet their SDL needs/interests. That can be a challenge too.
—Susan Foster, Mount Nittany Medical Center, State College, PA[1]

We live in the digital age. It is powered by technology, fueled by information, and driven by knowledge. The influence of technology goes beyond new equipment and faster communications, because changes in technology necessitate new skills to do the work and achieve results. In the information-based, skills-intensive economy of the twenty-first century, one thing is clear: knowing means growing. Workers who want to climb higher or realize their career goals while working conditions are changing must possess the competencies to do it. Lifelong learning for workers will become more important as a result.[2]

Lifelong learning is a means to an end of achieving career goals as working conditions and employers change. It is also important for building the competencies needed at every organizational level, since succession plans must lead the target of competencies needed in the future. Lifelong learning is worthy of discussion in this chapter precisely because it is through the learning process that individuals acquire the competencies they need to meet their career goals, as spelled out in their career plans, and prepare themselves for advancement, as organizational leaders need them to do to achieve the talent requirements spelled out in succession plans. It is, in part, through lifelong learning that career and succession plans can be integrated at the individual's level.

This chapter focuses on lifelong learning, addressing such issues as:

- What is self-directed learning?
- What is in a name—and, more specifically, what is the difference between training and learning?
- What are the characteristics of self-directed learners?
- What are the roles of trainers, coaches, and organizations in helping self-directed learners?
- What is an individual development plan (IDP), and how can IDPs help organize self-directed learning?

Four clearly identifiable skills clusters are needed for the digital age:[3]

1. Digital-age literacy—technical knowledge

   Basic, scientific, economic, and technological literacy
   Visual and information literacy
   Multicultural literacy and global awareness

2. Effective communication—skills

   Teaming, collaboration, and interpersonal skills
   Personal, social, and civic responsibility
   Interactive communication

3. Inventive thinking—thinking analytically/logically, problem solving, and original ideas

   Adaptability and managing complexity
   Self-direction
   Curiosity, creativity, and risk-taking
   Higher-order thinking and sound reasoning

4. High productivity

Prioritizing, planning, and managing for results
Effective use of real-world tools
Ability to produce relevant, high-quality products

To varying degrees, these skills are already being taught to our nation's children. But it is now imperative that every individual, not just today's youth, be prepared to thrive in a twenty-first-century economy.

The accelerating rate at which technology is evolving makes it difficult to stay current. However, it is crucial that we do, because technology changes the way we live, the way we learn, and the way we do business. Today's technologically charged environment requires individuals to plan, design, and manage in new ways. While an education was once something that culminated in a four-year degree, we now know that, to be competitive, workers must employ the desire to know as fuel for lifelong learning. They must maintain their curiosity and drive to stay current and informed.[5]

"Because change occurs constantly in our information-rich society, self-directed, continuous learning is no longer seen as an option for successfully workers in the Digital Age."[6] Today's workers are participating in more out-of-school learning to improve their job skills than at any time in the past, and they must continue to do so. The complexity of today's workplace makes competence with new literacy and new skills imperative.[7]

Self-directed learners can anticipate workplace changes and constantly upgrade their skills. Conversely, those who lack the ability to learn, and learn how to improve their learning, will find their employability jeopardized in the modern workplace.[8]

WHAT IS SELF-DIRECTED LEARNING?

Self-directed learning—in its simplest form—is analogous to performing a search for a topic on Google or Dogpile or Yahoo! or your favorite Internet search engine. You probably have done it hundreds of times. You hear an unfamiliar word, phrase, or concept, and your curiosity is overwhelming. Or maybe you have been given an assignment or work task to complete with a short turn-around. It is habitual now—simply log onto the search engine and within seconds you no doubt have more information ready for printing than you could ever imagine. Next, you must determine exactly what information will answer your question, solve your problem, or complete your task.

Compare the stages of the Internet search to a general definition of self-directed learning:[9]

- Set personal goals related to learning
- Plan for achieving those goals
- Independently manage time and effort, whenever and wherever necessary
- Independently assess learning quality and any products resulting from learning experiences

WHAT'S IN A NAME?

Two major concepts and two strategies discussed in this chapter are learning and training as well as lifelong learning and self-directed learning strategies.

Over the last decade or so, subtle yet significant changes have shaped how employers prepare their employees to accomplish work. Employers have become more sophisticated after realizing that the "spray and pray" or "sheep dip approach" of giving all employees the same training—en masse—does not achieve the desired training impact. Rather than the top (management) "pushing training down" to the employee level, the concepts of employee learning and learning organization have become more favored approaches. Training managers are becoming learning managers or chief learning officers, while training departments are refocused as learning or knowledge departments.[10]

Let us refocus on the definitions of learning and training:[11]

- *Learning* focuses on achieving permanent changes in behavior. Learning interventions are generally longer term, driven by the need to provide individuals with opportunities to achieve changes

through personal experience or practice. Interventions can include, but are not limited to, one-on-one coaching, mentoring, or 360-degree feedback.
- *Training* focuses on helping individuals acquire new competencies. Training interventions are generally event driven. Classroom-based workshops and learning modules still feature heavily in training.

See the comparison of the two shown in Table 10.1.

Senge defines the learning organization as "organizations where people continually expand their capacity to create the results they truly desire, where new and expansive patterns of thinking are nurtured, where collective aspiration is set free, and where people are continually learning together."[12] Self-directed learning and the learning organization philosophy are mutually supportive. It is the collective commitment of employees at all levels—using self-directed learning—that provides the competitive business edge while the organization's learning culture permits, and even requires, organizational leaders to listen, learn, and share relevant ideas with all employees.

With global competition and technology advancing at a light-year pace, it is now next to impossible to take the time to develop training using traditional methods. According to Guglielmino, "only the learning organizations will survive, and you cannot have a learning organization without self-directed learning."[13]

TABLE 10.1   A Comparison Between Training and Learning

Training	Learning
Skills development	Behavior change
Externally applied	Internally accepted
Short-term skill uplift	Long-term change
Equips for known challenges	Equips for ambiguous future
Meets current organizational requirements	Defines organizational future
Focuses on the group	Is focused by individuals
Primarily structured	Primarily organic
"Doing"	"Understanding"

Source: Structured training. Training versus learning. Retrieved from www.structured-training. com/asp/trainingvlearning.asp.

GE's former chairman and CEO, Jack Welch, is a true champion of the learning organization culture. Two of his leadership secrets explain why GE's success is due to its "keep learning" culture: "At the heart of this (learning) culture is an understanding that an organization's ability to learn, and translate that learning into rapid action, is the ultimate competitive business advantage."[14] Included in his 29 leadership secrets are three "Welch Rules" that summarize the necessity for a learning organization culture:[15]

- Make searching for new ideas a priority of every employee. In today's competitive environment, organizations cannot afford to leave anyone out.
- Hold idea-sharing meetings on a regular basis. Get a diverse group of managers together regularly. Make sure their ideas are translated into action.
- Reward employees for sharing knowledge. Find a way to reward managers and employees for sharing ideas and putting best practices to work at every level.

Additionally, employees in learning organizations are always encouraged to assume responsibility for their own learning. They are also encouraged to share knowledge. They are more personally satisfied to know that their contributions are helping to move their organizations forward to achieve competitive advantage.

Self-directed learning is not a new idea. People have always been self-directing their learning but did not call it that. Educational philosophers since Socrates have supported the idea that learning is individualized and that students should be center stage in the learning process.[16] However, with the explosion of knowledge, research, literature, and the Internet, interest in self-directed learning has mushroomed over the past 15 years. With its roots in adult education, the term *self-directed learning* has taken on various names in the past. For continuity, self-directed learning is used in this book. However, the following terms are nearly synonymous with it and may be used interchangeably:[17]

- Self-directed learner
- Self-direction in adult learning
- Self-direction in learning

- Self-directed instruction
- Self-directed teaching
- Self-directed training
- Self-directed lifelong education
- Self-conducted learning project
- Self-education
- Self-efficacy
- Self-planned learning
- Self-taught adults
- Self-acquired knowledge
- Self-guided learning
- Self-managed learning
- Self-regulated learning
- Self-taught

Before delving into self-directed learning in more detail, let us discuss some basic concepts of training and development and four overall learning approaches: informal, formal, self-directed, and other-directed. Deciding which approach to take depends on complexity of the knowledge and skill needed, timeliness of training, capacity and motivation of the learner, and availability of funds (see Table 10.2).

THE SELF-DIRECTED LEARNER

Unfortunately, not all employees will embrace self-directed learning as much and as rapidly as others. Those who have a propensity for self-directed learning will maintain a "preferred" approach to learning, while those who are less motivated and productive in a self-directed environment will exhibit a different approach to learning.

Inscape Publishing has produced an instrument, the Personal Learning Insights Profile, which is a unique resource that helps learners and facilitators gain insight into individual approaches to learning.[18]

Several other paper-and-pencil and online assessments exist that can help measure learners' readiness to adapt to self-directed learning. A learning style assessment to determine preferred ways of taking in and processing information—whether visually, aurally, through reading and

TABLE 10.2 Comparing Formal and Informal Training and Development

Informal Training & Development	Formal Training & Development
• Casual, incidental • No specific training goals • No formal evaluation • Occurs from experience on the job or informal discussion	• Needs assessment may be conducted • Learning objectives established • Learning method(s) used • A form of evaluation conducted at the end of training
Self-Directed Learning • Learner makes own training and development decisions and how they will occur • Learning is not documented by an individual learning plan or contract • Very low cost • Learner must have capability and be motivated • Training may take longer than other-directed	*Self-Directed Learning* • Learner makes own training and development decisions and how they will occur • Learner uses individual learning plan or contract to document learning: –goals –objectives –methods –evaluation
Other-Directed Learning • Someone other than the learner directs what training activities will occur • Learner must be highly motivated and able to conceptualize	*Other-Directed Learning* • Someone other than the learner directs what training activities will occur: –mandatory by organization –supervisor –licensing or certification training –employee development plans/goals –performance goals • Typically more expensive than others • Most reliable for desired knowledge and skill outcomes • Can be accomplished in a more timely manner

Source: McNamara, C. (1999). Ways to look at training and development: Training and development processes: Informal/formal and self-directed/other directed. Retrieved from: http://www.mapnp.org/library/trng_dev/ways/ways.htm. Reprinted with permission.

writing, or kinesthetically—is available at www.vark-learn.com/English/index.asp. Click on "Questionnaire" for "How Do I Learn Best?"

A learning preference assessment (LPA) that assesses learners' level of readiness for self-directed learning is explained at www.Guglielmino734.com (click on LPA).

Learners who are easily self-directed also tend to exhibit many special traits, including these:[19]

- A willingness to set goals
- A willingness to plan their learning strategically
- Positive self-images of themselves as learners and faith in their abilities
- A willingness to work to reach goals
- A willingness to develop interest in their work
- An ability to focus and maintain attention
- A constant willingness to teach themselves
- The ability to monitor their own performance
- An inclination to seek help when needed
- A desire to evaluate their work
- An understanding that hard work and perseverance lead to success
- A willingness to use what they have learned to adapt to new situations

Guglielmino lists specific learner *attitudes* that strongly support self-directed learning:[20]

- *Having confidence in themselves as competent, effective learners*—learners see themselves as "can-do" learners who enjoy being innovative
- *Accepting responsibility for their own learning*—primary responsibility for learning belongs to the learner, not the instructor, trainer, or professor; learners must recognize their own needs for learning and take responsibility for making it happen regardless of obstacles
- *Viewing problems as challenges rather than obstacles*—distractions and obstacles should be seen as opportunities to strengthen the learner and not to avoid or abandon a learning project
- *Creativity and independence in learning*—unstructured learning settings with no set directions or expected outcomes work best
- *Willingness to seek help*—use tools available and discovers tools that are not available
- *Valuing their own learning*—valuing the learning achieved on their own

THE INDIVIDUAL LEARNING PLAN

The individual learning plan (ILP) is simply a tool—like a road-map that guides from one place to another—used by employees or work groups that helps organize and plan self-directed learning activities. An ILP will focus primarily on building individual or group competencies. No single correct learning plan form or format exists. The format and look are less important than their functionality. What works best for learners is what matters the most. However, most ILPs provide a structure to help learners establish individual learning goals, track goal accomplishments, identify and locate the resources learners will use to reach the goals, and provide for some form of evaluation. Although an ILP is flexible, there are some major components or phases that comprise a robust ILP:[21] the initiating phase; the planning phase; the managing phase; and, the evaluating phase (see Table 10.3).

TABLE 10.3 Guiding Model or Plan for Self-Directed Learning

Initiating Phase	Planning Phase	Managing Phase	Evaluating Phase
What is the purpose or goal of the learning endeavor?	What questions are to be answered or what needs met?	What are the intended outcomes or personal benefits?	What learning resources are available or attainable?
What activities can best stimulate learning?	What are the criteria for successful accomplishment of any learning goals?	Has each learning activity been carried out?	How can the acquired information and knowledge be analyzed, interpreted, and incorporated?
What conclusions or personal change is obtainable from the experience?	Were the learning goals achieved?	Are there other goals that can be established?	How can personal proficiencies as a learner be improved?

Source: Stubblefield, H. W. (1981). A learning model for adults. *Lifelong learning: The adult years, 4*(7), 24–26. Retrieved from http://home.twcny.rr.com/hiemstra/sdilch6.html.

STEPS IN DEVELOPING AN INDIVIDUAL LEARNING PLAN (ILP)

Developing Learning Goals

Gather documents that will play an important role in devising an effective ILP: a statement of the organization's vision, mission, and values statements; the learner's position description; the learner's performance goal statement; the results of any assessments of individual or department competencies; and, any pronouncements about the organization's strategic plan.

Goals of an ILP

An ILP may be used to achieve one or several learning goals. Examples of ILP goals include:

- Developing or enhancing capabilities in the present job
- Planning for career achievement
- Developing skills and learning activities to support performance goals

Self-Assessment

Individuals must assess themselves (Figure 10.1). They must consider such questions as these: What competencies must they acquire or enhance to be successful in their present jobs? What competencies must they maintain to keep their present jobs? How will present competencies be applicable to future work? What advancing technology exists that will influence the need to learn? Learners should think ahead at least three to five years and assess their strengths and opportunities in their present or future positions either inside or outside their organization.

Determine the Preferred Learning Style

From the references listed earlier in this chapter, determine the individual's preferred learning style.

Scan the Learning Activities That Match Learning Needs and Styles

- Books, articles, magazines, journals
- CD-ROM, videotapes, and audiotapes

Identify the top 3 competencies required NOW in the present position	Identify the strengths (competencies) that the individual presently possesses
Identify the top 3 competencies that may be required in the NEAR FUTURE in the present position	**Identify the competencies needed for improvement or future development**

FIGURE 10.1 Individual self-assessment.

TABLE 10.4 Sample Entries in an ILP

Goals/Skills to Develop	Action or Learning Activity	Resources Needed	Target Completion Date
Improve computer skills to develop a fully functioning database	Register and attend classes	Community college, tuition	Spring semester
	Discuss appropriate database options	Meet with Roy's IT team	First quarter

- Computer-based and Web-based training
- Committee or self-organizing work teams
- Coach, mentor, cross-training, one-to-one peer coaching
- Lectures, talks, discussions
- Conference, workshop, seminar, formal training program
- Other resources—organization-specific developmental efforts such as people, places, positions, or assignments that will help to build needed competencies

The ILP

By evaluating the previous data, individuals can devise viable learning plans. In some instances, the short-term ILP will have an end date while other long-term ILPs may be a work in progress with floating completion dates. Table 10.4 depicts a sample of ILP headings and sample entries.

NOTES

1. Foster, S. (2004, April 17). Self-directed learning weblog. Comment posted to http://bobjackson.motime.com/.

2. U.S. Department of Labor. (1999). *Futurework: Trends and challenges for work in the 21st century.* Retrieved from http://www.dol.gov/asp/programs/history/herman/reports/futurework/execsum.pdf.

3. North Central Regional Educational Laboratory. (n.d.). *enGauge.* Retrieved from http://www.ncrel.org/enguage/skills/skill21.htm.

4. Learning Point Associates was founded as the North Central Regional Educational Laboratory (NCREL) in 1984. NCREL continues its research and development work as a wholly owned subsidiary of Learning Point Associates.

5. Chun, S. (2002, August). *Preparing Korean Americans for the 21st century workforce.* Symposium conducted at the Centennial Conference on Korean Immigration to the United States, Falls Church, VA.

6. Ibid.

7. U.S. Department of Labor (1992). SCANS study. Cited in http://www.ncrel.org/engauge/skills/invent2.htm.

8. U.S. Departments of Labor and Education. (1991). *Secretary's commission on achieving necessary skills (SCANS).* Washington, DC: Author.

9. North Central Regional Educational Laboratory. (n.d.). *enGauge.* Retrieved from http://www.ncrel.org/enguage/skills/invent2.htm. Copyright © (2003) Learning Point Associates. All rights reserved. Reprinted with permission.

10. Ibid.

11. Structured Training (n.d.). *Training versus learning.* Retrieved from www.structured-training.com/asp/trainingvlearning.asp.

12. Senge, P. (1990). *The fifth discipline: The art and practice of the learning organization* (p. 3). New York: Currency Doubleday.

13. Dolezalek, H. (2004, January). Building better learners. *Training, 41,* 31.

14. Slater, R. (2003). *29 leadership secrets from Jack Welch* (pp. 50–51). New York: McGraw-Hill.

15. Ibid., p. 53.

16. Rossi, D. (n.d.). *Self-directed learning: A strategy for lifelong learning.* Retrieved from http://www.library.cqu.edu.au/conference/papers/Rossi.pdf.

17. Hiemstra, R. (1996). *What's in a word: Changes in self-directed learning language over a decade.* Paper presented at the 1996 International Symposium on Self-Directed Learning. Abstract retrieved from http://home.twcny.rr.com/hiemstra/word.html.

18. Inscape Publishing. (1997). *Personal learning insights profile: Understanding personal learning approaches.* Minneapolis, MN: Author.

19. North Central Regional Educational Laboratory. (n.d.). *enGauge.* Retrieved from http://www.ncrel.org/enguage/skills/invent2.htm. Retrieved from http://www.ncrel.org/enguage/skills/invent2.htm. Copyright © (2003) Learning Point Associates. All rights reserved. Reprinted with permission.

20. Guglielmino, L. M., & Guglielmino, P. J. (2003). Becoming a more self-directed learner: Why and how. In G. M. Piskurich (Ed.), *Getting the most from online learning: A learner's guide* (pp. 25–32). Hoboken, NJ: John Wiley.

21. Stubblefield, H. W. (1981). A learning model for adults. *Lifelong learning: The adult years, 4*(7), 24–26. Retrieved from http://home/twcny.rr.com/hiemstra/sdilch6.html.

THE SELF-ASSESSMENT APPROACH: FINDING VALUE IN A NEW METHODOLOGY

Effective self-assessment of individual employees reduces turnover, increases job satisfaction, and can save a company millions of dollars per year. Organizations that effectively understand the self-assessment process and how it relates to competency acquisition and career training (and lends itself directly to succession efforts) and the subsequent increased returns on their business model have jumped in with both feet and are reaping the rewards today.

This chapter reviews:

1. The business case for employing a comprehensive self-assessment strategy
2. An explanation of a new individual self-assessment model that focuses on these steps:

   Step 1: Self-assessment initiation
   Step 2: Self-interest identification
   Step 3: Career investigation and experiential probing
   Step 4: Decision making

Step 5: Goal affirmation
Step 6: Actualization and revision

3. New career development self-assessment techniques

Any organization that embarks on creating or enhancing its career development and succession planning program needs to understand the complexity and importance of individual motivators through a self-assessment process. After all, if you do not know what you truly want to do with regard to your skill sets and strategic planning, how will your employees be able to best fit into that vision with what they would like to do with their abilities to make the organization successful?

Every year, a list hits the bookshelves of the best companies to work for. This list is a good public relations tactic and may attract talent to organizations that are fortunate enough to make the list. Satisfied employees will stay with that employer, which means that companies that are good to work for probably experience lower turnover. (It is also hoped that they will experience higher productivity.) This rating is meant to lead to the increases in employee productivity and efficiency in mission-critical organizational areas that have been demonstrated to increase shareholder value.[1] In today's business environment, it is critical to cross-train and develop flexible workers to meet business needs as they arise. The challenge lies in objectively assessing talent on hand to establish career plans and succession plans that contribute to achieving the organization's strategic objectives. People at the top must lead this charge.

THE INTERNAL AND MONETARY VALUE OF AN INTEGRATED CAREER DEVELOPMENT AND SUCCESSION PLANNING APPROACH

Employees look to leaders to assess the future they can expect with hard work and dedication to corporate objectives. That goes a long way to provide a sense of importance to what each individual contributes to the organization. Leaders must build confidence with employees, and (if they do) they are more likely to attract qualified candidates while reducing attrition by more than 50 percent.[2] Retaining qualified talent is

key to continued competitive success. To keep good people, an organization's leaders care for workers' needs and leverage their talents to meet business demands. People expect reciprocity from an employer, meaning that they expect the employer to exert efforts on their behalf that are about the same as the worker exerts on the employer's behalf. Job satisfaction surveys indicate that a major reason employees remain loyal to an organization is that they are continually offered opportunities for growth through organized training and career development activities.

A first step to encourage employee loyalty is to create a system that allows employee and employer to evaluate present skill sets (competencies) and strategic needs so that development gaps can be identified and addressed. When the organization provides a means to work closely with employees to develop their skills, employee loyalty increases. Further, it builds bench strength for the organization to tap as new business strategies are formulated and implemented.[3]

Employees want development programs. They know:

- Their skills are growing obsolete in the face of technological advancement.
- Their relationship with the employer is somewhat "contractual"; training builds the competencies that workers will need to succeed in present positions and qualify for future ones.
- Training can help them keep their jobs, qualify for new ones, and prepare for unforeseen threats to their long-term employability.

Effective succession programs have been shown to be directly related to competency acquisition and career training.[4] Organizations that have adopted this service for their employees include IBM, Intel, Sun Microsystems, and Motorola.[5] Organizations outside of the technology realm—such as The Vanguard Group, Lockheed-Martin, and Booz-Allen Hamilton—have also adopted extensive in-house development plans to meet present worker needs and prepare them for the future.

As many organizations are coming out of a recession-based model of operation, they face the challenge of remaining economically viable with fewer people (and weaker bench strength). To succeed, employers must optimize their talent pool and efficiently employ the knowledge capital of their workers to deliver business results. An efficient organization avoids the boom-or-bust, hire-or-layoff approaches to staffing in the face of swings in business cycles, maintains positive morale, and returns money to shareholders. One example of an efficient system (and a subsequent number-one Fortune 500 ranking in management quality) is Wellpoint, a leading health care company.[6] Wellpoint's integrated career and succession planning effort slashed attrition by about 6 percent, saved more than 21 million dollars in recruiting costs, and cut candidate search time by more than half.[7]

The internal and monetary benefits of integrated career planning and succession planning systems are clear. Employee self-assessment can help workers feel empowered and motivated.

EXAMINING THE ROLE OF SELF-ASSESSMENT

For any career or succession planning program to work, employees must work to develop themselves. Individuals lacking that motivation become turnover statistics in organizations that have established a corporate culture in which employee development is encouraged, expected, and rewarded. Encouraging employee self-assessment helps workers clarify their present career goals, their present competencies, and their development needs. In short, self-assessment is key to identifying individual values, interests, and abilities. It can encourage workers to reflect on the future, and that (in turn) can complement succession planning efforts. Moreover, self-assessment is a key building block for career planning. After all, if employees do not know where they want to go or how to get there, they will see no relevance to succession planning or career planning efforts.

THE INTERNAL ORGANIZATIONAL INDIVIDUAL SELF-ASSESSMENT MODEL

The Internal Organizational-Individual Self-Assessment Model was created to scope and sequence efforts by individuals to understand their workplace interests, abilities, and goals. The model can only be as successful as participants' willingness to be honest and objective with (and about) themselves (see Figure 11.1). The model deserves more elaboration.

FIGURE 11.1   Internal Organizational Individual Self-Assessment Model. *Source*: Knight, S. C. (2004). Unpublished manuscript. University Park, PA: Penn State University.

Step 1: Self-Assessment Initiation

Initiating self-assessment is a particularly difficult step to take. It is common for individuals to take this step only after experiencing a major, and usually negative, event—such as demotion or termination. This reactive approach to the self-assessment process typically results in less than desirable outcomes. A proactive approach, in contrast, allows individuals to make honest and objective value judgments to assist in establishing their career planning and future succession goals. As the global market continues to evolve from manufacturing and service to a more technologically and information-driven economy, individuals must position themselves to deal with many changes.

Many individuals select an occupation without fully, or realistically, understanding its demands or responsibilities. Often, people select occupations to meet their immediate needs. Those needs may be centered around finances, family situation, or even fear of the unknown. Whatever the reason for an individual's occupation choice, he or she is usually, and eventually, drawn to self-assessment to take stock of themselves. Once a person is comfortable with the need to self-assess, the second step in the process helps them discover what interests truly appeal to him or her.

Step 2: Self-Interest Identification

"Know thyself" was the dictum carved above the temple of the Delphic Oracle in Ancient Greece. Understanding oneself requires much courage, honesty, objectivity, and patience. Few people can sit down for one attempt at this process and surface all the answers. For organizations that provide self-assessment services for their employees, both employer and employee need to understand that it takes time. Self-interest identification is crucial for employees to understand who they are in relation to the organization—that is, how their interests, skills, and abilities align with the work tasks of the company. The individual's aspirations, goals, and dreams should also be explored.

Employees must ask themselves what they need to be happy in doing their present jobs and how they can be successful in pursuing their goals. Part of this process involves uncovering and examining natural talents compared to personal interests. For example, individuals who are naturally talented in graphic art technologies used to create promotional pieces may want to look at ways to apply this knowledge to their work. That is how organizations can uncover hidden talents of their employees.

In large organizations with full-fledged career centers, career counselors can confidentially assist individuals with this process. In smaller organizations that are beginning to incorporate a career development function, HR specialists may rely on consulting resources and guides to help individuals begin the initial process. This step in the self-assessment process serves as the launching pad for designing appropriate career pathways for individuals as well as identifying potential talent for succession planning efforts.

Step 3: Career Investigation and Experiential Probing

Once workers have tentatively decided on what career goals to pursue based on identified skills and interests, they can explore viable avenues to achieve those goals. This phase of the self-assessment model parallels the initial phase of corporate career developmental activities and succession planning efforts. From the perspective of career development, at this point individuals refine their professional goals through exploration. Exploration can take many forms and may rely on such activities as mentoring, job shadowing, and talking with peers about positions. This is a low-risk process that provides employees with pertinent information and cursory experiences to help define who they are and who they want to be professionally.

Employers who are supportive of investigative career exploration often support discussion groups or simulated work experiences to help employees find their niche. Many tools are available to simulate work-related functions in a low-risk/liability environment. For example, a financial services organization can actually simulate an equities trading floor without taking any serious financial risks. Purposeful exploration can help individuals sort out the myths and realities of potential jobs and offer organizational leaders valid ways to assess prospective talent.

Step 4: Decision Making

The fourth step in this process involves establishing a formal commitment to pursue a particular area of interest for development. To be successful, this choice must enjoy the support of the organization. This phase of self-assessment is where the action begins to implement a formal career development strategy that will build employee competencies in line with individual career interests and organizational needs. It is at this point in the career development cycle that employees participate in training sessions, obtain specialized training, and assume additional job functions to build their competencies. For succession planning, this step allows leaders to consider placing individuals into future roles as indicated by their career pathway plans. That ensures congruency between what talent the company strategically needs and what individuals want.

Step 5: Goal Affirmation

Successful companies and people leverage their competencies to meet customer needs and accurately predict what they will need in the future. In Step 5 of the self-assessment process, employees affirm their plans based on their own experiences and the company's strategic direction. Career development is a cyclical system that should be reviewed by both individual and the corporation periodically (every six months or so) to ensure proper continuity between individual development objectives and corporate objectives. As individual interests and corporate missions evolve, both parties must remain flexible in refining their plans. Linking a self-assessment tool with career development activities and succession efforts is critical to preventing goal misalignment. While that may seem burdensome, it can pay off for organizations with a planned process.

Step 6: Actualization and Revision

The final step of the self-assessment process examines relative achievement of development objectives. In this phase, employee and employer compare accomplishments to the action established at the outset of the development cycle. When planned activities are completed, employees should possess the competencies necessary to contribute further to the organization. The organization's leaders can clarify their succession plans and align qualified individuals to opportunities. High-achieving employees can then develop more competencies to directly benefit the business unit and themselves. Goals, interests, and subsequent abilities can change as a result of experience.

When employees fail to meet the needs of their development plans, individuals can be "recycled" through the model to redefine their career and developmental objectives. The organization's leaders may make a value judgment at this point about the viability of individuals to meet succession needs. The failure of an employee to meet his or her development goals creates several questions to be addressed:

- Does the employee possess the motivation, desire, and aptitude to handle an increased role within the organization?

- Are the developmental experiences provided by the organization adequate to meet varied employee needs?
- Are career and succession planning supported by senior leaders and aligned with the organization's strategic objectives?

NEW CAREER DEVELOPMENT SELF-ASSESSMENT TECHNIQUES

Many organizations do not have the budget to serve the entire workforce with intensive, individualized counseling. A mixed methodology for self-assessment is often necessary. Typical approaches to the self-assessment process combine some classroom training and individual counseling sessions with electronic and/or printed self-assessment tools.

Many options are available for organizations that wish to use off-the-shelf assessment tools. Many reasons exist to go this route. First, it is an effective way to address the issue of capacity. A standardized evaluation tool is an efficient method of soliciting and receiving self-assessment. Second, the reliability and validity of these tests provide accurate measures and reasonable interpretation of results, while a survey created in-house may lack proper quality controls. Third, a standardized testing instrument can save money for the organization. While testing materials may have a fee associated their use, surveying many people in a relatively short time mitigates this cost. Finally, a technology-based approach allows employees to administer their own tests at any time of day, minimizing productivity losses and offering convenience and some privacy to participants.

Testing materials available to individuals and organizations cover many topics, including these:

- Self-assessment of values, interests, and ethics
- Personality inventories
- Occupational exploration
- Computer-aided career guidance systems

Table 11.1 outlines some self-assessment services available.

TABLE 11.1 Standardized Self-Assessment Tools for Organizations

Personality Assessment Tools	Computer Career Guidance Programs
Myers Briggs Type Indicator http://www.myersbriggs.org	DISCOVER www.act.org/discover
Keirsey Temperament http://keirsey.com	SIGIPLUS http://www.ets.org/sigi/
Hogan Assessment Systems www.hoganassessments.com	FOCUS http://www.focuscareer.com/

Interest Inventories	Career Exploration Materials
Strong Interest Inventory www.cpp.com/products/strong	O*NET http://online.onetcenter.org/
Pearson Assessments www.pearsonassessments.com	America's Career InfoNet www.acinet.org/acinet/
Interest Inventory (COPS) www.edits.net/copysystem.html	JobWeb http://www.jobweb.com/

Source: Knight, S.C. (2004). Unpublished manuscript. University Park, PA: Penn State University.

It is worth noting that standardized testing alone is not sufficient for proper self-assessment. It is a way to efficiently address specific developmental needs. Organizations should use the four resource classifications outlined in Table 11.1 with a professional career counselor to achieve optimal impact.

To summarize, an organization's ability to assist employees in self-assessing their competencies has been shown to contribute to improved morale, lower attrition rates, and an increased return on investment for shareholders. This cannot occur without dynamic, and engaging, corporate leaders who rally employees to do their best for the good of the organization and their own careers. Proactive leaders encourage individual self-assessment.

Using the self-assessment model can greatly increase the synergy of an integrated career and succession planning system. To meet the needs of both organization and individual, most companies use a blended learning approach to minimize productivity losses and maximize flexibility. A well thought-out career and succession planning system infused with the self-assessment approach can leverage talent, resulting in increased profits and success.

NOTES

1. Harrington, J. (2003). Training adds up. *Incentive, 177,* 22.
2. Gubman, E. (2003). Engaging talent. *Executive Excellence, 20,* 11.
3. Griffith, C. (1998). Building a resilient workforce. *Training, 35,* 54–58.
4. Harrington, J. (2003). Training adds up. *Incentive, 177,* 22.
5. Griffith, C. (1998). Building a resilient workforce. *Training, 35,* 54–58.
6. Kiger, P. J. (2002). Succession planning keeps WellPoint competitive. *Workforce, 81,* 50–54.
7. Ibid.

TWELVE

OTHER APPROACHES

As with any effort relating to career development and succession planning, several key assumptions need to be in place to make it work to mitigate as many skill gaps as possible within an organization.

- First, the company and employee have a shared interest promoting oneself and the mission of the organization to the best of their ability.
- Second, accountability is the responsibility of all parties vested in this endeavor.
- Third, all succession and career development efforts should be tied to organization competencies as a means for movement (promotion, reclassification, lateral movement) and derived fair compensation practices.

To explain further, a case study is presented along with a model outlining how to effectively approach and mitigate skill gaps in relation to the individual, organizational management, and the organization. This model will provide the reader with the necessary tools and strategies to effectively manage the identified skill gaps present within the organization. Companies will be able to leverage this information to formulate a comprehensive developmental plan that will lend itself to efficient succession planning and execution.

While career programs build competencies for succession moves in an organization, some developmental gaps may not be addressed without more work. This chapter examines methods that can assist in narrowing developmental gaps to meet career and succession planning needs. It opens with an examination of an actual company's development-related issues.

CASE STUDY

This Fortune 500 organization is a leader in its field, producing cutting-edge equipment for government and private industry. It employs a workforce of 200,000 globally. Part of the organization employs 10,000, and that is the focus of this case. The organization is presently facing the need to hire 25 percent more people for the organizational unit (2500 new personnel) over the next year. The attrition rate tends to be about 15 percent per year, typically stemming from retirements and other human resource losses. The organization needs to hire about 4000 people annually to maintain its growth projections. It has recently experienced a dramatic rise in attrition (unrelated to retirement) of executive, managerial, and senior staff members; the CEO wants to know how to alleviate this issue and how to best retain and recruit star performers to meet strategic objectives.

Top-line managers see two factors contributing to the rise in attrition. First, the influx of new personnel necessitates constant reacclimation to new personalities and new skill sets. For some time, managers have expressed frustration about having to focus more on establishing effective work groups and "putting out fires" than meeting work deadlines. People are failing to show up for work on time, and many are missing multiple deadlines, affecting many departments. Managers also complain that new hires have little understanding of the organization's ethical standards and are pushing the envelope of acceptable competitive behaviors with other organizations and internal departments. There has been a noticeable drop in the quality of applicants. Many lack the competencies needed to succeed. Managers complain that they are starting to see a decline in the products that are being designed and distributed.

HR managers in the organization interpret the attrition in a twofold way. First, they claim that not enough qualified candidates exist in the available labor supply to meet the organization's needs. They simply cannot find individuals who match the competency profile for the available positions. As a result, they are forced to choose those who are "near fits." HR managers admit that they hire people who lack the required competencies, but they feel that it is preferable to hiring nobody at all. HR managers also place some blame for attrition on managers for failing to hold people accountable for implementing their developmental plans, which are determined at the beginning of every annual evaluation period.

While corporate policy requires annual performance evaluations, reevaluations at sixth-month intervals, and initial planning sessions for new hires, that policy is not being followed. Managers indicate that they are too busy putting out the fires created by the HR managers, who have hired inadequate staff to do the work—especially when the product is lacking in quality and deadlines are not being met in a timely fashion. HR managers claim that they process all new hires through an orientation session lasting for about an hour before the employees go to their assigned work groups. The HR department itself has also suffered attrition among recruiters and staffing professionals, which intensifies the pressure on those remaining. HR managers point out that recruiting and hiring 4000 people in a year with reduced staff is a daunting challenge.

Employees, when surveyed, indicate that many issues cause them to be concerned about the organization. Many employees feel that they are cast adrift in the organization and are shuffled from one project to another. They too feel that the new people joining their teams are ill prepared or even unqualified. That prompts senior employees to grow frustrated and, on occasion, to give up on projects with minimal support so that they can focus on what they can do best. They let projects evolve on their own. Employees also feel that their skills are growing obsolete due to inadequate time and attention devoted to professional development. They feel that renders them less useful to the organization. Few employees feel challenged, and managers admit they are too busy to evaluate people and work to help them develop their competencies.

While this organization is benefiting financially from large corporate and government contracts that total billions of dollars, the key problems facing it center on worker satisfaction and competitive sustainability. Reflect on the following questions about this case:

- What are the strengths and weaknesses of this organization as described in the case?
- What are, and what should be, the roles of individuals, managers, and others in implementing successful career and succession planning programs?
- What responsibilities should be shouldered by individuals, managers, and others to alleviate the problems described in the case?
- Within each job classification, what specific actions could be taken to meet the needs of individuals and more precisely address developmental skill gaps that exist in all levels of the system?

Table 12.1 presents a model of value in thinking about ways to close developmental gaps. Review it and think about how it may influence your answers to the questions posed above.

THE INDIVIDUAL APPROACH TO SKILL-GAP MITIGATION

Career Planning Through Self-Assessment

As discussed in Chapter 11, the individual self-assessment process is crucial to launching career planning efforts. Individuals who have reached an understanding of their interests, abilities, and career goals can advance through the formative stages of career planning. As career goals become clearer, individuals can make more accurate decisions about what training, or other planned learning events, can help them achieve their goals. Further, when individuals are clear about their career goals, they can provide a reality check on the organization's succession plans.

TABLE 12.1 Effective Approaches to Skill-Gap Mitigation in Relation to the Individual, Organizational Management, and the Organization

Responsibilities of the:	Accountability	Outcomes
Individual	Career planning through Self-assessment	Career goal alignment
	Internal motivation and initiation	Intrinsic desire to achieve
	Personal accountability	Creates obligation and structure
	Goal achievement and revisioning	Continual career development process
Organizational Management	Performance management	Methodologies for increased productivity and satisfaction
	360-degree feedback modeling	Provides clarity on knowledge skill assessment, performance, and increased focus on developmental succession efforts
Organization	Employee development	Creates talent on hand for strategic needs and succession evaluation
	Competency identification	Clarifies needed skill sets for job functions
	Orientation to corporate value, ethics, and mission	Demonstrates executive commitment to core business practices and goals
	Executive/managerial-level development	Develops competencies to effectively carry out defined objectives
	Total compensation packages	Ensures equity, relative competitive wages, and workplace satisfaction

Source: Knight, S. C. (2004). Unpublished manuscript. University Park, PA: Penn State University.

Conducting self-assessment of individual competencies and interests plays a key role in aligning individual career aspirations with organizational talent needs. Self-assessment opens up several possibilities:

- Employees determine that their interests and strengths align with the organization's mission and strategic objectives of the organization, and they commit to build competencies to position them for further advancement in the organization.
- Employees determine that their interests and abilities will not be leveraged by the organization, and they choose to leave to apply their talents elsewhere.
- Employees determine that their interests and abilities are not aligned with organizational needs, but they resolve to sit tight until they are forced to leave or to conform to what the organization needs.

Internal Motivation and Initiation

Most performers want to contribute to their organizations in any way necessary to ensure their viability. But the internal motivation of workers is their responsibility and not that of the organization. The company should provide opportunities for development and eventual advancement. However, if employees do not desire to develop themselves, then they will not develop.

If the employer is supportive and actively engaged in the career development process, employees' motivation to professionally develop their competencies to better serve the company can be contagious. The learning process can evolve into a reward-based system, providing incentives to achieve and contribute in as many ways as possible to help the company succeed. Rewards can come through verbal praise, public acknowledgement, promotion, or pay raises. Leveraging the internal motivation of employees can be very effective in narrowing skill gaps.

Personal Accountability

For motivated individuals, personal accountability creates a sense of responsibility to themselves, their team members, and their employers. Organizational expectations play a major role in establishing and maintaining accountability. However, individuals must embrace this accountability before managerial expectations can exert influence.

Personal accountability also creates a structure from which an individual can pace his or her professional development. It allows employees and employers to allocate resources and gauge workload balances to maximize workers' development. Most career development opportunities require some action by the learners. This sense of obligation increases the chances that successful learning will take place.

Goal Achievement and Revision

Recognition of goal achievement and the revision of developmental plans as needed are critical to the continual success of an organization. The successful completion of training assists in reducing development gaps identified in the planning process. Successful completion of a work goal benefits the organization with a more highly trained employee.

Since career planning is not a linear process, individuals must understand how newly acquired competencies can benefit the organization and then market those competencies appropriately. It is also the responsibility of individuals to revise their development plans if their career goals change. Employees must compare themselves to the competency profiles of higher-level positions to determine what they must do to prepare for advancement.

THE ORGANIZATIONAL MANAGEMENT APPROACH TO SKILL-GAP MITIGATION

Performance Management

The need for organizations to remain agile and flexible has necessitated reengineering of the evaluation and motivation of high performance. Performance management systems have become an integral component in the effective and efficient use of internal talent.[1] Frigo and Krumwiede note that more than 60 percent of organizations have completely revamped their performance evaluation processes to better meet their operational objectives.[2] A simple formula determines whether management was working properly prior to the implementation of performance management processes: Was the organization doing well on the financial bottom line? If so, the organization was functioning well; if not, changes need to be made. With the understanding that the world of work is becoming more intertwined and complex, old approaches are becoming ineffective for maintaining a viable business. Eccles[3] and Neely[4] note that a distinct need sparked performance measurement innovation.

Performance management can also minimize identifiable skill gaps. An effective performance management system facilitates evaluation of performance as it relates to production, relevant skill sets, and internal growth potential. The identification of deficient competencies within work units can provide opportunities to address issues with training initiatives. This strategy should be used to facilitate the development of an integrated career and succession planning effort.

360-Degree Feedback Modeling

Another strategy that can identify skill gaps is an assessment process known as 360-degree multirater feedback. Approximately 25 percent of organizations have utilized the 360-degree feedback process as a tool for assessing individual capabilities.[5] The intent of this process is to provide a comprehensive evaluation of individuals who lack key competencies. The process, in simple terms, provides the evaluator with surveys that are submitted anonymously by the person being evaluated, their coworkers, supervisors, subordinates, and in some instances, customers who have had direct contact with the employee.[6] The survey is composed of questions on many issues including performance, identification of areas of strength and weakness, and suggestions for improvement of deficient skill sets. Green notes that the tool is designed to pinpoint highly competent leadership abilities as well as developmental skill gaps.[7] This assessment also enhances an individual's understanding of performance and pathways for development while supplying managers with an identified talent pool to develop.

Employee Development

Employee development contributes to the effective implementation of succession planning efforts, maintains healthy recruitment and retention statistics, provides overall job satisfaction for employees, and increases bottom line profits. Successful organizations have accepted that employees should be continually developed to meet the dynamic needs of the international business climate. Development can take many forms, such as classroom training, computer-based career guidance systems, career counseling, mentoring, and problem-based learning approaches.

Competency Identification

Competency identification is a foundational process for any career and succession planning program. Competency identification requires that each individual job function be accounted for. Specifically, a competency model should minimally include the targeted group, a list of personal characteristics, and a list of behaviors that—when exhibited— will demonstrate the competency.

Competency assessment helps the organization's leaders understand what development needs may be required to ensure that employees are meeting the organization's strategic objectives. One direct result of a quality competency assessment should be a specific, needs-based development plan for an individual to close developmental gaps. Another result of a competency assessment should be an indication of how well-qualified individuals are to meet the competency model requirements of higher levels on the organization chart (or more complex levels on the continuum of professional responsibilities). Competency modeling provides a way to identify qualified candidates to meet future staffing needs of the organization.

Orientation to Corporate Values, Ethics, and Mission

The effective communication of values, ethics, and strategic mission is very important during the initial orientation process for new employees and at annual employee meetings. Effective organizational leaders realize that discussing their business processes and culture with new employees is essential. While hiring managers or human resources departments generally espouse corporate practices and expectations, the message is much more effective when it comes from top-level management. New and current employees who hear a message from the CEO concerning corporate mission and expectations can compare their personal professional beliefs with those of the organization. Individuals who feel that their philosophies and actions are congruent with the expectations of the company can continue to develop in ways that further strengthen the synergy between the two. For those who feel that their values are not in alignment with the expectations of the organization, an exit strategy can be developed.

Executive/Managerial-Level Development

Executive- and managerial-level training ensures that support at the top of the corporate hierarchy is being competently transferred to employees. Just as non-administrative workers have identified skill gap needs, managerial- and executive-level employees have developmental areas on which to focus. Proactive organizations continually focus on administrative team development as a means of delivering quality oversight to corporate objectives. Training often addresses how administrative staffs professionally manage themselves, the performance and effective management skills of their work groups, and leveraging and accounting for knowledge management. Executive- and managerial-level training creates a more talented administrative resource. Additionally, these individuals will feel more satisfied in their positions, and continually seek to maximize their succession potential.

Compensation Packages

Another effective tool for recruiting, retaining, and developing a workforce is the compensation package. A lucrative (but competitively gauged) financial compensation model can attract top talent to an organization. Often, the financial package offered is a direct result of talent supply versus demand for individuals possessing essential competencies. A compensation model can also play a dual role to encourage retention and mitigate development gaps.

If the compensation and benefits department of an organization can implement competitive wage structures as they relate to talent supply and demand, they will be successful in mitigating attrition rates. A final benefit of an adequate compensation package is that increased on-the-job knowledge (career development) provides expectations and the realization of increased responsibility (succession planning). This necessitates additional training and subsequent skill set mitigation as employees enter and move internally with the organization.

To summarize, while a comprehensive career development system can address many missing competencies, additional techniques and procedures to offset learning and developmental needs are sometimes useful. Mitigating skill gap deficiencies is an equitable three-party responsibility of the individual worker, management personnel, and a strategic and broad outreach by the organization and its practices. Utilizing successful methodologies in addition to the traditional career development and succession planning process can create a dynamic synergy that yields spectacular results.

NOTES

1. Kennerley, M., & Neely, A. (2002). A framework of the factors affecting the evolution of performance management systems. *International Journal of Operations and Production Management, 22,* 1222–1245.

2. Frigo, M. L., & Krumwiede, K. R. (1999). Balanced scorecards: A rising trend in strategic performance management. *Journal of Strategic Performance Management, 3,* 42–44.

3. Eccles, R. G. (1991). The performance measurement manifesto. *Harvard Business Review,* January–February, 131–137.

4. Neely, A. D. (1999). The performance measurement revolution: Why now and where next? *International Journal of Operations and Production Management, 19,* 205–228.

5. Waldman, D. A., & Atwater, L. E. (1998). *The power of 360 feedback: How to leverage performance evaluations for top productivity.* Houston, TX: Gulf Publishing Company.

6. Green, B. (2002). Listening to leaders: Feedback on 360-degree feedback one year later. *Organization Development Journal, 20,* 8–16.

7. Ibid.

PART IV

CONCLUDING THOUGHTS

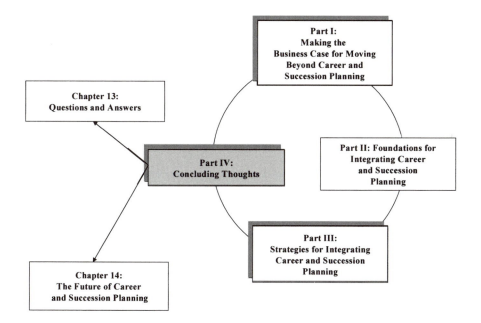

THIRTEEN

QUESTIONS AND ANSWERS

Why and how can we integrate and coordinate career planning and succession programs? These are vital questions and answers for people proposing new approaches to workforce planning. This chapter provides answers to strategic questions that should be part of the planning process for rolling out a program to coordinate career planning and succession programs.

W hen career planning questions are asked objectively, the answers can lead to immediate performance improvement. Similarly, succession planning approaches ensure properly trained and prepared leaders throughout the workforce. Having a leadership map in place involves knowing which employees possess the competencies to ensure that a department, unit, or organization will survive in the future. A succession plan can also work as a development program to train managers or identify competencies that must be imported to the organization through external recruiting. This chapter examines career and succession planning in a frequently asked questions (FAQ) format to provide a quick reference for creating synergy with career and succession plans.

QUESTION 1: WHY SHOULD CAREER AND SUCCESSION PLANNING BE ALIGNED?

Answer 1: It Is Key to Meeting Business Needs

Linking career and succession planning is about business. Making sure people know why they are doing what they are doing, and the organization knows how to continue doing what it does, is crucial. Careers are made by leveraging what an individual has learned in one job to the requirements and demands of next jobs. Most workers will have seven to ten different careers in their working lifetimes. Linking competencies from one job to the next can increase workers' satisfaction levels and earning capacity.

Succession plans ensure future capability. While meeting business expectations on a quarterly or annual basis may achieve performance goals, the long-term survival of a business requires that competent leadership be in the right place at the right times and doing the right things. After the unexpected death of the CEO of McDonald's Corporation, the company's succession plan put a CEO in place within 12 hours. Wall Street greeted this prompt response with a positive reaction.

Answer 2: Career Planning and Succession Planning Rely on Complementary Methodologies

Career plans and succession plans build on each other. Development of employee career plans complements the process of developing a succession plan. A methodology that incorporates long-term planning with shorter term and past assessment is used at both individual and organizational levels. For individuals, the process begins with assessing how a job is building skills and experience that can be used later in their careers, and then focuses on how performance has been evaluated against present goals. This methodology parallels the process of assessing how present capabilities have supported immediate goals, how those capabilities can be developed to improve performance, and how this can meet the organization's future leadership needs.

Answer 3: Career Planning and Succession Planning Require Systems Thinking

Career and succession plans are systems plans. HR adds value by linking individual parts of the organization to a central, core position. From this position, career and succession planning requires people to consider how their positions fit within a greater scheme. This greater scheme can be a long-term career plan or a departmental succession plan. In either case, the process requires examination of how the work environment can be improved.

Answer 4: Career Planning and Succession Planning Encourage Involvement

New employees, longer-term employees, managers, senior leaders, and downsized employees are interested in career planning. To managers and senior leaders, a succession plan reflects concern for the organization after they have left.

Answer 5: Integrating Career and Succession Planning Helps to Do More with Less and Strengthen Products

Aligning career and succession plans creates potential synergy. Historically, career and succession plans were developed in separate parts of the organization with separate objectives; alignment of the two means that individual and organizational plans are reviewed by a single source to identify common ground and goals.

Answer 6: Integrating Career Planning and Succession Planning Enables the Organization to Grow

Organizations can either enable or disable their own growth. By aligning career and succession plans, an organization ensures its growth by recognizing its employees' development. Not all employees will have a place in the organization's succession plan, but aligning career and succession plans can ensure continued leadership capabilities.

Answer 7: Both Career and Succession Planning Programs Rely on Learning Programs to Close Developmental Gaps

Career and succession plans require people to learn about themselves, their organization, and the future direction of both. Creating these plans begins with consideration of future goals and strategies, and how present performance and capabilities match long-term objectives. The learning that occurs when employees consider long-term goals impacts operational and strategic behaviors. The integration of individual and organizational planning results in a new, higher-value mind set.

Answer 8: Integrating Career and Succession Planning Facilitates Creative Thinking

When people consider their own careers in terms of an organization's succession plan, they are forced to think "outside the box." Such alignment requires that employees see their development and the organization's growth as codependent.

Answer 9: Integrating Career and Succession Planning Programs Facilitates Enhanced Accountability

Career plans and succession plans are aimed at increasing accountability to employees and management. By aligning these programs, employee recruitment, retention, and development can be improved by ensuring that current employees understand job succession, and managers understand the capabilities of the current workforce.

Answer 10: Integrating Career and Succession Planning Is Worth Doing Because More Organizations Are Doing It (First Beats Best)

New systems for organizing people, relaying information, and moving products and services require new ways of managing people. The alignment of career and succession plans can offer a better way to manage people through collecting and analyzing competencies and goals. The ideal organization constantly measures itself against goals, assesses performance against resources, corrects itself, and improves. By aligning career and succession plans, an organization can assess competence and capabilities at all levels to meet present and future business challenges.

QUESTION 2: HOW CAN CAREER AND SUCCESSION PLANNING BE INTEGRATED?

Answer 1: To Integrate the Programs, Engage Employees at All Levels

Organizations should communicate widely and develop shared responsibility and ownership for new programs. The approach a company takes to designing, developing, implementing, and evaluating a program reflects its culture. For example, one company may choose to assess each new hire for succession competencies, while another may wait until the first performance evaluation before assessing and developing. Some companies may require employees to program their self-assessment and development, while others may require managers to direct employee growth. Benefits of involving employees at all levels include the following:

- Cross-checking of results
- Shared responsibility for results
- Feelings of ownership at every level
- Employee ownership and acceptance of process results
- The view that employee development is positive and succession planning is fair

Answer 2: To Integrate Career and Succession Programs, Focus on Critical Competencies

Critical competencies are those behaviors that are essential to exemplary performance at leadership levels. Successful career and succession plans highlight key leadership areas and quality ratings associated with competency standards, allowing employees to differentiate between the best and the rest. This is one of the most critical steps in the succession planning process, and is supported by learning and development programs.

Answer 3: To Integrate Career and Succession Programs, Recruit and Screen Toward Success

Competency models are put in place to foster career and succession performance. Recruiting and screening with competencies facilitates high-level selection and employee screening to identify and foster leadership potential. Succession planning reviews should be incorporated into annual performance reviews to promote "next-level thinking." Employee involvement in self-developing along a leadership competency model can be very effective. Shared responsibility, employee feedback, and manager-employee partnering can ingrain the career and succession planning process into an organization's culture.

Answer 4: To Integrate Career and Succession Programs, Devise Comparable Ways to Measure Success

For career and succession plans to take root together, they must be measured in terms of employee growth and organizational leadership. Leading companies ensure program success at all levels by holding each unit (via department manager or HR officer) accountable for the effectiveness of its career and succession plans. Methods used by some organizations include these:

- Linking development to pay at the individual level
- Integrating development reviews into the performance review process
- Creating a performance matrix

Answer 5: Offer Learning Programs to Build Skills for Career and Succession Planning

Top companies ensure that employees are aware of their career planning options. Key methods for accomplishing this goal include the following:

- Implementing a thorough career development process that encourages empowerment
- Educating workers about their career development roles to facilitate advancement
- Empowering employees to take responsibility for their own career advancement

- Utilizing employee satisfaction measurements to develop improvement plans

QUESTION 3: WHAT ORGANIZATIONS ARE SUCCESSFUL AT INTEGRATING CAREER AND SUCCESSION PROGRAMS?

Answer

Organizations that effectively integrate career and succession planning use programs aimed at improving employee development, increasing the speed of leadership development, reducing workplace learning costs, and clearly defining career paths. Companies such as Microsoft, Lockheed-Martin, Merck, Apple Computer, Xerox, Hewlett-Packard, General Electric, and Motorola use career and succession planning throughout all levels of their organizations.

QUESTION 4: WHAT ARE SOME EXAMPLES OF COMMON CAREER AND SUCCESSION PRACTICES?

Answer

Companies that have successfully integrated career and succession planning have stand-alone programs as well as a "growth culture." Examples of effective practices include the following:

- Incorporating career path planning into performance development initiatives to effectively develop employees
- Aligning measurement areas to company strategy
- Communicating how and why metrics are used for employee and organizational development
- Providing employees with customer feedback
- Using competencies and behavior observation
- Establishing professional goals
- Reinforcing strategic direction
- Involving employee input in the process

QUESTION 5: WHAT ARE THE ADVANTAGES OF CAREER AND SUCCESSION PLANNING?

Answer

- A continuous supply of well-trained, broadly experienced, well-motivated people who are ready and able to step into key positions as needed
- A workforce with clearly measured workplace-tested skills that are integrated into the company with individually established positive goals
- Organization-wide distribution of capable people through various departments, with the goal of educating them in the culture and processes of the company
- Alignment of the organization's future needs with the availability of appropriate internal resources
- A documented workforce plan that can be used to sell the company to prospective employees and customers
- A workforce that is constantly reviewing, questioning, and refining procedures and processes, improving the quality of the company (both internally and externally)
- A tool to establish the workplace as an employer of choice

QUESTION 6: WHAT ARE THE CHALLENGES AND DISADVANTAGES OF INTEGRATING CAREER AND SUCCESSION PLANNING?

Answer

- Up-front investment in developing a formal written plan for each key person or position
- Perceptions of a fixed and structured growth plan that is not directed by employee or business needs
- Employee disappointment in the length of time suggested by the programs for advancement and promotion, potentially leading to early departure of high performers because of program complexity
- Lack of content in program approach, and subsequent lack of understanding by employees and managers

- Weak selection decision and involvement of unqualified people, initially; high-quality program participants and immediate success are critical to the effectiveness of the process

QUESTION 7: IS INTEGRATING CAREER AND SUCCESSION PLANNING WORTH THE EFFORT?

Answer

Given the speed of change in the business world, successful career and succession plans must be fluid. A responsive and flexible program requires the direction of well-trained, competent people. Many tensions and challenges must be faced:

- The need to be flexible
- The need to take on people who can and will make their own career decisions
- The need to increase the diversity of the talent pool (especially to ensure that the talents of minorities are properly developed)

While management training and development is one way to develop future leaders, it does not provide a map to ensure breadth of experience. Aligning career and succession plans provides a coordinated process for companies to deliver organization-specific, proactive career development for their most talented individuals. The highest performing organizations recognize career and succession planning as a vital part of their HR strategy.

QUESTION 8: HOW CAN AN INTEGRATED CAREER AND SUCCESSION PLANNING PROGRAM BE ROLLED OUT EFFECTIVELY?

Answer

The board of directors, CEO, and senior leaders play a critical role in lending support and priority to career and succession programs, insisting on high-quality, objective debate and follow-through. Unit leaders, line managers, and supervisors are the direct implementers of these programs. The first step is making it clear to senior and midlevel managers that career and succession planning is good for business. Success depends on program content, strong design, and complete senior leadership support.

The HR function has an equally critical role in the success of these programs. HR provides expertise in these areas:

- Workforce plans
- Program design and facilitation
- Reviewing and discussing plans
- Training managers on career counseling and job succession
- Information on how programs are linked to business strategy

HR reinforces manager knowledge of how integrated programs meet business challenges, improve performance, and provide growth at all levels.

SUMMARY

Changing how work is done requires workforce planners to know where employee competencies reside, and the ability to transition people quickly from one job to the next. To do this effectively, employees and managers need to work together. Business goals and targets change when new opportunities are presented. Careers are the same way; people work where the jobs are. When business goals, careers, and succession plans are addressed in the same system, all are strengthened. No one can plan for every event, but knowledge of an organization's present capabilities combined with a workforce that understands how present work fits within long-term plans can create a high-performance workplace.

FOURTEEN

THE FUTURE OF CAREER AND SUCCESSION PLANNING

How will organizations leverage their human resources to provide the competitive advantage to succeed? Why should an organization create a system that recognizes individual and organizational growth planning? What is the business reason for integrating individual planning and organizational programs? This book addresses the intangible assets of an organization by proposing a systematic approach to career and succession planning. This chapter boils down the changing environment of careers and leadership roles to five characteristics: mobility, fluency, agility, integrity, and opportunity. In this chapter, these five characteristics are described, which are central to individual and organizational growth.

Human resources, finance, marketing, and strategy are becoming more integrated; this integration of roles is creating new opportunities. HR coordinates with finance in using organizational competencies and capabilities to leverage employee staffing. Finance collaborates with marketing to fund new product design, development, and market rollout. Marketing and strategy work with HR to redeploy and upgrade organizational capacities, to produce goods and services in a timely manner. Organizational roles are coming together to create a seamless operational system.

These changes will force career and succession planning programs to align. Companies that coordinate their people management systems will reap the benefits created when individually centered programs are aligned with organizationally centered systems. A people-centered organizational development plan leverages motivation to achieve a visible plan for growth. The future of career and succession planning can be summarized in five characteristics of individual careers and leadership roles: mobility, fluency, agility, integrity, and opportunity.

MOBILITY

Changes in customer expectations, business processes, market locations, staffing styles, and workforce performance have increased the speed of business change. These changes necessitate the mobility of careers and succession plans. *Mobility* describes a mind-set for fast response, quick transition, and smooth exchange from one duty or business to the next. *Career mobility* means being ready for change, and open to applying individual skills and competencies whenever and wherever necessary. *Succession planning mobility* means knowing how markets are changing and where talents can be found in the organization that can propel it into new markets and position it to seize new opportunities.

FLUENCY

Business roles are converging rapidly. Total organizational awareness has replaced individual operational knowledge. Career and succession plans require systems thinking to align individual roles with the organization. Systems thinking entails seeing the whole organization, while remaining aware of individual contributions. *Fluency* is the ability to converse about the total organization, its business purpose, markets, and strategy, and the operational roles of finance, marketing, and human resources. *Fluency in career planning* reflects the ability to discuss and operate within multiple work environments. *Fluency in succession planning* means that people can move throughout the organization with higher-level knowledge of how each unit fits with others and understand what each unit is trying to accomplish.

AGILITY

Maintaining balance in changing times is a requisite for growth. New markets, business strategies, customer requirements, operating systems, reporting formats, and working relationships are continuously changing. The ability to listen, consider, digest, and implement change is described as workplace agility. *Agility* means ability to recognize new business challenges and environments, new tools and technologies, new systems and formats, and (perhaps most important) new employees and working relationships. *Career planning agility* is the ability to rapidly integrate into new work settings, learn and use new technology, and work with new staff under multiple styles of management. *Succession planning agility* describes alternative paths for increasing the depth of the talent pool. An agile succession plan offers multiple tracks of leadership to be reviewed and considered to fill any vacancy.

INTEGRITY

Ethics, accountability, and concern for open disclosure are key stakeholder concerns. Employees, managers, senior-level leaders, donors, investors, and regulators want to know that companies are doing the right thing. The Sarbanes-Oxley Act, passed in 2002, places a new emphasis on disclosure for publicly traded firms about their internal financial controls and their records management. Concern for balanced operational practices, fair compensation systems, and operational conduct that fits within a range of best practices are issues of integrity. *Integrity* describes an emphasis on responsibility and work behavior that uses systems, processes, and people in open, fair, and respectful ways. *Career planning integrity* reflects honesty, respect for others, and the involvement of management with personal issues that impact work performance and plans. *Succession planning integrity* reflects a corporate culture that values accountability and transparency in business processes. Succession plans that reflect integrity build higher levels of awareness in individuals for reporting on business processes, company practices, ethical standards, company values, and best practice measures.

OPPORTUNITY

The speed of change in business is presenting individuals and organizations with new opportunities on a daily basis. Preparation is the key to transforming change into opportunity. Career growth requires individuals to understand job expectations, performance levels, working relationships, and changing business demands. *Career planning opportunity* is gauged by how well a person can scan his or her immediate workplace and see higher-level work through work flow redesign, new deliverables through the use of technology, or new ways to meet customer expectations. Put simply, effective career planning is determined by how well individuals recognize opportunities to redesign their own jobs. *Succession planning opportunity* reflects an organization's use of internal staffing and learning programs to retain and develop key talent with a company brand. Succession planning, leadership development, and learning programs are effectively managed in high-performing companies. Effective succession planning programs allow organizations to develop their company leadership brand and strengthen the company's cultural awareness. Leadership branding through succession planning creates the opportunity to ensure future leadership through structured job promotion, rotating job assignments, and cross-functional positions.

To summarize, the way in which individuals and organizations view work and jobs is changing. It is imperative for individuals and organizations to recognize the speed of change in the workplace, and move to address this change to improve performance and results. High-performing organizations must coordinate career and succession processes to achieve market leadership.

APPENDIXES

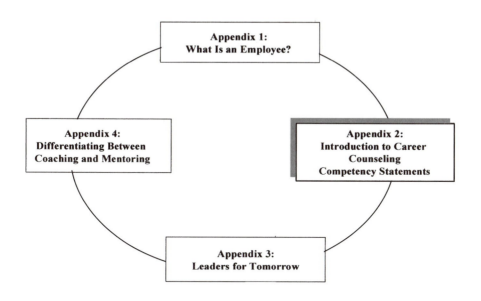

WHAT IS AN EMPLOYEE? THE ANSWER DEPENDS ON FEDERAL LAW

In a legal context, the classification of a worker as either an employee or an independent contractor can have significant consequences.

TABLE A1.1 Tests for Determining Whether a Worker Is an Employee

Test	Description	Laws Under Which Test Has Been Applied by Courts
Common-law test (used by Internal Revenue Service)	Employment relationship exists if employer has the right to control work process, as determined by evaluating totality of the circumstances and specific factors	Federal Insurance Contributions Act Federal Unemployment Tax Act Income Tax Withholding Employment Retirement and Income Security Act National Labor Relations Act Immigration Reform and Control Act

TABLE A1.1 *(Continued)*

Test	Description	Laws Under Which Test Has Been Applied by Courts
Economic realities test	Employment relationship exists if individual is economically dependent on a business for continued employment	Fair Labor Standards Act Title VII Age Discrimination in Employment Act Americans with Disabilities Act Family and Medical Leave Act
Hybrid test	Employment relationship is evaluated under both common-law and economic reality test factors with a focus on who has the right to control the means and manner of a worker's performance	Title VII Age Discrimination in Employment Act Americans with Disabilities Act

Source: Muhl, C. J. (2002, January). What is an employee? The answer depends on the federal law. *Monthly Labor Review*, 6.

TABLE A1.2   Factors Used to Determine a Worker's Status Under The Common-Law Test

Factor	Worker is an EMPLOYEE if	Worker is an INDEPENDENT CONTRACTOR if
Right to control	Employer controls details of the work	Worker controls details of the work
Type of business	Worker is not engaged in business or occupation distinct from employer's	Worker operates in business that is distinct from employer's business
Supervision	Employer supervises worker	Work is done without supervision
Skill level	Skill level need not be high or unique	Skill level is specialized, is unique, or requires substantial training
Tools and materials	Employer provides instrumentalities, tools, and location of workplace	Worker provides instrumentalities and tools of workplace and works at a site other than the employer's
Continuing relationship	Worker is employed for extended, continuous period	Worker is employed for a specific project for a limited time
Method of payment	Worker is paid by the hour, or other computation based on time worked is used to determine pay	Worker is paid by the project
Integration	Work is part of employer's regular business	Work is not part of employer's regular business
Intent	Employer and worker intend to create an employer-employee relationship	Employer and worker do not intend to create an employer-employee relationship
Employment by more than one firm	Worker provides services only to one employer	Worker provides services to more than one business

Source: Muhl, C. J. (2002, January). What is an employee? The answer depends on the federal law. *Monthly Labor Review,* 7.

TABLE A1.3. Factors Used to Determine a Worker's Status Under the Economic Realities Test

Factor	Worker is an Employee if	Worker is an Independent Contractor if
Integration	Worker provides services that are a part of the employer's regular business	Worker provides services outside the regular business of the employer
Investment in facilities	Worker has no investment in the work facilities and equipment	Worker has a substantial investment in the work facilities and equipment
Right to control	Management retains a certain type and degree of control over the work	Management has no right to control the work process of the worker
Risk	Worker does not have the opportunity to make a profit or incur a loss	Worker has the opportunity to make a profit or incur a loss from the job
Skill	Work does not require any special or unique skills or judgment	Work requires a special skill, judgment, or initiative
Continuing relationship	Worker has a permanent or extended relationship with the business	Work relationship is for one project or a limited duration

Source: Muhl, C. J. (2002, January). What is an employee? The answer depends on the federal law. *Monthly Labor Review*, 8.

APPENDIX TWO

INTRODUCTION TO CAREER COUNSELING COMPETENCY STATEMENTS

These competency statements are for those professionals interested and trained in the field of career counseling. For the purpose of these statements, career counseling is defined as *the process of assisting individuals in the development of a life-career with focus on the definition of the worker role and how that role interacts with other life roles.*

NCDA's Career Counseling Competencies are intended to represent minimum competencies for those professionals at or above the Master's degree level of education. These competencies are reviewed on an ongoing basis by the NCDA Professional Standards Committee, the NCDA Board, and other relevant associations.

Professional competency statements provide guidance for the minimum competencies necessary to perform effectively a particular occupation or job within a particular field. Professional career counselors

Revised by the National Career Development Association Board of Directors, April 1994. Reprinted with permission from the National Career Development Association. (c) 2003 National Career Development Association. Retrieved from http://www.ncda.org/about/polccc.html.

(Master's degree or higher) or persons in career development positions must demonstrate the knowledge and skills for a specialty in career counseling that the generalist counselor might not possess. Skills and knowledge are represented by designated competency areas, which have been developed by professional career counselors and counselor educators. The Career Counseling Competency Statements can serve as a guide for career counseling training programs or as a checklist for persons wanting to acquire or to enhance their skills in career counseling.

Minimum Competencies

In order to work as a professional engaged in Career Counseling, the individual must demonstrate minimum competencies in 11 designated areas. These 11 areas are: Career Development Theory; Individual and Group Counseling Skills; Individual/Group Assessment; Information/Resources; Program Management and Implementation; Consultation; Diverse Populations; Supervision; Ethical/Legal Issues; Research/Evaluation; and Technology. These areas are briefly defined as follows (competencies in bold italics must be met in to obtain the Master Career Counselor Special Membership Category):

- **Career Development Theory:** Theory base and knowledge considered essential for professionals engaging in career counseling and development.
- **Individual and Group Counseling Skills:** Individual and group counseling competencies considered essential for effective career counseling.
- **Individual/Group Assessment:** Individual/group assessment skills considered essential for professionals engaging in career counseling.
- **Information/Resources:** Information/resource base and knowledge essential for professionals engaging in career counseling.
- **Program Promotion, Management and Implementation:** Skills necessary to develop, plan, implement, and manage comprehensive career development programs in a variety of settings.

- **Coaching, Consultation, and Performance Improvement:** Knowledge and skills considered essential in enabling individuals and organizations to impact effectively upon the career counseling and development process.
- **Diverse Populations:** Knowledge and skills considered essential in providing career counseling and development processes to diverse populations.
- **Supervision:** Knowledge and skills considered essential in critically evaluating counselor performance, maintaining and improving professional skills, and seeking assistance for others when needed in career counseling.
- **Ethical/Legal Issues:** Information base and knowledge essential for the ethical and legal practice of career counseling.
- **Research/Evaluation:** Knowledge and skills considered essential in understanding and conducting research and evaluation in career counseling and development.
- **Technology:** Knowledge and skills considered essential in using technology to assist individuals with career planning.

Professional Preparation

The competency statements were developed to serve as guidelines for persons interested in career development occupations. They are intended for persons training at the Master's level or higher with a specialty in career counseling. However, this intention does not prevent other types of career development professionals from using the competencies as guidelines for their own training. The competency statements provide counselor educators, supervisors, and other interested groups with guidelines for the minimum training required for counselors interested in the career counseling specialty. The statements might also serve as guidelines for professional counselors who seek in-service training to qualify as career counselors.

Ethical Responsibilities

Career development professionals must only perform activities for which they "possess or have access to the necessary skills and resources for giving the kind of help that is needed" (see NCDA and ACA Ethical Standards). If a professional does not have the appropriate training or resources for the type of career concern presented, an appropriate referral must be made. No person should attempt to use skills (within these competency statements) for which he/she has not been trained. For additional ethical guidelines, refer to the NCDA Ethical Standards for Career Counselors.

CAREER COUNSELING COMPETENCIES AND PERFORMANCE INDICATORS

Career Development Theory

Theory base and knowledge considered essential for professionals engaging in career counseling and development. Demonstration of knowledge of:

1. Counseling theories and associated techniques.
2. Theories and models of career development.
3. Individual differences related to gender, sexual orientation, race, ethnicity, and physical and mental capacities.
4. Theoretical models for career development and associated counseling and information-delivery techniques and resources.
5. Human growth and development throughout the life span.
6. Role relationships which facilitate life-work planning.
7. Information, techniques, and models related to career planning and placement.

Individual and Group Counseling Skills

Individual and group counseling competencies considered essential to effective career counseling. Demonstration of ability to:

1. Establish and maintain productive personal relationships with individuals.
2. Establish and maintain a productive group climate.
3. Collaborate with clients in identifying personal goals.

4. Identify and select techniques appropriate to client or group goals and client needs, psychological states, and developmental tasks.
5. Identify and understand clients' personal characteristics related to career.
6. Identify and understand social contextual conditions affecting clients' careers.
7. Identify and understand familial, subculture and cultural structures and functions as they are related to clients' careers.
8. Identify and understand clients' career decision-making processes.
9. Identify and understand clients' attitudes toward work and workers.
10. Identify and understand clients' biases toward work and workers based on gender, race, and cultural stereotypes.
11. Challenge and encourage clients to take action to prepare for and initiate role transitions by:

    locating sources of relevant information and experience obtaining and interpreting information and experiences, and acquiring skills needed to make role transitions.

12. Assist the client to acquire a set of employability and job search skills.
13. Support and challenge clients to examine life-work roles, including the balance of work, leisure, family, and community in their careers.

Individual/Group Assessment

Individual/group assessment skills considered essential for professionals engaging in career counseling. Demonstration of ability to:

1. Assess personal characteristics such as aptitude, achievement, interests, values, and personality traits.
2. Assess leisure interests, learning style, life roles, self-concept, career maturity, vocational identity, career indecision, work environment preference (e.g., work satisfaction), and other related life style/development issues.

3. Assess conditions of the work environment (such as tasks, expectations, norms, and qualities of the physical and social settings).
4. Evaluate and select valid and reliable instruments appropriate to the client's gender, sexual orientation, race, ethnicity, and physical and mental capacities.
5. Use computer-delivered assessment measures effectively and appropriately.
6. Select assessment techniques appropriate for group administration and those appropriate for individual administration.
7. Administer, score, and report findings from career assessment instruments appropriately.
8. Interpret data from assessment instruments and present the results to clients and to others.
9. Assist the client and others designated by the client to interpret data from assessment instruments.
10. Write an accurate report of assessment results.

Information/Resources

Information/resource base and knowledge essential for professionals engaging in career counseling. Demonstration of knowledge of:

1. Education, training, and employment trends; labor market information and resources that provide information about job tasks, functions, salaries, requirements and future outlooks related to broad occupational fields and individual occupations.
2. Resources and skills that clients utilize in life-work planning and management.
3. Community/professional resources available to assist clients in career planning, including job search.
4. Changing roles of women and men and the implications that this has for education, family, and leisure.
5. Methods of good use of computer-based career information delivery systems (CIDS) and computer-assisted career guidance systems (CACGS) to assist with career planning.

Program Promotion, Management, and Implementation

Knowledge and skills necessary to develop, plan, implement, and manage comprehensive career development programs in a variety of settings. Demonstration of knowledge of:

1. Designs that can be used in the organization of career development programs.
2. Needs assessment and evaluation techniques and practices.
3. Organizational theories, including diagnosis, behavior, planning, organizational communication, and management useful in implementing and administering career development programs.
4. Methods of forecasting, budgeting, planning, costing, policy analysis, resource allocation, and quality control.
5. Leadership theories and approaches for evaluation and feedback, organizational change, decision-making, and conflict resolution.
6. Professional standards and criteria for career development programs.
7. Societal trends and state and federal legislation that influence the development and implementation of career development programs.

Demonstration of ability to:

8. Implement individual and group programs in career development for specified populations.
9. Train others about the appropriate use of computer-based systems for career information and planning.
10. Plan, organize, and manage a comprehensive career resource center.
11. Implement career development programs in collaboration with others.
12. Identify and evaluate staff competencies.
13. Mount a marketing and public relations campaign in behalf of career development activities and services.

Coaching, Consultation, and Performance Improvement

Knowledge and skills considered essential in relating to individuals and organizations that impact the career counseling and development process. Demonstration of ability to:

1. Use consultation theories, strategies, and models.
2. Establish and maintain a productive consultative relationship with people who can influence a client's career.
3. Help the general public and legislators to understand the importance of career counseling, career development, and life-work planning.
4. Impact public policy as it relates to career development and workforce planning.
5. Analyze future organizational needs and current level of employee skills and develop performance improvement training.
6. Mentor and coach employees.

Diverse Populations

Knowledge and skills considered essential in relating to diverse populations that impact career counseling and development processes. Demonstration of ability to:

1. Identify development models and multicultural counseling competencies.
2. Identify developmental needs unique to various diverse populations, including those of different gender, sexual orientation, ethnic group, race, and physical or mental capacity.
3. Define career development programs to accommodate needs unique to various diverse populations.
4. Find appropriate methods or resources to communicate with limited-English-proficient individuals.
5. Identify alternative approaches to meet career planning needs for individuals of various diverse populations.
6. Identify community resources and establish linkages to assist clients with specific needs.

7. Assist other staff members, professionals, and community members in understanding the unique needs/characteristics of diverse populations with regard to career exploration, employment expectations, and economic/social issues.
8. Advocate for the career development and employment of diverse populations.
9. Design and deliver career development programs and materials to hard-to-reach populations.

Supervision

Knowledge and skills considered essential in critically evaluating counselor or career development facilitator performance, maintaining and improving professional skills. Demonstration of:

1. Ability to recognize own limitations as a career counselor and to seek supervision or refer clients when appropriate.
2. Ability to utilize supervision on a regular basis to maintain and improve counselor skills.
3. Ability to consult with supervisors and colleagues regarding client and counseling issues and issues related to one's own professional development as a career counselor.
4. Knowledge of supervision models and theories.
5. Ability to provide effective supervision to career counselors and career development facilitators at different levels of experience.
6. Ability to provide effective supervision to career development facilitators at different levels of experience by:

   knowledge of their roles, competencies, and ethical standards determining their competence in each of the areas included in their certification further training them in competencies, including interpretation of assessment instruments monitoring and mentoring their activities in support of the professional career counselor; and scheduling regular consultations for the purpose of reviewing their activities

Ethical/Legal Issues

Information base and knowledge essential for the ethical and legal practice of career counseling. Demonstration of knowledge of:

1. Adherence to ethical codes and standards relevant to the profession of career counseling (e.g. NBCC, NCDA, and ACA).
2. Current ethical and legal issues which affect the practice of career counseling with all populations.
3. Current ethical/legal issues with regard to the use of computer-assisted career guidance systems.
4. Ethical standards relating to consultation issues.
5. State and federal statutes relating to client confidentiality.

Research/Evaluation

Knowledge and skills considered essential in understanding and conducting research and evaluation in career counseling and development. Demonstration of ability to:

1. Write a research proposal.
2. Use types of research and research designs appropriate to career counseling and development research.
3. Convey research findings related to the effectiveness of career counseling programs.
4. Design, conduct, and use the results of evaluation programs.
5. Design evaluation programs which take into account the need of various diverse populations, including persons of both genders, differing sexual orientations, different ethnic and racial backgrounds, and differing physical and mental capacities.
6. Apply appropriate statistical procedures to career development research.

Technology

Knowledge and skills considered essential in using technology to assist individuals with career planning. Demonstration of knowledge of:

1. Various computer-based guidance and information systems as well as services available on the Internet.
2. Standards by which such systems and services are evaluated (e.g. NCDA and ACSCI).
3. Ways in which to use computer-based systems and Internet services to assist individuals with career planning that are consistent with ethical standards.
4. Characteristics of clients which make them profit more or less from use of technology-driven systems.
5. Methods to evaluate and select a system to meet local needs.

NCDA opposes discrimination against any individual on the basis of race, ethnicity, gender, sexual orientation, age, mental/physical disability or creed.

LEADERS FOR TOMORROW

The U.S. Department of Transportation's (DOT) Leaders for Tomorrow formal mentoring program is a midlevel program that provides workforce development for emerging leaders. The program adds value to the organization by enhancing professional leadership skills within the organization, increasing employee job satisfaction, and transferring institutional knowledge and corporate expertise, thus establishing a pipeline of trained professionals who are prepared to handle organizational challenges and equipped to meet future goals of the U.S. Department of Transportation.

DOT MENTORING PROGRAM OBJECTIVES

The program is designed to engage and propel its participants into heightened levels of learning and organizational development. Program objectives will include skills and management development training,

Retrieved and adapted from http://dothr.ost.dot.gov/HR_Programs/DOT MEN_1/dotmen_1.HTM.

developing a career plan and networking opportunities. The DOT program manager will pair a GS 15 (federal grade level) manager, supervisor, or executive (mentor), with an employee at the GS 13 or 14 grade level (protégé) for the primary purpose of knowledge management through hands-on experiences and classroom training. Ongoing communication between pairs will take place to achieve mutually agreed upon outcomes. In this partnership, both individuals share in the growth and professional career development of one another.

PROGRAM BENEFITS AND TIME COMMITMENTS

The 10-month program has been designed to provide the framework for institutionalizing a structured program for developing mentors and protégés within DOT. This program is aimed toward fulfilling workforce development gaps by building new leaders and securing a superior dedicated staff, with a minimum level of cost and time investment. The Leaders for Tomorrow program will benefit those directly involved in the program as well as other department employees.

Managerial Benefits

- Supports secretarial emphasis on professional development for DOT employees
- Increased managerial and supervisory leadership effectiveness
- Builds teamwork and a shared sense of commitment to DOT's mission
- Improves overall organizational performance
- Produces a cadre of confident and competent future leaders
- Mentors may receive continuing leadership unit credit for participating

Employee Benefits

- Facilitates cross-modal learning and development
- Encourages cross-training opportunities
- Enhances and expands skill levels that improve business performance

- Focus is directed toward achieving self-identified professional goals in alignment with organizational objectives
- Assists individuals in making critical career transitions that can significantly impact professional growth and organizational improvements
- Protégé experiences are viewed favorably by senior management

Time Commitment

Participants must commit to meeting with their mentor/protégé a minimum of two hours per month. It is during this time when mentor/protégé pairs discuss reading materials, share outcomes and concerns as well as other developmental issues. In addition to this, there will be interactive workshops and roundtables designed for mentor/protégé participation. Various networking activities will be hosted for both mentors and protégés to exchange thoughts, experiences and ideas, and to become more acquainted with one another. The Department will host a mentor/protégé kickoff orientation activity at the beginning of each new session as well as separate orientations for each group.

MENTORS

Mentoring has long been applauded as the most time and cost-effective way to build a skilled workforce onsite. For mentors, it is a thorough way to develop an individual's career by honing professional skills and supporting organization objectives.

Mentors' responsibilities include:

- Exposing protégés to new experiences not currently available in their immediate work environment
- Advocating on behalf of their protégés to help meet professional goals
- Designating and fulfilling time commitments required to develop the mentor relationship

Mentor characteristics include:

- Knowledge of organizational goals, policies, functions, communication channels and training programs

- A willingness to share personal experiences relevant to the needs of the protégé
- Having tact, diplomacy and sensitivity in working with others who may belong to a different culture or are physically challenged
- Demonstrated proficiency and initiative

Mentors also need to have the ability to nurture and motivate protégés, be skill-savvy and be willing to dedicate time to the program.

PROTÉGÉS

Protégés will have mentors that are on average two grade levels above them.

What Do Protégés Do?

Protégés are people who elect to receive mentoring to facilitate and accelerate their professional progress. Protégés can expect to receive support, learn new interpersonal skills, develop career advancement strategies and obtain a better understanding of organizational processes that enhance career mobility. Protégés will need to allocate time, develop an agenda and meet with their mentor at least twice a month. All protégés are required to complete a developmental assignment that adds value to the protégé's career and to the Department. Protégés are required to complete and submit an application to the OST Program Manager.

Goal-Setting and Skills Evolution

Career goal setting by protégés should include a variety of professional enrichment aspirations. Each goal must be specific, have a time frame and be results-oriented, relevant and reachable. The Leaders for Tomorrow program will not only assist in the process of selecting interested mentors for the protégés, but will provide career assessments, ongoing workshops and challenging workplace assignments.

Characteristics of a Protégé

Protégés need to be enthusiastic participants, active learners and willing communicators. They must be able to express career desires and follow-up on suggestions and assignments given by mentors (including through a sign language interpreter). Protégés should be able to demonstrate the following skills:

- Ability to work independently
- Ability to develop and maintain rapport with persons of various levels
- Effective communication skills
- Ability to set goals and develop plans
- Ability to receive and act on constructive advice
- Commitment and responsibility for own personal and professional development

APPLICATION PROCESS

All mentors and protégés must complete an application to become a participant in the Leaders for Tomorrow program. Applications can be accessed via the Internet and e-mailed to the program manager. This agency provides reasonable accommodations to applicants with disabilities. If you need a reasonable accommodation for any part of the application process, please notify the agency. The decision on granting reasonable accommodation will be on a case-by-case basis. Interviews may be conducted to determine final participant selections. The application contains identifying information and a brief self-assessment. The application also consists of four questions that ask the candidate to write a brief narrative with regard to organizational contributions and the candidates' expectations of the program. Application information will be reviewed, processed and used to assist decision-making during the matching process.

PROGRAM GOALS AND OUTCOMES

The Leaders for Tomorrow mentoring program is designed as a structured initiative to engage participants in meaningful career growth and development experiences that will be of great value to them and DOT. Program benefits are oftentimes not seen immediately. However, there is a gradual transference of professional skills and increased confidence—invaluable skills that are hard to measure. Significant qualitative measures should be captured over time.

Goals

- Enhanced self-awareness and acquiring new skills
- Ability to cultivate effective partnerships
- Motivation toward career exploration and advancement
- Developmental opportunities
- Identify and implement career goals
- Increased positive workplace morale

Outcomes

- Improved communication and feedback skills
- Organizational recognition/exposure
- Unique learning opportunities in various DOT organizations
- Networking opportunities
- Transferable skills
- Larger pool of trained and competent future leaders

PROGRAM STAFFING AND OVERSIGHT

The OST (Out Service Training) program manager primarily manages the Leaders for Tomorrow mentoring program. However, because this initiative is designed as a Department-wide partnership, all operating administrations are expected to be actively involved to reap program benefits. Organizational business goals must be clearly articulated by senior executives and managers as this program evolves so that modifications and adjustments can be implemented as quickly as possible.

The program manager will work closely with a professional contractor to administer assessments and evaluations to help employees identify interests, values, skills and professional needs. With the support of internal resources offered by the OST Office of Workforce Planning and Learning, this program will provide ongoing assistance to managers and employees in identifying and utilizing performance development resources. All participants will have the opportunity to experience individual career counseling that will provide the framework for determining career goals, evaluating needs and identifying obstacles and enablers for progress in their profession.

A DOT Mentoring Community Intranet site is being developed to provide career development information and to promote ongoing communication between OST and operating administration counterparts.

DIFFERENTIATING BETWEEN COACHING AND MENTORING

Dr. Matt M. Starcevich sought to learn (from mentoring protégés) if there was a difference between mentoring and coaching. In 1998, he conducted an online survey, and the results were solid—there is a difference.[1] The following is an abstract of the results of that survey.

FOCUS

Mentors in either a formal mentoring program or informal relationship focus on the person, their career and support for individual growth and maturity while the coach is job-focused and performance oriented.

> A mentor is like a sounding board, they can give advice but the protégé is free to pick and choose what they do. The context does not have specific performance objectives. A coach is trying to direct a person to some end result, the person may choose how to get there, but the coach is strategically assessing and monitoring the progress and giving advice for effectiveness and efficiency.

Mentoring is biased in your favor. Coaching is impartial, focused on improvement in behavior.

In summary, the mentor has a deep personal interest, personally involved—a friend who cares about you and your long-term development. The coach develops specific skills for the task, challenges, and performance expectations at work.

ROLE

Mentoring is a power-free, two-way mutually beneficial relationship. Mentors are facilitators and teachers allowing the protégé to discover their own direction.

They let me struggle so I could learn.
Never provided solutions—always asking questions to surface my own thinking and let me find my own solutions.

A coach has a set agenda to reinforce or change skills and behaviors. The coach has an objective or goals for each discussion. In our study, the top four terms chosen to best describe the mentor's dominant styles were friend and confidant, direct, logical, questioner.

RELATIONSHIP

Even in formal mentoring programs the protégé and mentor have choices—to continue, how long, how often, and the focus. Self-selection is the rule in informal mentoring relationships, with the protégé initiating and actively maintaining the relationship. If I am your mentor, you probably picked me. In an organization, your coach hired you. Coaching comes with the job, a job expectation, in some organizations a defined competency for managers and leaders.

SOURCE OF INFLUENCE

The interpersonal skills will determine the effectiveness of influence for both coach and mentor. The coach also has an implied or actual level of authority by nature of their position. Ultimately, they can insist on compliance.

A mentor's influence is proportionate to the perceived value he or she can bring to the relationship. It is a power-free relationship based on mutual respect and value for both mentor and protégé. A job description might contain the word "coach," or you might even have that job title—it is just a label or expectation. "Mentor" is a reputation that has to be personally earned; you are not a mentor until the protégé says you are.

RETURNS

The coach's returns are in the form of more team harmony and job performance. The mentoring relationship is reciprocal. There is a learning process for the mentor from the feedback and insights of the protégé. "The ability to look at situations from a different perspective. I am a Generation X and he is in his 60's."

The relationship is a vehicle to affirm the value of and satisfaction from fulfilling a role as helper and developer of others. Mentors need not be all-knowing experts—such a position could be detrimental. In our study, the most significant thing the mentor did was "listened and understood me" and "built my confidence and trust in myself; empowered me to see what I could do."

ARENA

A great deal of informal mentoring is occurring with at risk youth, in our schools, as well as in volunteer, not-for-profit, and for-profit organizations. If I am your mentor, chances are you have chosen me to be of help with some aspect of your life. Coaching even in the sporting arena is task related—improvement of knowledge, skills, or abilities to better perform a given task. Mentors are sought for broader life and career issues. The protégé is proactive in seeking out mentors and keeping the relationship productive. The coach creates the need for discussion and is responsible for follow-up and holding others accountable.

CONCLUSION

Coaching and mentoring are not the same thing. Our results and experience support the conclusion that mentoring is a power-free, two-way mutually beneficial learning situation in which the mentor provides advice, shares knowledge and experiences, and teaches using a low-pressure, self-discovery approach. The mentor teaches using an adult learning versus the teacher-to-student model and is willing to not only question for self-discovery but also to freely share their own experiences and skills with the protégé. The mentor is both a source of information and knowledge and a Socratic questioner.

If I am your coach, you probably work for me and my concern is your performance, ability to adapt to change, and enrolling your support in the vision/direction for our work unit. If there is still doubt in your mind, visualize how the conversation and relationship would be different if your manager scheduled a coaching discussion at two o'clock this afternoon to discuss your roles, responsibilities, and expectations, rather than if you called your mentor to discuss some things that you have been thinking about.

NOTE

1. Dr. Starcevich is the founder of the Center for Coaching & Mentoring in Bartlesville, Oklahoma. Results of the online survey are available at http://coachingandmentoring.com/surveyresults.htm.

INDEX

ABOUT THE AUTHORS

William J. Rothwell, PhD, SPHR, is Professor-in-Charge of the Workforce Education and Development program in the Department of Learning and Performance Systems on the University Park campus of the Pennsylvania State University. He is also President of Rothwell and Associates, Inc. (see www.rothwell-associates.com), a full-service consulting firm that offers services in succession planning and management. As a consultant, he has worked with over 30 multinational corporations. As an academic, he heads up the number two-ranked graduate program in Workplace Learning and Performance in the United States.

Before arriving at Penn State, Dr. Rothwell had nearly 20 years of experience as a human resources practitioner in the private and public sectors. He was previously Assistant Vice President and Management Development Director for the Franklin Life Insurance Co., a wholly owned subsidiary of a Fortune 48 corporation. Before that, he was Training Director for the Illinois Office of the Auditor General.

Dr. Rothwell is author of *Effective Succession Planning: Ensuring Leadership Continuity and Building Talent from Within*, second edition

(Amacom, 2000), regarded by some as the "corporate bible" on succession management practices. He was also National Thought Leader for a Linkage-DDI (Development Dimensions International)–sponsored study of 18 multinational corporations in 2001 that examined corporate best practices in succession planning and management. The technical report from the latter study appeared as *Effective Succession Management: Building Winning Systems for Identifying and Developing Key Talent* (The Center for Organizational Research, 2001.) He is also coauthor of such books related to succession management as *The Strategic Development of Talent* (HRD Press, 2003), *Building In-House Leadership and Management Development Programs* (Quorum Books, 1999), and *The Competency Toolkit* (Human Resource Development Press, 2000), and author of *The Action Learning Guidebook* (Jossey-Bass, 1999). Among his latest books are *The 2004 ASTD Competency Study: Mapping the Future* (ASTD, 2004), *The Workplace Learner: How to Align Training Initiatives with Individual Learning Competencies* (Amacom, 2002), which is about the competencies of workplace learners and methods of measuring the developmental learning climate in organizations, and *What CEOs Expect from Corporate Training: Building Workplace Learning and Performance Initiatives That Advance Organizational Goals* (Amacom, 2003). He has also authored, coauthored, edited, or coedited more than 50 books and has consulted on succession planning and management with a broad array of organizations in business, government, and nonprofit settings both in the United States and internationally. He can be reached by e-mail at wjr9@psu.edu or by phone at 814-863-2581 (office).

Robert D. Jackson is a Senior Consultant with the Pennsylvania Department of Transportation. In that role, he manages the career development systems program for the Center for Performance Excellence, PENNDOT's internal consulting bureau. He is responsible for the development and execution of leadership development programs for 12,000 employees. He directs the PENNDOT Leadership Academy for Managers and the associated academy for supervisors.

Robert specializes in managing and evaluating PENNDOT's employee coaching initiatives and other career-enhancing programs for 11 engineering districts throughout Pennsylvania and 24 bureaus and organizations within PENNDOT's central office in Harrisburg. He is also responsible for administering the new employee orientation program for the central office. As a relationship manager to the department's corporate university, Robert is responsible for researching and benchmarking excellent training and development organizations and corporate universities to determine best career development practices.

He is also an adjunct instructor at Penn State Harrisburg, where he teaches three courses in the Training and Development master's degree program.

Prior to joining PENNDOT, Robert held several training and development consulting agreements in both the public and private sectors. He consulted with the (Pennsylvania) State System of Higher Education to foster the public/private cooperative efforts of Pennsylvania's 14 public universities and IBM Learning Services. He has made numerous presentations on the topic of the manager's or supervisor's role in employee retention.

Additionally, Robert was the State Recruiting and Retention Superintendent for the Pennsylvania Air National Guard, a component of the United States military reserve. He was responsible for all Air National Guard recruiting and retention activities in the Commonwealth as well as an operations staff of 18 recruiters and retainers.

Robert also served in other career advisor and retention positions to execute and support a variety of career development and employee retention initiatives at the unit level in the Air National Guard. He managed and administered all aspects of employee retention including an $110,000 incentive program. He frequently counseled and advised unit commanders, supervisors, and employees on career concerns and opportunities as well as personnel issues within units.

In 1997, Robert was initiated as a life member of ASTD (formerly known as the American Society for Training and Development), Central Pennsylvania Chapter, for his devoted leadership at the chapter, regional, and national ASTD levels. He served as chapter president in 1991 and 2001. Additional service to the profession includes service on the Advisory Council for the Master's Degree in Training and Development program at Penn State University, Harrisburg, Pennsylvania.

Robert is completing his PhD in Workforce Education and Development at Penn State University and is focusing his research on career development. He has a master of education degree in Training and

Development from Penn State University and a bachelor of science degree in Business Education from Bloomsburg University (Pennsylvania). He is also a certified DDI learning systems facilitator.

Shaun C. Knight is currently a Business and Career Solutions Associate for Penn State's School of Information Sciences and Technology. Shaun has responsibilities for the deployment of career development services for graduate and undergraduate students within the school who are seeking postgraduate employment and educational opportunities.

He has had extensive experience in career development counseling, planning, and placement with many diverse populations and has addressed international, national, and statewide audiences through speaking engagements and consulting experiences. Shaun has worked extensively developing corporate relationships with many organizations falling into the classification of Fortune 50, 100, and 500 firms.

Shaun has also worked with organizations that focused on delivering effective career development services to executive-level clients through the utilization of developmental coaching and strategic career planning.

Additionally, Shaun has been involved with program development and management activities, as well as providing administrational guidance on state-funded projects addressing public and private sector business needs. Shaun is also serving as an independent consultant for a multinational career development corporation involved with delivering career development services through a variety of technological applications.

In addition, Shaun has also served as a career development specialist, which included assisting dislocated corporate executives, technical and nontechnical workers, low-income individuals, and at-risk youth in formulating strategic programs that will enable them to become gainfully employed or successfully navigate the promotional tracks of an organization. Shaun also assisted in the design and implementation of a career exploration and community service summer at-risk youth program that was recognized by the Commonwealth of Pennsylvania as an exemplary career development model for services to this population.

Shaun serves on many local and state committees and boards addressing workforce and career development trends within business and educational organizations. Shaun is near completion of his PhD in

Workforce Education with a focus on career development and associated technologies from the Pennsylvania State University. He has completed his master's degree in Workforce Education with a focus on training and career development and finished his bachelor of science degree in Secondary Education from the Pennsylvania State University. He is certified through the NCDA as a Career Development Facilitator and is also a certified DDI learning systems facilitator.

John E. Lindholm, PhD, SPHR, is the Director of Total Rewards at Legal Sea Foods, Inc. He has 15 years of experience working in financial, educational, and food industries, where his work has involved commercial credit analysis, performance and compensation management, human resources development, and visioning and workforce planning. He consults in the areas of job design, total rewards, and workforce learning and performance programs. John has presented papers at national conferences on the topics of competency modeling, facilitation, and enterprise profitability. He has coauthored with William Rothwell and William Wallick on *What CEOs Expect from Corporate Training* (Amacom, 2003), and his most recent publication is on the topic of career and succession planning. John earned his PhD in Workforce Education and Development from the Pennsylvania State University and is a faculty member at Clark University in Worcester, Massachusetts. His areas of interest are job analysis, performance development, total rewards, organizational learning, and leadership studies.

Wei Aleisha Wang is a PhD candidate at the Pennsylvania State University, pursuing a degree in Workforce Education and Development with a specialization in employee training and development. A graduate of Nankai University in China, she has experience as a consultant in human resources in China. She has also published and presented about training in China. She has coauthored the articles "Why 21st Century Is China's Century" and "Training Trends in China." Her career goal is to become a human resources professional.

Tiffani D. Payne, a Bunton-Waller fellow at the Pennsylvania State University, is a PhD candidate, pursuing a degree in Workforce Education and Development with an emphasis in training and development. She received a master of arts in Organizational Management from Antioch University in 1999, and graduated from Hampton University in

1996 with a bachelor of science in Marketing. She began her career in sales and marketing, specializing in sales training and online advertising program management. Her most recent experiences are in change management and organization and workforce development in the not-for-profit sector.